TH
WHOLE WORLD
WILL
LOVE ME

"**E**TERNAL FATHER, *since Thou hast given me for my inheritance the Adorable Face of Thy Divine Son, I offer that Face to Thee, and I beg Thee, in exchange for this* coin *of infinite value, to forget the ingratitude of souls dedicated to Thee, and to pardon all poor sinners.*" —St. Therese

St. Therese of the Child Jesus and of the Holy Face
1873-1897
Canonized in 1925. Declared a Doctor of the Church in 1997.

THE
WHOLE WORLD
WILL
LOVE ME

THE LIFE OF SAINT THERESE
OF THE CHILD JESUS
AND OF THE HOLY FACE

By

Dorothy Scallan

Edited by
Fr. Emeric B. Scallan, S.T.B.

Companion Book to
THE GOLDEN ARROW and THE HOLY MAN OF TOURS

*"O God of hosts, convert us: and show
thy face, and we shall be saved."*
—Psalm 79:8

TAN BOOKS AND PUBLISHERS, INC.
Rockford, Illinois 61105

NIHIL OBSTAT: John M. A. Fearns, S.T.D.
                   Censor Librorum

IMPRIMATUR: ✛ Francis Cardinal Spellman
                   Archbishop of New York
                   New York
                   July 28, 1953

The Nihil Obstat and Imprimatur are official declarations that a book or pamphlet is free of doctrinal or moral error. No implication is contained therein that those who have granted the Nihil Obstat and Imprimatur agree with the contents, opinions, or statements expressed.

Copyright © 1954 by Emeric B. Scallan. First published by The William-Frederick Press, New York, 1954, under the author's pen name, Doris Sheridan.

ISBN 0-89555-818-1

Images of St. Therese and of the Holy Face of Jesus:
Copyright © Office Central de Lisieux.

Printed and bound in the United States of America.

TAN BOOKS AND PUBLISHERS, INC.
P.O. Box 424
Rockford, Illinois 61105
2005

IN RECOGNITION AND IN GRATITUDE

for teaching her youngest sister SAINT THERESE

TO EMBRACE

The Devotion to
The Holy Face

THIS BOOK IS HUMBLY DEDICATED TO

MOTHER AGNES OF JESUS

PRIORESS OF THE CARMEL OF LISIEUX

WHO EXPIRED IN THE ODOR OF SANCTITY
JULY 28, 1951

THE HOLY FACE OF JESUS

Painting by Sister Genevieve of the Holy Face (Celine Martin), based on
the photograph of the Holy Shroud made by Secondo Pia in 1898.

HOWEVER TENDER WAS THE DEVOTION WHICH
SAINT THERESE HAD FOR THE CHILD JESUS,
IT CANNOT BE COMPARED TO THE DEVOTION
SHE HAD FOR THE HOLY FACE.

— MOTHER AGNES OF JESUS

Publisher's Preface

"The whole world will love me," predicted St. Therese near the end of her life. (See p. 303.) This is certainly a startling statement from a Saint, and one can presume that these words were well scrutinized for undertones of pride and egotism during the Process of her Canonization.

Yet these words were simply a prophecy of the truth, stated with humility, and in a few short years they came to pass. Therese had not touched many souls directly during her lifetime, but as she neared death, she stated, "I feel that my mission is about to begin: my mission to make others love the good God the way I love Him." She would touch souls mainly through her now-famous book, *The Story of a Soul*, which has sold millions of copies in many languages the world over. This phenomenon is an extraordinary event in the field of publishing as well as in the life of the Church.

St. Therese had said, "After my death I will let fall a shower of roses," and she kept her word. So many favors were obtained through her intercession that people worldwide clamored for her canonization. The Bishop of her diocese, "despite his lack of enthusiasm"[1] for it, opened Therese's cause in 1910. The miracles continued. Between 1907 and 1925, seven volumes entitled *Showers of Roses* were published, recounting the multitudes of heavenly favors received through Therese's intercession.[2] Today St. Therese is probably the most popular Saint in the world.

---

1. Pierre Descouvement & Helmuth Nils Loose, *Therese and Lisieux* (Toronto: Novalis, 1996), p. 317.
2. *Ibid*, p. 316.

One of the singular merits of this book, *The Whole World Will Love Me*, is that it brings out St. Therese's devotion to the Holy Face of Jesus. "It was the Little Flower's devotion to the Holy Face which drove her to her unparalleled heights of sanctity," states Fr. Emeric Scallan.[3] Here the reader learns of the beginnings of this devotion in Tours, its uncanny spread to Lisieux, and its crucial importance in the life of St. Therese and in her mission to save the souls of unbelievers. The author particularly brings out the role of the Holy Face of Jesus in enabling St. Therese to triumph over temptations against faith in the long and excruciatingly intense "dark night of the soul" which she endured for the last 18 months of her life.

Written in a "story" form, *The Whole World Will Love Me* is nonetheless a well researched biography by an author steeped in her subject and is very likely the best biography of St. Therese yet to appear. It brings out many facts about her life that are usually overlooked or barely mentioned in most accounts. These include the providential circumstances of her parents' meeting, the Martin family's financial circumstances, Louis Martin's refusal to work on Sunday, his efforts to work with the Church's "bureaucracy" in Rome to get a hearing for his daughter's aspiration to Carmel, the daily challenges of life in Carmel, St. Therese's last illness and death (not described, of course, in *The Story of a Soul*), and the remarkable spread of her fame soon after her death.

Even readers very familiar with St. Therese's life will find their eyes opened to many new insights in Dorothy Scallan's book. And those who have previously appreciated the Little Flower as St. Therese *of the Child Jesus* will come away from this book with a new understanding of St. Therese of the Child Jesus *and of the Holy Face*.

—The Publishers, 2005

---

3. Page viii of *The Golden Arrow: The Autobiography and Revelations of Sister Mary of St. Peter (1816-1848) on Devotion to the Holy Face of Jesus*, translated by Fr. Emeric Scallan (1954; TAN, 1990).

THE
WHOLE WORLD
WILL
LOVE ME

"O JESUS, *Thy Face is the only beauty that delights my heart. Impress on my soul Thy divine likeness, so that Thou mayest not look at Thy spouse without beholding Thyself. O my Beloved, for love of Thee I am content not to see here on earth the sweetness of Thy glance, nor to feel the ineffable kiss of Thy sacred lips; but I beg Thee to inflame me with Thy Love, that it may consume me quickly, and that soon* Therese of the Holy Face *may behold Thy glorious Face in Heaven.*"
—St. Therese

1

"THERE IS no need for me to inquire how things turned out for Zelie at the convent," said Captain Guerin as he entered his well-lighted house and closed the cold, wet outdoors behind him. "I can tell at a glance from the way you look that you've been disappointed."

"I could have told you even before we left this morning," answered his wife, "that the nuns wouldn't accept Zelie as a postulant. But, then, whenever I say anything, you tell me I am too pessimistic!"

The captain pretended not to hear her answer. Stroking Zelie's silken dark hair, which was neatly parted in the center and displayed a strikingly fair forehead to real advantage, he asked sympathetically, "Did they give you no hope at all, my child?"

"Sister Superior said I had no vocation," the daughter replied, valiantly holding back the tears in her large brown eyes.

"But I don't understand! You always had your heart very much set on entering a convent, and if I am any judge of my daughter, I would say that you would make a good nun. Tell me, what reason did the Sister Superior give for refusing you?" Although Captain Guerin had retired from his commission in the army many years before, he had never lost the characteristics of a military officer. In his opinion those in authority ought to be at all times ready to give reasons for their official acts. Now he wanted to know why his daughter, who had been so anxious to wear the veil since she was thirteen, was turned away from the religious life as unsuitable.

NOTE: To distinguish the two Carmelite Saints, both of whom bear the same name, Teresa, the French version "Therese" is used throughout this book for the Saint of Lisieux, and "Saint Teresa" for the Mystic of Avila.

"Sister Superior did not give us any reason," interposed Madame Guerin. "She simply said that Zelie had no religious vocation — and there the matter ended."

"So!" The gray-haired captain looked affectionately at his daughter. Then he asked her pointedly, "What will you do now, Zelie?"

"I wasn't thinking of myself just now, Papa."

"No? And of whom are you now thinking?"

"Of Louise. My being turned down this afternoon may also hurt her chances of being accepted as a postulant. And you know how much she hoped to become a nun some day."

Just then Louise, the younger of the two Guerin daughters, red-eyed and dejected, entered the room without a word.

"You see what I mean, Papa. Louise now feels that all is lost for her as well . . . . "

"Nonsense," replied the captain. "Louise, as well as you, shall have your fair chances of selecting the kind of life to which you feel yourselves called. There are other cities in France besides Alençon. And there are numerous convents scattered over the country where perhaps you may be very welcome. Nothing has been lost!" Then, turning to his wife, he added, "Come, let us sit down to supper. We will have no more talk of barred convent doors and disappointed daughters."

The captain was a gentle father and a man of refined tastes, as his home and surroundings testified, but he could be very practical as well. Retiring from Napoleon's army, he had chosen to settle his family in Normandy, selecting the charming city of Alençon — whose very name was symbolic of the gossamer lace for which it had gained world renown. Here he purchased a two-story house situated directly across the street from an imposing seventeenth-century mansion which had once housed a duchess, and which was now occupied by the Prefecture of the city. True, the captain's dwelling had none of the dimensions of the grand mansion opposite, but it had a quiet dignity nonetheless, being strongly built of brick with wrought-iron trimming. The ground floor consisted of a living room, dining room, kitchen and a hall with a spiral staircase that led to a second floor which had three bedrooms. "A good house in a respectable neighborhood is a basic necessity to right Christian living," the captain had commented, on handing over the purchase price equivalent to a small fortune.

Born in a moderately well-to-do family, which knew how to guard its fortune, and even add to it by saving part of its earnings during every year, Captain Guerin came into a modest inheritance from his parents. Even after paying for the new house, therefore, he still retained enough to set aside in the family vault for dowries for his three children when they came of age and were ready to start a life of their own. However, after the family was settled and had become familiar with their new surroundings at Alençon, Captain Guerin became somewhat concerned at the small pension he received from the government as a retired army officer. Clearly, it was altogether insufficient to meet the current living expenses of the family. Determined not to draw from the bank any of the money reserved for his children's future, he began earnestly to look for some remunerative work. But this was not easy to find. Educated for the military, he found no opening where he could exercise his specialized army training in quiet and peaceful Alençon.

After repeated efforts proved fruitless, he purchased equipment and opened a small café, leaving his wife to manage the business, hoping in this way to help defray some of the household expenses. But Madame Guerin soon showed signs that she obviously had none of the genial manners nor the competence necessary for even a small business. The venture failed completely and the family's investment was a total loss.

What was the captain to do now? He knew he had to make a decision — one, as it were, on the battlefield of life, and this must be done swiftly. A position had to be defended, and it was *not* a strategic hill, nor an attack on an enemy supply base. It was his home and his family.

"Perhaps it was unwise to buy such an expensive house . . . ." ventured Madame Guerin. "If you had bought a cheaper one, we would have more now to live on until you could find a suitable position . . . ."

"If you had only helped out a little more energetically with the restaurant, as other women do to help their husbands during a crisis, all would have turned out well," replied the captain in his usual quiet, even voice.

"Will you go on blaming me for failing with the business as long as we live?"

"No, I shall be careful never to mention it again. It's no use crying over spilt milk."

For a time things ran smoothly and the two were silent. But soon their financial condition was in such straits that both knew a drastic step had to be taken.

"What will you do now?" the wife pressed her husband. Even during this trial he seemed as much a captain of his own soul, as he had once been a captain of the army. "Will you draw from the dowries reserved for the children?"

"Surely you are not serious?"

"Well, what else is there to do?"

Captain Guerin was accustomed to his wife's helplessness whenever a problem arose and would have preferred to remain silent, but he felt he had to make himself clear on this issue, which was to him most vital.

"Whatever we do, we shall certainly not use the children's dowries. Like all God-fearing parents, I believe we owe our children a decent start in life and I intend to exert myself to the limit to achieve this end or stand accused of failing in my duties as the father of a family. The children's dowries will remain untouched, and that is final!"

"But we need money for living expenses. Will you sell the house, then?"

"Sell the house? Sell the roof over our heads? That would make us truly homeless paupers!"

"Very well, tell me, then, just what do you intend to do?"

"I am going to work!"

"But you have already tried everywhere for a suitable position and you didn't succeed."

"I am no longer waiting for a *position*. As of today I will get a *job*! I'll become a carpenter . . . ."

"But you can't mean that!" It was her turn to be amazed. Could her accomplished husband forget his high rank in the military? Could he forget his insignia and stoop to work at the ordinary job of a mere carpenter?

The captain did not tarry for further explanations. Donning work clothes and taking hold of a saw and a hammer he began from that day onward to work at one carpenter job after another. People soon found that the skill of his hands well matched his cultural accomplishments. His services became much in demand. He was never to be without work. Moreover, everyone still continued to call him *Captain* Guerin, despite the fact that he exchanged his brass-trimmed officer's uniform for a suit of work clothes.

But, most important, the Captain himself knew he had won: not only a battle, but a war — a war against false human standards — when he had willingly set himself to a life of manual labor rather than jeopardize his family's welfare. It paid off remarkably well, too. He still lived in the good, two-story red brick house opposite the imposing Prefecture. He sent his children to good schools. But, above all, he had gained the inner satisfaction that he not only managed to keep his children's dowries untouched, but had even added to them substantially from his steady earnings as a carpenter.

And now that both his daughters were grown young ladies soon to settle into a life of their own, he was happy that they would not leave their parental home penniless. Thus, with security and honor, they could start out on a life of their own. And Captain Guerin, as head of his house, having prudently attended to all the needs of his family, felt his soul at peace, as only the souls of the just know peace in this life of turmoil and strife.

2

THERE WERE new and happy interests clamoring for attention
in the Guerin household. Five years had elapsed since the day
the captain had assured his daughters they could dry their tears,
that there were numerous convents in the country where they
would be welcome. And now Louise, the younger Guerin girl,
had been accepted; not at local St. Vincent's, but at the Visitation Convent at Le Mans.

"Papa, the nuns have given me this requisition list, even,
telling exactly what I will need to bring to the convent when I
enter next year," beamed Louise, clutching it like a priceless
treasure. By the end of the year her trunks were packed, containing only the necessary linens, clothing, sewing materials, and
the required devotional books and breviaries. Twenty-two-year-
old Isidore, the son, returned to Alençon to spend a few days
with his parents and sisters, and especially to see Louise off for
Le Mans. Only Zelie seemed more pensive than usual.

"What will *you* do, Zelie, after Louise goes to Le Mans?"
her brother asked affectionately.

"I don't know," was the disconsolate answer.

"Well, it doesn't matter. Papa says you have nothing to
worry about since he's going to leave you this house. And what's
more, since you have made such a grand success of lacemaking
in these past five years, there is no fear for your future. It seems
assured."

In their upstairs room the night before her departure, Louise
offered Zelie her version of parting advice: "After I am settled
at Le Mans, and when you come to visit me, who knows but

year after she had been turned down at the convent. Not knowing how to occupy herself, she had prayed earnestly for light
to know what to do. Having finished a novena to the Blessed
Virgin with this intention, she was on her way home from
church when she heard a clear voice say: "Go and make point
lace."

Overcoming the objections of her family, Zelie heeded this
prompting, took a two-year course in lacemaking, and was
finally awarded a certificate to fill orders for the traditional
laces as one who would uphold their reputation for historic
excellence. Then followed those happy years of surprising success for Zelie, who as a manufacturer of handmade Alençon lace
developed a thriving business that gave her a steady income and
a secure place in the world.

In the light of this past evidence it was not easy for the captain to shake off Zelie's present story of the incident on the
bridge as a mere whimsy of her imagination. From all appearances she was certainly not viewing the matter lightly. She
seemed determined that it was something that would decide her
future life. God's ways were not always our ways. The captain
began wondering whether there was not something he ought to
do in this matter which called for delicate handling. After
all, here it was not a question of a voice urging Zelie to make
lace. His daughter was considering marriage to a man whose
name she did not even know. The Guerins had always held
their heads high and Zelie had a reputation for shying away
from all men.

Supper finished, Zelie was anxious to retire to her room but
her father took her aside. "Zelie, I don't want you to pay too
much attention to that voice you say you heard on the bridge
this afternoon." But even as he spoke he knew that Zelie was
not paying any attention to his advice. Some other higher coun-
selor had replaced him. "Promise me you will do as I ask you."

"I cannot promise that, Father. You will recall that you gave
me a similar warning when I heard a voice some years ago
urging me to make laces."

"But that was something far less important."

"No matter! I simply cannot disregard the voice and make myself plan something counter to its promptings."

"I am not asking you to disregard the voice altogether, Zelie. I merely want to advise you not to set your heart on marrying anyone."

"Have you known me ever to set my heart on marrying anyone, Father?" Zelie asked.

"No, that's just it! I wouldn't want to see you change now."

"This is an entirely different matter. I will do whatever God indicates as His will for me. Certainly, I had nothing to do in the matter of meeting the young man on St. Leonard's bridge this afternoon. But I believe that if Our Lord indicated to me by a voice that the man who passed me on the bridge was he whom Our Lord had prepared for me, then I must not disregard it."

"But, girl, you don't even know if the man you met on the bridge is single. He may be married and have a family of his own . . . ." Captain Guerin stopped. He saw Zelie abruptly turning away and walking up the spiral staircase as one determined to end a conversation that had reached a climax of absurdity.

Perplexed, the captain now turned to his wife for comfort. "Really, I didn't mean to hurt her," he fretted. After a few minutes of brooding silence he looked up again. "Tell me, can you repeat the exact words Zelie said the voice spoke to her?"

"Yes, I believe I can. The words were: 'This is he whom I have prepared for you.' "

Silently the captain weighed the meaning of the words, and then, brightening up, said, "We shall say nothing about this to anyone, do you hear? I'll handle this thing my way," he finished, looking relieved.

"Captain Guerin, what in the world are you up to?" his wife asked formally.

"Well, you see, it's like this. Alençon is not so large a town that all its inhabitants should not somehow be identified by someone. I'll make inquiries and find out who the stranger on the bridge really is!"

"But . . . . Be careful! Don't let on why you are interested. Think of Zelie's reputation, you hear?"

"Don't worry! I promise you I'll be on my guard."

3

IN THE DAYS that followed, Captain Guerin managed a casual inquiry here and there about a young man who lived in the vicinity of St. Leonard's bridge, dressed well and was about thirty years old. He soon learned from a friend that, undoubtedly, the gentleman referred to was none other than the expert watchmaker and jeweler, Mr. Louis Martin.

"Did you say he was a watchmaker?" prodded Captain Guerin.

"Yes, and there's none better in town, for this Martin studied watchmaking abroad. So, if it's a watch or a clock you want, go down to his store at 15 Pont-Neuf and you're sure to be well satisfied with your purchase. He does a jewelry trade, too."

"Well, well," came indifferently from Captain Guerin, careful to conceal any interest in the young man beyond his activities as a jeweler or watchmaker. After all, what would people think if they knew he was weighing the qualities of this stranger, this Louis Martin, as a possible future son-in-law?

From there on it was a simple matter for Guerin to find out all he cared to know about the watchmaker's personality, for almost everyone knew Martin, as people generally do a small-town merchant conducting a business in their midst. So it developed that he was single and lived quietly with his aged parents in the building where he conducted his jewelry trade.

Not long afterward, discreet arrangements were made with friends to invite a group of young people to a social, and thus it happened that Zelie Guerin was formally introduced to Louis Martin. From the first moment Zelie opened her lips to speak with him, her personality made a deep impression on him.

And as he studied the serene, compelling loveliness of her eyes with their depth of expression as she conversed with him, he knew this was the first time in his life that he was eager not to lose a single word that was said. In side glances he found himself appraising also her luxurious dark hair, the fairness of her complexion, and her winning smile. Louis, of course, recognized her at once as the girl he met and admired on the bridge as she passed him by, but he was too reserved to mention the incident. Moreover, something in Zelie's quiet manner prevented any discussion of the momentary, passing attraction they had both registered on that occasion.

In less than three weeks after their meeting on the bridge of St. Leonard, Louis Martin, tall and handsome, was calling on Zelie Guerin in the red brick house on St. Blaise. Forgetting his usual reticence, Louis soon found himself telling Zelie the story of his life.

"I always liked working with my hands," he was saying one Sunday afternoon. "Perhaps that's why I took up watchmaking."

"It's an excellent profession, Louis. And besides requiring skillful hands, it calls for specialized training, which means mental exertion. I heard you studied abroad."

"Well, I studied for two years in Strasbourg where I stayed at the home of a friend of my father's. Then I went to Paris where I studied watchmaking for three more years before I became what one might call a *fair* watchmaker."

"Fair? I think you're quite an expert. So does everybody else in Alençon."

The few measured words of praise coming from her meant more to him than any he could ever have received in the past.

"But why speak only of my watchmaking, Zelie?" he said, taking advantage of this opening to express his admiration for her. "You are the one who should be complimented on your skill, and for your artistic talents in lacemaking. All Alençon admires your work. And everybody says you have contributed a great deal towards reviving the lace industry for which the city is famous. Did it take you long to learn the art?"

"Two years of study" she answered. "But it's fully five years now that I've been in the lacemaking business." Zelie's face lit up with special enthusiasm whenever she spoke of point lace.

As a watchmaker, he understood and appreciated the skill required in the precise handling of minute objects. They seemed to have so much in common. Certainly, if skill and knowledge were needed to assemble the tiny and intricate mechanism going into the making of a fine timepiece, laces, such as Zelie manufactured, also called for it. But to achieve in this difficult artistic enterprise a prosperous industry and business, such as Zelie had, was unique. It not only attested to Zelie's rare ability but practicality in business matters, an affability and courtesy in dealing with various types of customers, and the art of satisfying them at every turn.

Zelie now picked up a small unfinished piece of lace and, as they spoke, began daintily pitting her shiny steel needle against the white fabric before her. Louis was quick to notice how flawless were the movements of her exquisite hands. Unconsciously he compared her with himself. How alike they were! How many years he had spent cultivating the deftness of his fingers which seemed now so much like hers, fashioning delicate lace. Zelie would indeed be the perfect life partner for him, he thought. Then, suddenly, analyzing his thoughts, he colored.

This was the very first time he had ever considered a partner in life. Marriage had never entered any of his deliberations. Everyone of his acquaintances in Alençon knew this, and Louis Martin knew it even better. He was thirty-four and settled permanently into a quiet and useful pattern of bachelorhood. He had his profession and his business. A good home with his aged parents, and the outdoors and fishing for recreation. And, most important to Louis Martin, there was his daily Mass, daily visits to the Blessed Sacrament, attendance at evening devotions when these were scheduled and good reading. All formed the religious background of a life, contributing toward a fullness of happiness that seemed complete to him. Louis Martin felt no lack, there was no need pressing him to alter his condition. Everything made for peace, security and contentment, and he was always quick to tell this to his mother, who from time to time diplomatically suggested the possibility of marrying and his settling down. "But I am settled, Mother," he invariably answered.

Yet now, watching Zelie's deft fingers delicately running over the snowy batiste, Louis — without any prodding from anyone — was musing over Zelie Guerin as one to share his life. Somehow he felt that marriage with Zelie promised him the hope of some higher goal. But, then, he knew Zelie only a few weeks, and he must not say anything now that he might later regret. However, even as he was considering the need for prudence, he knew, inwardly, that his future life was somehow indissolubly tied with that of Zelie.

On his next visit Louis again found himself exchanging confidences, telling her things never mentioned to anyone before.

"Zelie, there's something I'd like to tell you," he began, and laughed. He had caught himself laughing a great deal these days since he had made Zelie's acquaintance. "Would you believe me if I told you I became a watchmaker only as a second choice . . . ?"

"That's interesting. What was your first choice then, Louis?"

"If I tell you, I'm afraid you won't believe me."

"Why shouldn't I believe you?" she asked, smiling broadly.

"Well, it does sound rather incredible . . . ." he hedged.

"Suppose you leave that for me to decide. What was your first choice?"

"I had thought of becoming a Benedictine monk. I actually applied at the Monastery of St. Bernard when I was in Switzerland."

"Really? You wanted to become a priest?"

"Yes! I was twenty-two at the time."

"What happened?"

"Oh, I was turned down. The Prior told me I had to learn Latin before I could be admitted."

"But I don't understand. Why couldn't you learn Latin as a novice?"

"That's what I thought, too. Perhaps, it was a more gentle way of telling me I had no vocation. Anyhow, I took private lessons in Latin for quite a while, but later I dropped it and went back to watchmaking . . . ."

On hearing this Zelie felt she could hold out no longer. She confided to Louis how she, too, once longed so greatly to enter a convent, had applied, and was not admitted. Their dual disappointment tended to cement their future destiny.

At home that evening, when he had finished telling his mother all he knew and felt about Zelie, she lost no time in bringing the matter to a point.

"She is the girl for you, my son!"

"Yes, I know it, Mother."

"When will you ask her to marry you?"

"Don't you think it's still a little too soon? After all, we met only about two months ago . . . ?" he said anxiously.

"Nonsense! It is not too soon in your case. You are no child. You are past thirty-four, and Zelie's twenty-seven. You have waited long enough, and now that you have met your real partner, do not delay your marriage. It is high time you started out on your own. I have been praying and hoping for this day, son, and now that I know Zelie is the one, I am very happy. You will have a good wife and a happy home."

⁂

The following Sunday, when Louis again called on Zelie, she noticed at once that there was something important on his mind.

"Zelie, I'd like to take you over to my Pavilion this afternoon," he said as if preoccupied.

"And what is your Pavilion, Louis?"

"Oh, it's a nice strip of land on the outskirts of town which I bought some five years ago. It is neatly walled in, and in the center of the grounds there is a sort of narrow tower — a kind of shelter. It has been a favorite haunt of mine, especially on Sundays. During the summer, when the weather turns very hot, I take off from work and go out there to enjoy the out of doors. Since it's close to the river, I keep my fishing tackle there. Recently I planted a few nice fruit trees and built a small shrine to the Blessed Lady on my grounds. Now . . . will you come?"

Once at the Pavilion, Zelie realized it was everything a small private picnic ground should be. Some of the fruit was ripe and there was a rolling lawn shaded by two tall trees. At one end of the garden she noticed the statue of the Virgin standing on a pedestal, beaming gracefully and lending an air of peace to the scene.

"I brought you here to ask you to marry me, Zelie," Louis said without any other introduction to the subject. Swallowing deeply, Zelie quietly accepted.

"I ought to give you more time to make up your mind, I know, but as for me, Zelie, I am sure that I want nothing more in life than to marry you. I can't, of course, expect that you should be equally as sure as I am at this early date."

"But, Louis, I too am sure," she told him unhesitatingly, realizing that this was the proper time for her to reveal to him what happened on St. Leonard's bridge that first afternoon as they passed each other. "Furthermore, there is a very special reason why I am so sure about you, and now that you've proposed marriage and I have accepted, I feel I ought to tell you all about it . . . ."

Zelie started talking and was amazed all at once to see that it cost her nothing to shun her customary reserve and to initiate her betrothed into the secret of the voice on the bridge. Altogether unprepared for this turn of events, Louis listened with rapt attention to Zelie's story and its unexpected climax — in which he came into play as the principal figure in the drama . . . .

[19]

" . . . Then it was that I heard a distinct voice tell me, 'This is he whom I have prepared for you,' " she finally concluded.

For a few moments an indescribable stillness settled over the place so that Zelie's final sentence seemed to vibrate through the air, and remain suspended there as if carved in visible letters in the midst of space.

To him the knowledge of her mystical experience shed an entirely new and significant light on their whole future together. The next time he called on her, he begged her not to delay their wedding.

"Since you told me about the voice you heard, I feel more than ever that I don't deserve you. Yet I am convinced that God wants us to be joined in marriage and I hope you will select an early wedding date."

4

THE FOLLOWING MONTH, on July 13, 1858, after a short court-
ship of only three months, Zelie Guerin and Louis Martin were
joined in holy wedlock in the Parish Church of Notre Dame in
Alençon.

"Where will you make your home?" his neighbors asked
the groom.

"In my house on Pont-Neuf, together with my parents," answered Louis. "Zelie wants no change of residence at this
time."

Taking advantage of the weeks that yet remained to summer,
the newly married couple leisurely settled into their new pattern
of life together. They gave several dinner invitations to relatives,
and invited friends to their home on Pont-Neuf. They also
made excursions to the Pavilion, and went for long walks in
the country. Before the summer was over, Louis took his bride
for a short trip. He had always liked traveling and the prospect
of a visit to another city invariably appealed to him as thrilling and adventurous.

With September and its first spell of cool weather, Zelie was
eager to resume a more useful daily routine.

"Now that vacation time is over, Louis, I want to go back to
my work of making lace," she announced without ceremony
one morning after breakfast.

"By all means, Zelie. It will be an agreeable pastime for you,"
he answered, not attaching much significance to her remark.

"But, I don't intend making laces just as a pastime, Louis. I
plan to resume filling orders for laces and going on with my
business just as I did before we were married."

"But, Zelie, I don't want you to feel that you must work for an income, not now that you are married to me," he announced in the manner of a proud, young husband.

"That I know, Louis. You earn more than enough for us," she nodded with understanding. And the new bride was too competent a business woman not to realize that Louis, as a jeweler and expert watchmaker, could well provide for all that would be needed. She knew, moreover, that the financial standing of their new household was such that it promised security for the future. To begin with, her husband had a modest fortune of his own, part of which he had received from his parents and part from his earnings. In addition to the house, jewelry store and the summer cottage, Louis' bank account showed some $9,000 to his credit. Newly added to this was Zelie's contribution of $5,000, on the day of her marriage, $2,000 of which was dowry, and $3,000* representing her own savings during five years of lacemaking. From all indications the Martins were starting out well together, and it seemed certain that they would never know want.

If Zelie wanted to resume her lacemaking career at this time, she had high motives for doing so. "There will be many hours, Louis, and days, when I shall be glad to have something profitable to do. A woman is happiest when her hands are busy. I never imagined marriage would entitle me to a life of ease or indulgence. It seems I have added reasons for working now that I am married. With your mother helping at home, I have all the time in the world to sit at my parlor window and fill orders for lace. It will make me happy."

"Very well, dear. Just so that you understand I don't expect this of you at all!"

"I know you don't, Louis. It's my own idea entirely. Except, if I may add just one thing . . . ."

"What is that, Zelie?"

"Well, you know, the voice that once told me to make point lace has never told me to stop making it now that I am married," she finished with an amused smile.

*These figures must be multiplied many times in order to approximate their equivalence in today's currency. —*Publisher, 2005.*

Her husband smiled happily. "Go and do just as you wish, my Zelie. I shall never stand in your way . . . nor stop you from your lovely work."

*   *

There was so much to learn from Zelie's original outlook on life, her spontaneous enthusiasm, affectionate disposition, and her inclination toward the mystical, that Louis found his life filled with new and absorbing interests.

But what was most important to him was that from the very beginning of their marriage, he felt that he and his wife could continue the life of virginity which they so much esteemed. Such was his rare virtue at the age of thirty-five, when he became her husband, that he was most reluctant to part with his virginity. Handsome, educated, and in the prime of his manhood, Louis had been exposed to the usual temptations encountered in youth. In fact, he had had an added measure when he lived in Paris for three years to study watchmaking. But he faced and overcame these temptations by adhering strictly to his habit of frequent confession and Holy Communion.

So, for the present, he was happy to live in continency with Zelie who was equally satisfied to remain a virgin, for the love of God. They lived thus, retaining their virginity, for the first ten months of their married life. This was no spontaneous decision, but, with Louis, a planned way of life. In this, Zelie seemed completely at one with him. That his conduct was based on sound principles, in a notebook Louis copied down, at this time, certain passages from his spiritual reading, which served to confirm his views on chastity. It was titled "The Doctrine of the Catholic Church on the Sacrament of Matrimony."

"The bond which constitutes the Sacrament of Marriage is independent of its consummation. A striking proof of this truth is shown in the life of the Blessed Virgin and of Saint Joseph, for although they were truly married, they remained chaste and continent. Numerous saints have imitated them. Though married, they continued to live as virgins, limiting themselves to a chaste union of the heart. Such marriages had everything necessary to make them valid."

If Louis Martin had been deficient in Latin, he proved himself more than moderately proficient in spiritual science. With theological precision, he could elicit a judgment supported with proofs from Scripture, reason and tradition. But most remarkable about Louis Martin was his inherent modesty, which comes to light through the penned pages of his notebook. Not his the method of freely discussing intimate conscience matter with whomsoever! He confides his clear-cut decision regarding chastity to a hidden page in a notebook, meanwhile keeping his conversation with others high above any level that allowed room for the callous to introduce their indiscreet and objectionable opinions on so delicate a subject as virginity.

Then one day, two months before their first wedding anniversary, Louis and Zelie were talking about the days before their marriage. Opening her heart to him, she spontaneously told her husband of the yearning she had for children of her own. "After we were engaged, I used to pray that God would bless our marriage with many children, all of whom would be consecrated to His service. I even wrote about it to my sister at the convent . . . ."

It was out! Louis looked up surprised. But he was also gratified. "Did you say you used to pray that God might give us a large family of children?"

"Yes, I did, hoping, however, that they might *all* be someday consecrated to God!" she repeated. "Since both of us had once aspired to become religious and were not accepted, I had hoped God would give us many children who might spend their lives in His service."

The simplicity, faith and detachment revealed in Zelie's face as she spoke these words (destined to glorify church history), made, at once, a deep impression on Louis. He seemed unwilling to speak or think of anything save the possibility of the new and glowing future which her words had opened up.

"Zelie, let us go to Father Sertillanges and explain this plan of yours to him. Let us ask him if, after all, it would not be more in conformity with God's plan, that, as a married couple, we should raise a family!"

" . . . All of whom might one day be consecrated to God . . . ?" Zelie asked. But her voice had more the reverent tone of a prayer of petition than of mere human interrogation.

Father Sertillanges lost no time in endorsing the contemplated change. A new, hopeful horizon now loomed before them.

As the priest watched the couple go off toward their home on Pont-Neuf he realized that the Martins were indeed not only one pair in a million, but, perhaps, the *only* modern couple in the world who, after nearly a year of married life spent in continency, were now prepared to change their lives for the sole purpose of bearing children all to be consecrated to the service of God.

(In the light of twentieth-century indulgence and excess, culminating in unprecedented separations and divorces; in the light of shifting responsibilities attendant on providing the needs of the family — or avoiding children altogether — the Martins were indeed the most *un*predictable. Sophists might well smile wryly at their "puerility" and the know-it-alls nod with complacent tolerance. But the fact was that the Martins of Alençon had now begun to blaze a trail that was to immortalize their heroic deeds and singular virtues.)

In February of 1860, their first child, a girl, was born.

"What will you name her," asked a friend, "or haven't you decided yet?"

"Oh, yes, we've decided the first name of all the children God may be pleased to give us!" answered Louis.

"You have?"

"Yes, it will be Marie, in honor of the Holy Virgin. Our first child will, therefore, be named Marie Louise."

Shortly after, calling at the rectory to make out the baptismal record, Louis Martin said, "Father, this is the first time you see me here for a baptism. But, I assure you, it will not be the last. From now on you will see me here frequently!"

The ideal proposed by Zelie, and endorsed by Father Sertillanges, namely, a family of children who were *all* to be dedicated to God's service, became a shining beacon for Louis and Zelie Martin — nor were they to be disappointed.

When Marie was two and one-half years old, she was presented with a baby sister, whom they named Pauline. The following year a third child, Leonie, was born, and the year after that a fourth daughter, Helene, was welcomed into the family circle. The Martins now had four lovely little girls, ranging from Marie, the eldest, aged four years and eight months, Pauline aged two years, Leonie not quite ten months, and Helene, the newly baptized infant.

As a virtuoso skilled in gems, it was natural for Louis soon to begin comparing his children to the precious stones he handled in his velvet-lined jewelry cases. Marie, the eldest, was of course a priceless diamond, and Pauline became the precious pearl. As for the two little ones, still in their cradles, he had, perforce, to wait a while before he found appropriate nicknames. If love and devotion were the primary qualities of a father, Louis certainly had them. At home, beside his wife and in the midst of his children, he found a peace and contentment which he would not have exchanged for any other society in the world.

Some of his friends, noting his fast-growing family, felt obliged on this point to offer him advice.

"Why don't you arrange to open your jewelry store for a few hours on Sundays, especially now that you have such a large family to provide for?"

"Well, I'll tell you, my friend, my little Helene's milk bill is not so huge an expenditure that I should be unable to meet it working six days a week. We'll get along . . . ."

"Evidently you still think it wrong to open your store on Sundays, don't you, Louis?" further this anxious neighbor pressed; but receiving only a smile in return, he continued, "I assure you most of us merchants in town do keep open for a while, because on Sunday folks come into town from the country, and if you stay open, you're right in line for some brisk business. I know, Louis, because I'm always open for a while on Sundays and I've learned from experience it pays off well. Besides, I asked the priest about it in confidence, and he told me the extenuating circumstances were such that I could be dispensed. So you see, it's perfectly all right. That's why you could at least keep a side door conveniently opened, so customers could saunter in. Let me assure you it is not a sin. You can ask your Father Confessor . . . ."

"I did ask him."

"And what did he say?"

"Just what you say!"

"Well, there you are! Then you'll open on Sundays . . . for a while? Eh, Louis?"

"No! I prefer, you see, to have God's blessing by keeping the Lord's Day holy."

So it was with Louis Martin.

One evening two years later, after work, Zelie greeted her husband with the proposal that they all unite to make a special novena.

"I was thinking how wonderful it would be if we only had a boy in the family who might some day become a priest — maybe even a missionary. So I decided that you and I and the children should begin a novena asking Our Lord for a son."

"Oh, yes, Papa, we want to pray for a little brother who might become a priest," echoed Marie who was now six, and then Pauline after her, who was about four.

Louis was unable to repress a smile. He could not help recalling the solicitous friend who only recently admonished him to keep his store open on Sundays as a sort of final alternative to preserve his growing family from the disaster of encroaching poverty. Evidently no such worry over money matters clouded the outlook of Zelie, his wife. She was already thinking of another child, a possible son this time, who could become a priest. But then Zelie, who kept the family accounts, and knew as well as he did the secure foundation of their household, could hardly be expected to harbor the anxieties of his solicitous neighbor.

As for Louis, he felt the merchant's unhealthy enthusiasm for Sunday business — as a last resort of escaping bankruptcy — in itself seemed a serious indictment of the man's economics. Something was indeed remiss if a man could not provide for his family by working six days a week. Moreover, to Louis, God's Third Commandment: *Remember thou shalt keep holy the Lord's day*, seemed to have a special significance. To his mind, the very word "Remember" seemed to add a tone of singular warning since to no other of the remaining nine commandments did God attach this word of caution — only to the Third . . . .

Yet a merchant, Louis reflected, had appointed himself an adviser, and, under the pretext of advising prudence, cautioned the jeweler that he, too, ought to keep his store open. Louis was never able to forget dreading hearing the merchant say, with such apparent flippancy, "Louis . . . I learned from experience that it pays off well." He always felt like answering: "As for me, dear friend, I *never* stay open on Sundays and *I* learned from experience that *it* pays off well." But knowing how difficult it was to make others understand his point of view, he would say nothing.

As for himself, Louis had had ample opportunity to learn from experience the rewards that came as visible blessings for keeping the Lord's Day holy. To be sure his wife and he had always exercised only ordinary, human means of getting ahead, utilizing modern methods of achieving success. Considering their industriousness and uncommonly sound judgment in business matters, their prosperity was not surprising. As a watchmaker always on the job, his excellent service earned him a steady increase of customers. Zelie, unwilling to abandon her money-raising project, found ways of surmounting every difficulty to keep up her business, despite the fact that in their eight years together four children had been added to the family. From her substantial earnings she was able to pay for domestic help, which permitted additional hours of remunerative work with her needle. Seated at the front window of her parlor, stitching lace, she was, moreover, always on hand to survey what transpired in her home and insure its smooth and tranquil upkeep.

From the combined commerce of so hard-working and hustling a couple, enough abundance followed as a normal consequence. According to all prudent standards of normal, gradual progress, the Martins knew that during the eight years they had prospered very well. Outside of the real estate at their marriage, besides their modest fortune of some $15,000* when they first fused their savings and dowry, now Zelie and Louis were gratified that their bank account showed they had tripled their initial wealth.

But if there was more than ordinary financial security in the house on Pont-Neuf, this never tended to unsettle the family's equilibrium, nor make them ostentatious. They managed to keep the knowledge of their domestic prosperity to themselves. They continued in the same house Louis owned when they married, and outside of a few pieces of tasteful new furniture bought for their needs from time to time, and the well-made clothes worn by the family, especially for the High Mass on Sundays, no one ever suspected how graciously the Martins had prospered.

But, then, neither could the ordinary run of people suspect what tireless and sustained efforts Louis and Zelie made to achieve the well-being of their home, nor the price in heroic virtue these efforts had cost — from which lesser heroes would have shrunk with repugnance. With the Martins, their home's security and happiness was the consequence of their unique plan of family life, earned as the direct blessing of God. Zelie was

*See footnote on p. 22. —*Publisher*, 2005.

a member of the Third Order of St. Francis, whose set purpose kept the spirit of poverty keenly alive in their home. This, not only by her constant fidelity to manual labor, in the spirit of the poor who must earn a living, but in her observing all the fasts of the Church despite the fact that her health was never robust.

From this faithful keeping of the Church's laws of fasting and abstinence, Zelie and her husband, carefully measuring their allotted meatless food — particularly during the seven weeks of Lent — learned how well they could get along on what *was* allowed. Of their household it could be truly said that in their family circle there was waged an endless war on idleness, and on waste in eating and drinking. Adopting the regimen of moderation, they prospered materially, and spiritually came away fired with lofty ideals.

So, now that his wife, and his children, pressed him to join in a novena to storm heaven for a son — who might some day become a priest — Louis counted himself indeed privileged to head such a family.

When, in the fall of that year, Helene was obliged to relinquish her place of honor as the baby to a new-born brother, named Joseph, the happiness of the Martins knew no bounds. Five months later, however, Joseph took ill and died. This was the first real sorrow to mar the happy home life of Zelie and Louis, now experiencing the poignant grief of burying their own child.

Resigning themselves, they again prayed — for another son, to replace the one they had lost. They might still have a boy who would become a priest, they hoped. And again their joy burned brightly when, the following year, another son was born. Him they named John. For a few months all went well; then this one, too, became ill and died — when he was only eight months old.

The Martins saw in this the manifestation of God's will. Zelie vowed never again to pray for a son. She would indeed be grateful for the children it would please God to send them, but never seek her own will by asking for a son, even from the motive of hoping to see him at the altar. No, neither Louis nor Zelie prayed for a son again. They would still cherish and desire children — all to be consecrated to God's service — but would never show any preference for either a boy or a girl.

5

It was natural for Zelie to now turn with increased devotedness to Helene who, at three, was still the baby in the family. Moreover, there was always something indefinable about the child, a rare kind of sweetness and charm which, as Zelie put it, seemed not of this world.

Looking into its blue eyes, she invariably recalled that pleasurable occasion when Helene, as an infant in the cradle, for the first time recognized her mother as apart from the rest. Looking up, the child had smiled with such a profound depth of meaning that Zelie was never to forget the thrill of joy this experience had brought her.

In fact, she always was embarrassed when her brother Isidore, who was now a pharmacist in Lisieux, playfully teased her with a letter he had received in which Zelie described the exceptional charms of Helene. It was true. She had. The letter was there to prove it — "Little Helene is a lovely jewel. I cannot realize that I have the honor of being the mother of such a charming creature. I don't remember ever having felt such a surge of happiness as when I picked her up and she smiled at me. I felt I was looking at an angel. I cannot express what I felt. I believe that no one has ever seen or ever will see such a charming little girl . . . ."

It was no wonder that Isidore, himself the father of a little girl, should be amused at the ardor of his sister's effusion about Helene's charms. Protesting mildly, Zelie would insist that her unrestrained praise in the letter was based on an extraordinary experience. "I tell you, Isidore, I felt I was looking at an Angel . . . ." she'd insist. Then, always, noting her embarrassment, Isidore would genially give in. But he really never pretended to understand the intensity of Zelie's reactions, nor was he ever able to grasp what she had caught in her baby's disarming smile that defied her powers of description. Not until that fateful day in the spring of 1869 when such dreadfully conflicting news came from Alençon.

The Martins had just attended the baptism of their newly born daughter, Celine, thrilled with the advent of another child. But hardly had Celine, strong and robust, made her presence felt at 15 Pont-Neuf, than God required a tremendous sacrifice. Helene, whose lovable personality was so keenly discerned even in infancy, took violently sick, and she died within a few days. She was four and a half years old.

When Isidore Guerin learned of his sister's grief he buried his face in his hands, in deep thought. Now it became clear to him why the infant had appeared to her mother as an angel the day she smiled to Zelie for the first time from the cradle. Now Isidore understood why Zelie felt that exceptional surge of happiness on picking her up and receiving that smile so like a creature of another world. Perhaps, in that brief moment, looking at her smiling child and avowing she had never seen nor ever hoped to see such a charming little girl again, the mother had been granted a rare favor, a future glimpse of Helene's soul as one of Heaven's blessed. Isidore, like the rest of the family, by now knew that Zelie was gifted with the grace of a mystical nature. They accepted it as a matter of fact. There was the "voice" she had heard, urging her to do lacemaking— which became her life's occupation. She was also told by a "voice" who her husband was to be, although she did not even know his name. And now her brother felt that Helene's rapturous smile, which had stirred Zelie with such marvelous emotion, indicated in a singular way, beforehand, that this child of special predilection would take an early flight to Heaven.

But if the devoted and religious uncle could discern the mystical in the circumstances surrounding the death of his four-year-old niece, for the parents there was only the consciousness of a grim and dread loss. Louis, who had mourned the burial of their two infant sons, now knew that it was a far more excessive grief to bury a daughter of nearly five. But on seeing Zelie pale and worn he learned to forget this sorrow and hastened to console her.

"Stop grieving. Helene is happy in Heaven, praising God. You know that. You are the spiritual giant in our family. It is not like you to pine . . . ."

It was true, Zelie agreed. They must be resigned, and, for the sake of the family's welfare, allow their grief to be assuaged by remembering that they still had four living children.

When, during the succeeding weeks the infant, Celine, with her arresting dark eyes began to weave her spell of charms on the family circle, Zelie soon found herself smiling, and her life full.

But perhaps nothing contributed more to jolt her into her usual serenity and cheerfulness than an incident which occurred when she chanced to meet a neighbor in a street of the town.

As a whole, nearly everyone who knew the Martins showed them a great deal of respect and even fondness. Among their business acquaintances — as in their social group — they were very well liked. But it was inevitable that there should also be a few who, partly from envy at their prosperity and happy family life, should seek occasion to inject something unpleasant. Meeting Zelie on the street, the neighbor under pretense of sympathy opened the conversation:

"It is so good to see you out again, Madame Martin."

"Thank you, Madame," answered Zelie.

"Permit me to tell you how sorry I was to hear of your misfortune. It was really sad to learn about your little ones dying that way . . . ."

Zelie looked up, conscious of a peculiar insinuation, but she only said, "Well, we must be resigned. Besides we still have four nice little girls to look after, who make us very happy."

The neighbor, feeling cheated by Zelie's quiet reply of resignation, hastened to make a second try to steer the conversation into an unpleasant channel, and thereby place the bereaved mother at a disadvantage. "But, still, all those three children dying that way . . . . It seemed something awful to us when we heard it. In fact, I was saying to my husband that perhaps it would have been better for you if you had never had all those children . . . ."

And this was just the jolt Zelie needed to restore her to that perfect state of balance from which she felt she would never again be unsettled, neither by a death or other trial. The idea that an outsider should take it on herself to arbitrate directly to her face as to what was best for the private life of the Martin family, how many children it was good for them to have, and whether it would have been better not to have had them at all — rather than to lose them through death — produced in Zelie, that moment, a fighting reaction for Life. The meddling neighbor had not been solicited to offer any sympathy in behalf of her dead children, nor to lend any assistance in behalf of her living ones. She and her husband had always managed very competently to shoulder all their family responsibilities, and Zelie now intended to bring this vital information to the attention of the lady meddler standing before her.

"Madame, just what are you alluding to?" Zelie asked, not attempting to cover her annoyance. Recognizing a tone of indignation in Zelie's voice, the woman saw her mistake, and was ready to retreat before it was too late.

"Oh, I didn't mean anything. I only mentioned that it was sad about your children dying . . . ."

"You also said, if I remember well, that you told your husband you thought it would have been better for us never to have had those children."

"Well yes, I did say —"

"Never mind repeating it, Madame, and, what is more, be careful never to say such a thing to me again in your life. Remember, people can marry and hope for children, but only God can create them and give them to parents . . . . And who are you to pose your questionable theories between God and His deeds of creation? . . . Who are you to question or disparage God's wisdom where the destiny of immortal souls is at stake? I am, indeed, amazed to learn that you and your husband should find it opportune to discuss between yourselves how many children my husband and I should or should not have. Surely, you don't ever expect to be consulted on the matter, do you? Really, Madame, your intrusion into our family affairs is deeply resented, to say the least!"

"But I meant no offense, believe me," the woman parried, trying to excuse herself. "I simply wanted to say that it was *too bad* about your children dying . . . ."

"It was *not* 'too bad,' Madame. Nothing that God does is ever 'too bad.' What *we* often do, however, is very bad . . . too bad to even mention!"

"I see you are annoyed with me, when, as a matter of fact, I had no intention of doing anything wrong," came the further excuse. But, even as she was talking, she knew very well that she had purposely introduced this topic to wound Zelie Martin by putting her at a disadvantage, in exposing someone who was not, after all, too much of a success, and, perhaps, even somewhat worse off than many others. But seeing her defensive position entirely crumbled by Zelie's logical replies, she sought for shelter in a new position.

"I suppose there is no use in my trying to explain, for you're determined not to hear my point of view," she complained, assuming the role of one hurt.

"On the contrary, if you do have a justifiable explanation, I am ready to stay here all afternoon to hear you out. Nothing would give me greater pleasure than to learn that I misunderstood you."

"That's just it, Madame. You misunderstood me," she repeated, catching at it desperately, like a drowning man at a straw.

"Then go on and explain. I shall be very happy to apologize."

"Well, I only meant to say that having children and rearing them is not only a joy, but it also entails work and suffering.

And now since three of your children died off that way, I was thinking it was a shame you had to suffer all that for *nothing*."

" '*For nothing*,' did you say?"

"Yes. Since they are gone, certainly all that suffering was for *nothing* . . . . Wasn't it?"

"But you are more mistaken than ever, Madame. My sufferings were not for *nothing*. The fact is that the few temporary anxieties and pains which I endured can never be compared with the eternal happiness of my little ones in Heaven . . . . Good day, Madame!" Zelie finished. Then she turned and walked away, leaving the neighbor staring after her, and not realizing exactly what had happened that she should have deserved to be so unmistakably scolded by the jeweler's wife whom everybody regarded as a person of quiet, retiring and generally cordial manners.

That evening Madame Martin seemed so happy, and even radiant with joy, that her husband noticed it.

"You are getting younger every day, Zelie."

"The children make me that way. They really *do* amuse me, at times."

"I think it is something more than the children, if you ask me," he remarked, throwing her a knowing glance.

"Well, maybe you're right at that, but the children had a lot to do with it," she countered, and Louis, noting a concealed irony in her voice and a witty look stealing into her eyes, shook his head. There were things about Zelie he would never learn if he lived with her a hundred years! She was indeed apt to turn up with a surprise or two, and always when one least expected it. Taking advantage of the first chance moment alone together, when the children went off to the garden, Zelie told her husband the story of the meddling neighbor.

"Zelie, I am amazed at you! Did you really tell that woman off that way?"

"Of course I did . . . . And I never enjoyed anything more . . . . And, besides, I never felt so happy over anything after, as

I did over that. Somehow, I found myself! After refuting her foolish remarks, I came to realize in a very special way how good God has been to us, and how much we have to be grateful for in our married life. Not only for the four children we have still with us here, but also for the three little ones who are now praying for us in Heaven—and who are for all eternity to enjoy the sight of God."

The following day, when Zelie went to her usual place to kneel for a while before a statue of the Virgin which they had placed on a pedestal, she unconsciously found herself thinking of what she had said to Louis about their three children being happy in Heaven. Suddenly she felt a doubt asserting itself in her mind. As for the two boys who died in infancy, it was certain they were there; but what about Helene who was nearly five when she passed away?

Could she be sure that she had gone straight to Heaven?

In her subconscious mind Zelie always remembered one particular incident connected with Helene which gave her a feeling of anxiety, and now this buried memory burst suddenly upon her in all its unmistakable reality. She now remembered every detail of it: the incident when she caught little Helene telling a small lie. The tiny misdemeanor loomed before her like some fearful specter, and Zelie suddenly felt very sick at heart. True, she had promptly punished her child for the fault. But who knows the strict judgments of God? Perhaps her Helene was at present suffering the fires of purgatory? All her joy had been bred from the hope that their whole family life was one of happiness in God — their four living children safe with them at home, and their three departed ones rapturously happy in Heaven; yet now the doubt about Helene struck dread terror in her heart.

Zelie could hardly bear the thought, and so, steeped in black anxiety, she began to pray as she knelt before the Virgin's statue. Then, suddenly, she was aware of something marvelous. Seeming to come from the direction of the statue, Zelie distinctly heard the following words: *Helene is here with me.*

Her lips parted in a grateful smile. She felt that she had just been granted another of her mystical favors, and at a time when it meant everything in the world to her. Helene was also in Heaven! She had been assured.

6

THE FOLLOWING SUMMER, in July of 1870, war broke out between France and Prussia. Three short months later, Prussian military penetration into France proved to Frenchmen on the home-front that the enemy was obviously prepared for every step of the conflict, in marked contrast to themselves. Successive war bulletins told them all too clearly that France was fast losing the struggle. Dazed French magistracies now regretted the money they had squandered, and deprecated their military unpreparedness.

In the meantime Bismarck's victorious divisions marched steadily on. Nothing was lacking to his huge war machine purchased by a strategically planned thriftiness and an enforced labor movement imposed on the German people at the cost of untold privations to their home life.

Nor did the Prussian Army resort to looting the nation they were conquering, for their plans, laid well in advance, were directed toward a more profitable objective than mere spoils plundered through the primitive device of looting. It was only a matter of months till France would be brought to her knees. Then, as conquerors, the Prussians would name the price of the tribute of victory and exact it from Frenchmen who only a short while before felt unable to afford the most basic war matériel indispensable to insure their national self-preservation. How would they fare when, conquered, they would be forced to pay Prussia for war indemnities?

Frenchmen in administrative posts preferred for the time being to escape considering what military disaster would mean to the nation for whose well-being they were responsible. On the other hand, the people of France, taking a realistic view of the war, felt there was no time to waste on profitless fault-finding, either of the enemy or their own government officials. The war, with its horrid consequences, had touched their homes, spilling French blood. Husbands were killed, sons and brothers were cruelly maimed, and otherwise the peace of thousands of homes in cities and in villages was in some way or other directly affected by the conflict.

Louis and Zelie from the very beginning had felt that a great peril had befallen Europe with the outbreak of the Franco-Prussian War. With the advantage of more than average education, and moreover, with their deep religious insight, they grappled with the basic problems which entered into the war. Surely, millions of Frenchmen as well as Germans were Catholics, and *their* faith had not produced the ill-fruits of hatred and its resulting war. They felt that only materialism breeds struggle. Faith always expresses itself in love. It was impossible to believe that millions of persons in different countries, united in a bond of charity through their Christian faith, and their Christian lives, should be locked in a death struggle with each other through any fault of their own. There were families in the enemy camp who were much like the Martins in Normandy, yet by some force of circumstance, unscrupulous and misguided rulers, bent on aggression, had plotted their strategic moves to instigate war.

The Martins were not pacifists. They would have been the last family in France to accept "peace at any price." There were certain priceless things in life for which they would have willingly fought and died. Zelie and Louis deemed their liberty to exercise their faith, as chief among those priceless entities for which they would unhesitatingly sacrifice their mere physical well-being.

True, at the time, there seemed to be no question of any threat to the religious liberties of Europeans. The Franco-Prussian War seemed, on the surface, just like any other war that came to Europe from time to time during hundreds of years in the past. Neither could the Martins be expected to see, in 1870, the repercussions to all humanity from its aftermath, although their off-spring was to witness deeds of horror following close in its wake.

Yet it is important to note that Zelie and Louis, as did thousands of religious Frenchmen, sensing, as it were, a dawn of doom, began to hope for deliverance aside from that which they knew was not to be anticipated through any stroke of French military prowess. In one final gesture of trust in the power of prayer, they now turned their eyes to Bernadette, the seeress of Lourdes, to hold off military disaster for France. Could the nun of twenty-six, whose name was a household word throughout Europe, save her country from conquest?

Frenchmen now hoped against hope that she could and would . . . . Zelie and Louis were among these until that fateful day when news reached Alençon that Prussian troops were already inside the city of Nevers, where Sister Bernarde was stationed at the Motherhouse. Louis took a grim view of the situation and made no attempt to conceal his disquiet.

"Zelie, there is bad news from Nevers," he announced, rushing into the parlor to acquaint her with the latest development on the front.

"How bad?"

"The Prussians have occupied the city."

"Oh, Bernadette did not save us . . . ." moaned Zelie, tears gathering in her eyes. "Are there any details about her?"

"Yes. Reports are that our commandant went to the Motherhouse and asked to speak with Bernadette. He said: 'Sister, the Prussians are now at the gates of our city. Tell me, are you not afraid?' "

"And what did Bernadette say?"

"She answered: 'Sir, I fear only bad Catholics!' "

"Oh Saviour, have pity on France," cried Zelie. For a while neither spoke and only the clock on the wall ticked away loud seconds. Zelie was unwilling to say more in the presence of the children who stood around listening. Marie aged ten, and Pauline eight, could sense bad news and would worry over it.

But on retiring that night, Zelie picked up the thread of their conversation.

"What do you suppose Sister Bernadette meant when she told the commandant that she feared only bad Catholics?"

"I don't know. It is a very difficult matter to understand."

"But I think I have an explanation. She must have meant that if Catholics as a whole kept the laws of God and served Him as they should, they would bring about many conversions and also establish a sort of balance between good and bad. In this way the evil deeds of the erring and misguided would be counteracted by the good deeds of the right-living. But, when Catholics themselves— who know better — join the ranks of those who through ignorance offend and abuse God's laws, what can even a living Saint like Bernadette do?"

"You seem to explain this very well, Zelie. Surely, war is a punishment for sin. Good Catholics could avert it by serving God as they've been taught. Evidently that is the conclusion the saintly Bernadette came to draw for us."

That night Louis reflected that the Church counts on the prayers and merits of the good within her fold, but when an overwhelming number of Catholics remain indifferent to God, then even a Saint or a small group of devout Christians here and there are quite powerless to stay the hand of God. No, Bernadette was not able to avert military disaster for her country. Evidently too many wills opposed hers. The scales of justice were not balanced, and so it befell that the war broke out and many of the good had to suffer along with the bad.

A few days later, French resistance everywhere continuing to decline, Prussian occupation troops were seen marching into peaceful Alençon. Making a hurried survey of the town, the captain soon enough found his way to the house at 15 Pont-Neuf to acquaint Louis Martin with the requirements of the Prussian billeting program.

"Your residence shall quarter nine Prussian soldiers. You will see to it that they are well provided with food and shelter."

The Martin children looked on frightened as they saw nine men in strange uniforms make themselves at home in their house — the war had indeed come to the family fireside.

Louis soon learned how unbearably long a day can be when lived under foreign domination, and he watched with suspicion the nine soldiers in the house eating his food and sharing his roof. Then, one day, coming into his store, he caught one of the stocky soldiers making off with a small tray of jewelry from his counter. Seizing his arm, Louis escorted the German to the occupation headquarters to report the offense.

But when he returned home finally and told Zelie what had happened and how he settled the matter, she was almost frantic.

"Louis, you shouldn't have done that!'

"But why? Soldiers are forbidden to steal. If I allowed him to get away with this, the town might soon be overrun with other crimes, and there might be no end of it . . . ." he started to explain. But he stopped when saw his wife, in a gesture of hopelessness, cover her face with the lace on which she was working. "But did I do something wrong, Zelie?" he asked worriedly.

"Yes, Louis, you did, and you must undo it at once," she said, announcing that only the day before she had heard that the Prussian commandant had had one of his own soldiers shot because he had been caught stealing some merchandise of practically no value. Louis needed no further explanation. Catching his hat, he fled from the parlor out into the street, and ran all the way until he again arrived at the Prussian commandant's police headquarters. Breathless, he begged to speak to the captain.

"Yes, Mr. Martin, what can I do for you?" the captain asked, puzzled to see him back so soon.

Louis, visibly perturbed, began to plead in behalf of the soldier under arrest. He interceded so earnestly and convincingly that the captain felt constrained to yield.

"Well, you are the one who reported the soldier. If you now say that you want to withdraw your charges, I suppose there is no further reason to hold him. Sign these papers and we will consider the case closed."

The papers signed, the soldier was ordered released, and Louis, obviously worn out from the ordeal, returned home.

But it took fully two weeks for Zelie to recover sufficiently from the shock to be able to speak of the near-tragedy without fear.

"Just think how horrid war is! Here in Alençon we have seen them shoot one of their own soldiers because in a moment of weakness he stole some trinket. Maybe the unfortunate man had a family? He could have repented for his fault . . . and gone on living, serving God and man. Instead he is dead. Dead at the hands of his own comrades. It is too dreadful . . . ." groaned Zelie.

"Yes, really, there is no greater punishment than war. Who can ever count the victims?" agreed Louis, wondering, as he studied his wife, whether the Franco-Prussian War would not also have claimed her among its fatalities if the soldier who had stolen from their store had not been released but shot also like that other.

Two long weeks later, the French saw the utter futility of resistance with hastily ill-outfitted garrisons against the offensives of an enemy who had every available means of modern warfare down to detailed maps of their terrain, and even explicit marching orders. Then Napoleon III surrendered and left France, never to return.

While the conquered French awaited the terms of peace, the Prussian diplomat Bismarck set in motion his plan of strategy that was to change drastically the map of Europe. The first step came in the form of the officially announced peace terms which Bismarck had drawn up for France, which was waiting in grave suspense. To Bismarck the winning of the war would be a conquest only if it brought the reward of territorial annexation. Therefore, in addition to exacting from the French one billion dollars in gold as indemnity for losing the war, Bismarck demanded that the French cede their two large provinces of Alsace and Lorraine.

It seemed an exorbitant price for losing a war that lasted five months, was waged on French soil, and with minimum casualties to a Prussia singularly well prepared for it in advance.

On learning the bitter news, Louis rushed home to acquaint his family with the tragic developments.

"Bismarck just announced the peace terms, Zelie. They are fearful!" he fairly shouted, in a husky voice.

"What are they?"

"A billion dollars in gold plus Alsace and Lorraine!"

"You mean, you mean we must give Prussia our French territory?"

"Yes, all of Alsace and Lorraine. Nearly one tenth of the territory of France itself," he answered gravely.

"What an *unjust* tithe!" Zelie could not avoid the Scriptural allusion. It seemed so wryly fitting. "What do you think will come of this?"

"Nothing good, I'm afraid. This shuffling of national boundaries is bound only to bring trouble between nations."

" . . . And suffering to many French families living in Alsace and Lorraine," added Zelie, her womanly insight grasping at the problems of home life.

"Family welfare, Zelie, means very little to men with a flare for power. Don't forget, my dear, that for some ninety years past the Prussian regime has continued to dominate a third of Poland, with no qualms as to the welfare or likes of the Polish people whom it despotically subjugated."

"Yes, you're right. Poland has disappeared from the map of Europe."

"Swallowed up by three foreign powers, Russia, Austria and Prussia, each of which annexed a third of her land and continue to hold it as a pawn of their greed."

For a while the two were quiet. Then Louis resumed, "But think, now, of this new aggression, Zelie. Prussia already swelled to overflowing with the looted ground of Poland, a third of which she now claims as her own, reaches out for a tenth of France through Bismarck's infamous peace terms. This momentous shifting of power in its favor can brew nothing good for the world."

The private family discussion at 15 Pont-Neuf, conceived in the logic of the moral law, and not the opportunist logic of history, which became for contemporary unscrupulous leaders the norm of judging, contained the solution to many of the basic problems at stake. Surely, the inglorious partition of a country like Poland, rated as one of the six major powers of Europe, and its absorption by foreign nations — if perpetuated — could but give rise to the plotting of similar aggressions reaching world proportions.

Some days later came more world-shattering news. Actually it seemed to Louis that some ominous plan foreseen by nobody had been set into motion, and it looked as if no one could halt its destructive advance.

"Zelie, the whole world as we knew it seems to be crumbling," he said hopelessly.

"What do you mean? Surely, it can't be that bad."

"But it is. Bismarck just made another move to add more territory . . .!"

"Besides one third of Poland which they already have, and the tenth of France just taken by annexing Alsace and Lorraine?"

"Yes, in addition to that . . . ."

"But how? Surely, they haven't won *another* war somewhere?"

"Oh, no, it was not by any military stroke that they maneuvered to get their latest territorial booty," said Louis, going on to explain Bismarck's most recent land gains which were calculated to follow immediately on Prussia's annexation of Alsace and Lorraine — since he had planned it that way. It now developed that the small Germanic states, like Bavaria and Saxony, impressed by Prussia's sudden rise to power through her latest acquisitions in France, felt the time was ripe to capitalize on a situation that would offer them strategic advantages: they unanimously volunteered to join their lands with that of enlarged Prussia to form one Great German Empire.

However, the real truth was that Bismarck had for many years kept a watchful eye on the neighboring small Germanic states with the intention of annexing them to Prussia to form one powerful German State. With this in mind he had spent many years influencing the Germanic princes ruling these states to get them to see the strategic material gains, and prestige, that would accrue to them from the proposed national merger. In due time Bismarck was convinced that the small sovereigns could be counted on to agree to his plan of fusing with Prussia when the opportunity presented itself. He had but to bide his time and await the propitious moment.

And now that their hereditary foe, the French, had suffered swift and crushing defeat from Prussian troops, the Germanic princes made that historic overture to merge with Prussia. King Ludwig of Bavaria took the initiative in the momentous bargain, by writing a circular letter to the several sovereigns of the lesser states.

Louis adjusted his glasses and began to read from the bulletin before him while Zelie listened attentively:

"Most serene and powerful Prince, dear Friend, Brother and Cousin — Victoriously led by Prussia's heroic King, the German tribes who for centuries have been united in language, manners, science and art, now celebrate a brotherhood of arms. We now have glorious proof showing how important it is for us to merge our lands with Prussia in order to form a united Germany. I, therefore, address myself to you, the German Sovereigns, and I propose that you should together with me urge the King of Prussia to exercise over us full presidential rights. Moreover, I urge that he should now be given the title Emperor, etc. [Signed] Ludwig, King of Bavaria."

Louis looked up from the paper. "Now, Zelie," he said, "you can see that this letter is designed to give the impression that no Prussian coercion has been exercised over the Germanic rulers to join Prussia . . . . "

"Yes, it is made to look as if the small German rulers voluntarily wish to fuse their lands with Prussia on the grounds that they speak the same language, and share the same customs and art . . . ." she answered thoughtfully.

"Right, and I say, very well then, if Prussia deems it just to annex these countries because they speak the same language and share the same customs as she, then by the same logic, let Prussia make a gesture to return their third of plundered Poland to the Polish people with whom the Prussians have nothing in common — neither as to language, customs, culture nor religious aspirations." Louis paused and moved his chair up closer to the table. "Moreover," he added, "by the same token, let Bismarck restore Alsace and Lorraine to the French, because neither do we claim anything in common with the Prussians in language, customs or culture . . . ."

Zelie shook her head helplessly. To her it seemed that all differences could be resolved in the light of logic, and the moral law. "About that letter," she said, "which the King of Bavaria sent, is there any further news on its developments?"

"But of course. Let me read you the address the King of Prussia made to the German armies in consequence of this initial move of the Bavarian ruler. Ah, here it is . . . : 'On this day ever memorable to me and my House, I take with the consent of the German princes and the German people in addition to my rank as King of Prussia that of German Emperor. Let it always be remembered that brotherly feeling, bravery and obedience have rendered the army victorious . . .!' "

A few weeks later the drastic changes introduced by Bismarck became history. William of Prussia was no longer a petty king. He had become *Kaiser* Wilhelm, the First Emperor of the new German Empire. And so, virtually overnight, the whole balance of power in Europe swerved overwhelmingly in the direction of Germany.

Unfortunately, this period in world history witnessed such momentous changes that these were never quite assimilated and not without serious repercussions. Geographically and nationally, civilization had attained a state of vigorous maturity and ripeness which could not tolerate such abuses.

In Europe given peoples and given nations had each developed their special habits, languages, customs, culture and religious temperament to such a degree that each was marked with its own distinguishing characteristics. These particular groups had, moreover, during the centuries, come to inhabit definitely localized territories, with clearly delineated boundaries.

And soon, progress, peace and security came to be closely associated with the safeguarding of these national identities. But after one of Europe's six largest independent nations, Poland, which was unsettled temporarily by internal strife, became a pawn of Prussia, Austria and Russia, and was divided among themselves into three sections, then modern history witnessed a violent plunge into chaos. This was inevitable. A people such as the Poles, with its own rare culture and history, its unique religious temperament, could never be dissolved without world-shattering repercussions.

With Bismarck's conquests the very map of Europe foreshadowed momentous cataclysms: modern history was witnessing the rise of revolutionary men. These were exploiting their official government positions, injecting a spirit of pillage into national affairs on a world scale, with the objective of eventual world conquest.

It seemed inevitable, therefore, that such historic upheavals, unpardonable in a civilization possessing a highly developed moral mind, should drag in their wake two world wars.

The undoing of past political crimes, as a first step in reorganizing world statesmanship, had escaped the logic of Bismarck. As a consequence there was inaugurated a school of

diplomats dedicated to perpetuating a policy of unjust aggran-
dizement.

The Martin family, which experienced the Franco-Prussian
War and saw the shadow of nine Prussian soldiers at its fireside, could never forget the crushing historical adventure.

7

SEVERAL CHANGES took place in the Martin household in the year following the war. Zelie came into an inheritance from her father when he passed away. He left her the family home on the street of St. Blaise.

"This presents an opportunity for change," she suggested. "Why not sell your store, here on Pont-Neuf, and move to the house my father willed me? It would leave you free, so you could help me manage the lace business. It has grown too large for me to handle by myself."

Louis needed no further encouragement. He saw the logical advantages of his wife's plan. It was no longer necessary for them to hustle to keep two businesses going.

Three months later, having sold the store to a nephew, Louis moved his family into the comfortable two-story residence which they soon redecorated and refurnished. There was a small but noticeable alteration, too, on the outside: on the front of the house was a marble sign: LOUIS MARTIN, MANU-FACTURER OF ALENCON POINT LACE.

The new arrangement ushered a still more prosperous well-being into the Martin household. Zelie's lacemaking, begun some twenty years before as a small individual enterprise, had grown into a thriving industry keeping many employees con-stantly busy filling orders. Now with Louis in full charge of the agency, attending to new business, calling on customers and making trips out of town, the Martins were surprised at the steady growth of their trade. Fusing their business abilities and skill, Louis and Zelie found the reorganization of their home and business life to their mutual taste.

"The new arrangements are ideal," remarked Zelie pleasantly one afternoon. "They give you more time at home with the children, and that's very important."

"Yes, and I also have more time now to read my favorite author, Dom Gueranger. I used to read his *Liturgical Year* only on Sundays, and never realized how much I had missed. The numberless feasts falling on weekdays all have the most interesting and stimulating histories. Dom Gueranger explains them all. And then there is a short résumé of the different Saints' lives for every day of the year. The other day, for example, I read a very inspiring story . . . . It was about a Saint named Hedwig, who sanctified herself in the married state. And do you know, Zelie, as I was reading, I couldn't help comparing her with you."

She looked up and smiled.

"But, Louis, Saint Hedwig was a princess, if I remember right."

"Yes, she was of royal blood, but the important thing is that she attained sanctity by being a model wife, by helping her husband in his difficult work."

"Yes, I know. It is told of her that on one occasion, having learned of the oppression of the poor by some unscrupulous landowners, Saint Hedwig appealed to her husband the Prince, begging him to undo the injustice, which he did. After forcing the greedy lords to return the crops that were extorted from the poor, the Prince asked her if she was now happy, to which she sadly replied: 'You have restored to the poor the crops that were stolen from them by the greedy, but, my Prince, who shall restore to them the many tears they had shed during their trial?'"

"Very beautiful!" agreed Louis, shaking his head in admiration. His Zelie seemed to know the lives of most of the Saints. "But now I want to tell you what struck *me* concerning this Saint described by Dom Gueranger. It is the Lesson from the Bible taken from the Book of Proverbs, adopted for today's reading. In my judgment it applied so strikingly also to you!" Louis began to read:

" 'Who shall find a valiant woman? The heart of her husband trusts in her. She renders him good and not evil all the days of her life. She had worked with her hands and her fingers have taken hold of the spindle. She looked well to her house and she has not eaten her bread idle. She made fine linen and she sold it. She opened her hands to the poor and needy. She shall not fear for her house in the cold. She sewed herself clothing of tapestry, fine linen and purple. Her husband is honorable sitting among the senators in the land. Her children rose up and called her blessed; her husband also rose up and he praised her. Many daughters have gathered together riches; but you have surpassed them all.' "

Louis finished and laid down the book. "Those words of the Bible, Zelie, describe in a few words *your* own soul. Since we've been married these fourteen years, I've seen you do all these works for which the valiant woman is extolled in the Book of Proverbs."

Somehow his wife found herself with nothing to say in reply. It was true she left nothing undone to help her husband in the way of advancing the material and the spiritual welfare of their family, but then this seemed to her the only happy way of life. During the fourteen years of their marriage she had had eight children, four of whom were living, and of the four who had passed away, the last, Melanie, born two years before, had lived only a few weeks. During these many years she had managed, moreover, to be continually occupied at lacemaking and increasing their income thereby, for the sake of the children. The two eldest were now attending boarding school at the Visitation Convent at Le Mans where Sister Dosithea, her own sister, was stationed.

Then another half-year ran out, and Zelie, as usual seated at the front window, was again busy with her lacework. Unconsciously she found herself hoping for another child. The baby,

Celine, was three years old at this time, and Zelie could think only of how desirable and welcome another child would be. For Zelie children were the goal of her marriage and the sole reason for her unyielding industriousness. Unable to shake off this longing, she wrote a long letter to her sister. Sister Dosithea had been for years her spiritual confidante, always telling her her hidden hopes even as she had once shared them in her happy childhood. Zelie also knew that the Sister never counted it a loss of time to answer these letters. For these replies Zelie always waited with keen interest, finding in her sister's penned words a source of courage and illumination.

As for Louis, he knew his wife's longing for another child, but he felt that four children to cheer their family hearth were all they could hope for now. He was already forty-seven, and Zelie about forty, and she was not at all well. For some years past a tumor in her breast had been giving them all deep cause for concern, but with her accustomed cheerfulness Zelie dismissed these anxieties over her physical ailment.

There was only one sentence on her lips, one hope in her heart: "Ah, Louis, I would so much like to have another child, one last one, if it should please God." She would say it over and over and there was a significant tone of petition in the sentence. She would not give up this hope though it seemed unlikely that her desire would be fulfilled.

The year ran out and it was Christmastime. Marie, aged thirteen and Pauline, eleven, were home from boarding school to celebrate the holidays. Never had St. Nicholas been more munificent in his gifts to the four Martin girls than that year. They were all at an age when they could appreciate the joys of Christmas.

Besides, the family reunion had other highlights. The two younger ones, Celine and Leonie, had long stories to tell their big sisters, Marie and Pauline, to acquaint them with all that had happened while they were away at school. One incident Leonie turned to tell Marie:

" . . . Then one day a poor man and his wife and their little son came begging and they had no place to sleep and Papa and Mama took them in and kept them upstairs in your room for nearly a whole week. And later Papa found a place for them in a boarding house, and Mama gave the lady money to buy food, and then Papa found work for the man, and now they're all right . . . . "

If for the two youngsters it was exciting to tell about the distraction of visitors at home, to thirteen-year-old Marie this news brought uneasiness. Her mother was perhaps overtaxing her strength by carrying her idea of charity too far. It was one thing to give people alms so they could go forth and purchase their needs, but quite another thing to take them into the house and be burdened with the dozen extra troubles and work which an added person always costs the woman of the house. Marie worried about this for a few days but she said nothing, until the late afternoon of New Year's Day on visiting her mother's room.

"Mother, Leonie and Celine were telling me," she began quietly, "about the family you took in a few months ago. Really, I worry over how much you can continue to add to your work and still be able to stand . . . . "

"Oh, that, Marie. We had to do it, dear. The people were deserving. Life is like that. Suddenly you see another human being suffering . . . . "

"But, you, too, are suffering and enduring as much as you possibly can," reasoned Marie.

"Perhaps, but I was going to add that when you see another human being suffering and you realize you can relieve that suffering and that God is looking on and wants you to give your help, you *can't* refuse . . . . "

"But who helps you when you are weak and the pains in your chest increase?" Marie asked, wiping her eyes.

"Who helps me? Why, you do, dear, right now. I've had you and Pauline nearly two weeks at home doing everything for me. Isn't *it* wonderful to have a big girl of thirteen run up and down stairs to fetch things, and isn't it a comfort to hear Pauline downstairs calling out to Celine not to do this and then, again, to do something else, taking my place so well that I need not even be there!"

"Nobody can take your place, Mother." Marie kept sponging her eyes.

"Now, come, my precious, I am not dying yet," she said, and then, in a visible effort to change the subject, Zelie added, "Did Leonie also tell you how well it turned out for that family we took in for a few days? Your father found a steady job for the man, and they are getting on fine. Doesn't that make you happy?"

"If you were well, and not sick in bed, that would make me happy," answered Marie. "I feel that you will always go on sacrificing yourself for others. Don't I remember how two years ago you took in Emily and nursed her in our house for three full months."

"But, my dear, Emily had been such a good little worker. She had washed so many clothes for us and watched over the children, and cooked, when Louise was off. Then, when she took ill with that dreadful rheumatic fever and I saw how deserted she was, with neither doctor, nor medicine, nor even the proper food she needed, with her parents altogether too poor to provide, I had to take her into our home and nurse her. The doctor said Emily needed care and a special diet of fruit juices, oranges, milk, fresh eggs and chicken broth. When I visited her and saw a plate of beans and salt pork left untouched by her side, I had to do something for her. She was really destitute and her pains were terrible."

"I know, Mother, and I was sorry for Emily, and I was really proud of you when you nursed her back to health by waiting on her day and night for three full months. But your own health, Mother, your own health . . . ."

"Now, now, Marie, God does not ask us for such extraordinary services every day. Not very often. But when He does place in our path a suffering person like Emily, surely He expects us to do something about it — if we can. But, cheer up, Marie, this is New Year's Day. I want you to go downstairs and plan a little party for the children. Do it for your mother. I will be here listening to you laugh and be merry. Go down and play a game with the children."

The following day was to be a memorable one not only for the Martins of Alençon but for the whole Catholic world. It was January 2, 1873. On this day was born Therese, the ninth and last child of Louis and Zelie Martin. That one additional child for which Zelie had hoped so vehemently had been given her!

Two days later the predestined child was baptized in the parish church of Notre Dame, and Marie, extremely self-confident for her thirteen years, was the jubilant godmother. Returning from the christening, the whole family gathered round the newly baptized infant, pulsating with inexpressible joy.

As for the children, Pauline, Leonie and Celine hovered in breathless admiration at the new sister, now the center of attraction in her rich baptismal attire on which Zelie had secretly worked for many weeks. It being midwinter, Therese wore a white woolen garment trimmed with ermine. The baptismal dress itself was elaborately embroidered and trimmed with Zelie's own matchless point lace. To the Martins the baptism of this their last child was the crowning event of their life, and they spared no effort or expense to enhance its solemnity. In their prosperous and well-ordered home externals were never neglected but were always adapted to the occasion.

As for Louis and Zelie, there was never a happier moment than when their children were handed over into their arms for the first time after baptism.

To Zelie, especially, this was the supreme moment, the moment that made everything different. Now, only now, when the blight of sin which all parents transferred to their offspring was removed by the waters of Baptism, was human existence ennobled and a path for hope and happiness opened. Embracing her baby, Zelie kissed her forehead for the first time after Baptism, softly whispering, "God bless you, Therese!"

Then reflecting deeply, she thought: "I wonder how *this* little one will turn out . . . . God knows!"

8

A FEW DAYS after the christening, Marie and Pauline returned to the school at Le Mans and Zelie gave herself over completely to the care of the newly born child. Unmindful of the increasing pain in her breast, she thought only of Therese's well-being. It was no wonder, then, that in her solicitude, she should soon discover that Therese was not faring very well. The family physician was consulted. Having made his examination, he said, "Madame Martin, your infant is undernourished and needs breast-feeding. Since you are unable to suckle her, you must arrange as soon as possible to get her a wet nurse."

Zelie knew she had to act quickly. As her husband was out of town on business, she decided to go herself in search of one. In her dilemma she thought of Rose Taille who lived on a farm outside the city limits, and, though it was midwinter, Zelie set out hastily in the direction of the small farmhouse.

"Rose, you have helped me before. You must help me now. My little Therese may die unless you suckle her!" Zelie pleaded.

But Rose Taille was not very eager. She looked pensively out over their small farm, noticed from her place at the window her husband who was just then feeding the animals. Next she surveyed her own four children who were gathered around her, the youngest a son less than a year old. Finally she shook her head.

"Madame, how can I help you? You can see I have more than enough of my own."

But Zelie began to plead so earnestly that Rose felt constrained to yield to her appeal.

"I am going over to the Martins', to look after their infant who needs feeding," she called out to her husband. "Do you think you can manage without me?"

The farmer, not given to easily allowing others to inconvenience him, was about to say that this was out of the question. But there was something so disarming about Zelie's expression, who now approached him so anxiously, and, besides, she began to plead her cause so warmly and so humbly that he felt ashamed to turn down a lady so refined and wealthy who was almost on her knees before him.

"Well, I guess you can go," he stammered lamely and soon the two women were off in the direction of the city. But they had not gone far when they were overtaken by the eldest Taille boy.

"Pop says you gotta come back. He said to tell you to come right back. He can't get along in the house without you . . . ."

"Go home and tell your father to make the best of it. He told me to go and I'm going! We won't be changing our minds every few minutes!" Rose's mind was made up. She would do what she could for the Martin infant.

After the very first feeding Therese seemed to have gained strength. It was evident that there was only one thing to do: since Madame Taille could not very well remain away from her own large family, Zelie would have to surrender her infant to the care of Rose on the small farm at Semalle. And so Therese, born into a home of abundance and refinement was destined, as an infant, to be reared in the poor and simple atmosphere of a cottage where she was surrounded with beasts of the field and strangers, in place of her own family and parents. Yet, in this atmosphere, in many ways resembling the stable of Bethlehem, Therese was destined to imitate even in externals that Divine Childhood which she was later to emulate with such excellence that she would make of this interior imitation of the Christ Child a sure way of spiritual perfection.

Zelie, in the meantime, returned from each visit to the farm at Semalle more and more grateful at seeing Therese grow into a strong and well-developed child. As for Therese herself, as the months flew by, she began to carve a destiny of her own in the farmhouse. The four Taille children had a charming rival. They could not guess the reason why their own father, who was generally brusque, yet found time to hover playfully over the infant in its crib, or why their mother should so often leave her chores to play with the baby who was not their own. But then the Taille children could not have understood that Therese was different. At every opportunity she tugged at her foster parents with her tiny hands, clutching at their sleeves, and, unconsciously, at their heartstrings. When she began to walk, she laboriously trudged after her wet nurse, casting affectionate glances in Rose's direction. It soon became evident that Therese loved her foster mother with a rare devotion, and the farmer's wife, who had never received any such devotion from her own four boys, was compelled to yield to the charm of the baby's love.

By the time Therese was a year old she was so attached to her nurse, that it was quite impossible for Rose to shake the child off at *any* time of the day. If the farmer's wife had to go to the fields, Therese had to be nestled in a small stack of hay close by. And when it was time to milk the cow, promptly Therese had to be bundled into Rose's large apron and strapped to the back of the placid animal. But if these ingenuous arrangements had been thrust upon Rose by the power of Therese's disarming affection — and precluding any hint of separation — this daily routine also had its share of advantages. For one, Rose never had to worry that harm would befall the precious Martin baby for lack of attention. The infant's personal safety seemed assured. The astonishing fact, however, is that Therese had seen to that herself. Before she was able to utter one articulate word to ask for anything, she had managed to secure what she wanted most — Love. This she accomplished through her affectionate glances, the grateful smiles given when one paid her the slightest attention, and, finally, by her heartbreaking cries when those she loved attempted to leave her by herself.

Therese, in her cradle, had begun a career of which she would never let go. Because that career was love and not anything less, Therese would never have to retrace a single step on her upward climb. Rather, perfecting her career of love, she would find ever better and better short cuts to the summit of her goal.

But to Therese, not quite a year and a half old, short cuts to the summit of love could mean nothing. Not hers to begin, as yet, the pursuit reserved for later years when mature reason would unfold the nature of the short cuts, and give them a name — self-sacrifice. For Therese, at seventeen months, could give herself only to the fullest demonstration of her heart's deepest longings. When, one morning, she noticed Madame Taille with two baskets, one on each arm, dressed for a trip to town, she guessed correctly that her nurse was going somewhere, and intending to leave her behind. Promptly clutching at Rose's long, flowing skirt, Therese held on desperately, while the woman tried to appear indifferent. After all, she simply had to go to the market to sell her produce of eggs, butter and cheese, and that was all there was to it. Shaking the youngster off, Madame Taille walked to the door and darted quickly toward the gate, when she was frozen to a halt by the piercing screams which she quickly recognized. Retracing her steps she went into the cottage.

"Therese, be a good little girl and play with the other children. I will be back in a short, short while." But her words fell on deaf ears. Therese continued shaking with uncontrollable sobs, looking through her tears as though her heart would break. Rose realized that she would never muster up enough courage to allow the tears of the sorrowing child to go unheeded.

"Come on, then, come on. Let me get your bonnet," she said, giving in and hastening to get the child ready. "You should stay at home, here, where it's nice and comfortable, but then it's no use for you to be comfortable if your heart's in misery. . . . ." she concluded. Therese suddenly became serenely happy, her tears entirely a thing of the past.

When the farmer's wife arrived finally at the market and had displayed her produce to the best advantage, she proceeded to establish Therese Martin on an improvised bench surrounded by the eggs, the butter and the cheese, and at last gave herself over to bargaining with her prospective customers. As for Therese, to a casual passer-by with a sense of humor she might have appeared as one of the items for sale, there in the midst of an array of vegetables and dairy products. But she stayed perfectly serene, entirely oblivious to the jokes and comments she aroused. She was to always remain too little to be concerned about anything so complex. Simple love was her fondest concern, and, nestled close to her cherished nurse, she had what she had longed for and nothing else mattered.

Anyone coming upon her in the market place that day, prattling away and as contented as the day was long, would never have guessed that she was the daughter of the retired watchmaker, Mr. Louis Martin, or that her mother was the prosperous manufacturer of Alençon lace. But, then, it was part of Therese's destiny to turn up with a gentle surprise for any and all who tried to pass judgment on her from mere external appearances. For just when her critics became absolutely sure that they had pigeonholed her correctly, they were always to discover that the joke was on them. From earliest infancy she was to star as the heroine in a drama of many unique surprises. Mistaking her for a country urchin in the market place that morning was to be the smallest of these errors compared to the stupendous mistakes that would be ventured in regard to her spiritually . . . . And so embarrassing, historically, to those imprudent enough to make them.

9

"YOUR MAMA made you this lovely blue silk dress, which you must wear today because we are going to pay her a visit," announced Rose one Sunday morning, feeling sorry, if not guilty, that she was concealing the full truth. For Therese was really going home that day to stay permanently. Plump and vivacious, her face tanned by the outdoors, she seemed entirely out of danger, and the Martins saw no reason for keeping her away from the family circle where she was wanted and she belonged.

Unconscious of any deception, Therese was happy at the prospect of an outing. But Rose was filled with conflict as she dressed the child. She realized this parting would cost her much more than it would cost the child. For many months now, Rose had returned the child's affection, giving love for love. True, originally she had been attracted by the pay involved in nursing and keeping Therese, but now she could scarcely remember that day. She would gladly have spent her last *sou* to buy the little one the delicacies she liked. The fact that the Martins paid her three times over for Therese's upkeep had come to mean little, even to frugal, penny-pinching Madame Taille, accustomed to thrift because of the exigency of her condition. One just could not deny the lovable baby anything. Her capacity for responding to any sign of affection was boundless, and the grateful eyes she turned to one for the slightest friendly gesture was as disarming as her petitions were compelling. She had begun to conquer others, by love and love alone. Now even Rose's husband watched her departure with regret.

After Therese was warmly welcomed back to the bosom of her family, Rose stole quietly away to Mass at the Church of

Notre Dame. About a half hour later, recognizing that she had been abandoned by her nurse, Therese burst into such fretful weeping that the Martins were at a loss as to what to do to quiet her down.

" . . . Rose will be back, darling. She only went to Mass. She will be back soon . . . ." Zelie tried to console her little one but it was no use. To Therese this was not the house to which she was accustomed, nor were the inmates the familiar ones she had come to know and love in the cottage. When tiny Therese continued weeping bitterly for another quarter hour, Zelie became alarmed. She found it necessary to dispatch Leonie to the church to fetch Madame Taille at once.

Finding her somewhere in the center of the congregation, Leonie whispered something urgent in her ear. On this, the woman, promptly closing her prayerbook, got up, genuflected and sped out of the church for the Martin home although Mass was not quite finished. When Therese saw the familiar figure in the doorway, though dimly for she was blinded by profuse tears, her face lighted up, and peace was gradually restored. After the exhausted weeping, the nurse found it easy to rock her charge into a deep sleep. When she awoke refreshed, and found herself surrounded by the merry circle of her family, who made a concerted effort to keep her distracted and entertained, she forgot her misery of the morning. From then on she came to be reconciled and to accept the love of her own family, particularly of her mother whose surpassing personality she soon discovered.

That summer was one of the happiest the Martin home had ever enjoyed. Marie and Pauline were home from school for their long summer vacation, but what was most conducive to the family's constant merriment was the vivacity descending on them in the person of Therese. Though not quite two yet, her expansive heart embraced them all. Surrendering to her artless outpourings, it was no wonder that her father was soon riding her through the house and garden astride his large black boot, while Therese, rearing with joy, coaxed him to go faster and faster.

"You will spoil her, I am afraid," cautioned Zelie.

"I don't think so. At least, it doesn't seem to have affected her so far," protested Louis, grinning.

"But it may affect her in the future," cautioned her mother; then, remembering how increasingly ill she had been feeling lately, she dismissed the charges about spoiling Therese. Only God knew what the child would have to endure in the future. Perhaps she would soon be motherless? But why think of that now, when they were all so happy together!

In the fall Pauline went back to school at Le Mans and Marie, having already finished, remained at home and started giving elementary lessons to Celine who was now about seven. Home life at the Martins had quieted down, and Zelie noticed that Therese was suddenly less vivacious, even pensive. Several times a day, when she came upon her, Therese seemed buried in thought. Zelie couldn't remember such behavior in her other children at such an age, so she decided to find out what Therese might be thinking. Did she *mean* "thinking"? Was it possible for a child not yet two years old to be so deeply absorbed as to really present her mother with the problem of interrogating her about her pensive moods?

At first this seemed absurd to Zelie, suddenly remembering that so far her admonitions to Therese were always in the matter of curbing the baby's excessive activities and exuberance. But now she was confronted with its obvious contradiction. Therese was alarming her not by some new activity but because, pensive as a forty-year-old, she was "thinking" so deeply *about something* that this mood became Zelie's concern.

"Therese," Zelie finally broke in, though cautiously, "tell Mama what you are thinking about."

"Paween, Paween."

"Pauline?"

"Yeth, Paween," Therese repeated, a distant look in her eyes.

"Oh, you darling! You're pining away for Pauline, lonesome because Pauline is away at boarding school. Come with Mama to the garden," she said, laying down her lace and picking up

Therese. She decided to spend the rest of the day in amusing her baby and helping her forget Pauline.

But the days that followed proved to Zelie that she had not succeeded in making Therese forget. Coming upon her, sunk in a meditative mood, Zelie might say: "Therese, what are you thinking about?" and the answer would invariably be the same: "Paween." Though surrounded by her parents and three sisters, the two-year-old continued to long for the one absent member of the family.

Finally Zelie asked Marie: "Have you noticed how Therese continues going off into a corner several times a day, looking pensive? When I ask her what she is thinking about, she tells me Pauline. Do you think she misses her, not seeing her around?"

"Well, yes. But, you know, Pauline had been putting her to bed at night and telling her stories about Jesus. I think Therese took a special liking for her because of it."

"Well, you wouldn't think that a mite not yet two could show an inclination toward the things of religion, would you?" And, not waiting for an answer, Zelie ran on. "But, then, I suppose that is what spiritual writers try to tell you when they say that the supernatural is built on the natural. Those who are enthusiastic about this life have it in their power to be equally zealous also for the next life," and Marie, listening, suddenly looked at her mother admiringly, but Zelie failed to notice it for she was already turning to go downstairs to resume work on her laces. She paused halfway down and, looking up, said in a casual way, "Marie, suppose you take over where Pauline left off, and begin telling Therese stories of Jesus when you put her to bed at night . . . . Will you do it, dear?"

"All right, Mama, but I can't promise that I will do as well as Pauline — though I should because I'm two years older. But, then, everybody knows Pauline's got a vocation, and she's surely going to be a nun some day."

"And you, Marie, what will you be?"

"I'm not sure, Mother. I don't know yet."

"At sixteen you don't have to make up your mind. You have plenty of time . . . and don't fret," came encouragingly from her mother. "Meanwhile you can begin instructing Therese about Our Lord, and perhaps awaken in her a desire one day to become a nun also."

Zelie did not then realize it, but Therese, at two, having heard people say that Pauline would be a nun, had already started to imitate Pauline and wanted to become a nun herself. Of course she was unable to understand what being a nun meant. Yet, Therese was certain that if Pauline, who spoke to her so convincingly of Jesus every night, would become a nun, then being a nun had something to do with Jesus, and, therefore, this, too, was what *she* wanted in life. [1]

---

1. *St. Therese of Lisieux,* edited and translated by the Rev. Thomas N. Taylor: "God in His goodness did me the favor of awakening my intelligence when I was still very young, and He has so deeply engraved in my mind the impressions of childhood that past events seem to have happened but yesterday (p. 33).

    "When I was just learning to talk, Mama would ask me: 'What are you thinking about?' and the invariable answer was: 'Pauline.' Sometimes I heard it said that Pauline would be a nun and without quite understanding what that meant I used to think: I too will be a nun" (p. 36).

    Hereafter this volume will be referred to as *Autobiography.*

10

IN PAULINE'S absence, Marie, encouraged by her mother, wholeheartedly took over the task of teaching her precocious baby sister the priceless lessons of religion contained in the life of the Saviour. Beginning at the crib and ending at the cross of Calvary, Marie told Therese in simple language the historical truths of the Redemption to which the child listened wide-eyed and intelligent. She was taught to kiss the Crucifix reverently, and now began to lisp her daily prayers.

Her mind being nourished with these stirring teachings, she no longer pined for the absent Pauline. She grew happy and indicated a child's active career once more. She had only begun to live, and if she did take time out for "thinking," there was no decline in her practical achievements.

One bright morning little Therese took it into her head to climb the stairs leading up to the second floor. The problem of surmounting some two dozen heavily carpeted stairs was a trying ordeal for a two-year-old. Her plump little legs were much too short to carry her upward with flying colors. A difficult stunt, but she was bent on doing it.

Awkwardly, and laboriously, but successfully, she landed on the first step. She was thrilled with success. But her ready intelligence registered also a note of caution. There were still some twenty-three stairs looming ahead, leading to dizzy heights. Realizing with what effort the first step had been conquered, she needed bolstering.

"Mama, Mama," she loudly called out. Not looking up at Therese's plight, her mother answered casually, "Yes, darling."

So, encouraged by her mother's voice, Therese tried the second step, which was also reached. Again she called out to her mother and waited for the voice. "Yes, darling." Then she climbed the third step. And so, a fourth and a fifth step were conquered by the same method.

In the meantime, hearing further shouts of "Mama," Zelie dropped her lace and stepped into the corridor to see what the child was up to. Seeing Therese smiling happily and safe enough atop the sixth step, Zelie decided to stand by. "Yes, darling," came the signal. As she watched, Therese made one successful step after another and still continued to call out before each renewed attempt, until she finally reached the top. From that day on it became a daily setting-up exercise for Therese, but always accompanied by her unvarying method of calling to her mother and waiting for the signal which would bolster her courage.

But there were also occasions when Zelie worried over her baby's unpredictable behavior. For instance, when Therese was trying to get into Marie's room. Still too small to reach the doorknob, the child simply lay down on the floor and stayed there a long time without saying a word. Zelie let the incident pass and said nothing, but when she saw Therese repeat the performance the next day, she called Marie to task.

"What is Therese doing there lying down on the floor?"

"Oh, did you notice it, too?" asked Marie playfully.

"Why, of course. I noticed her do it yesterday and now she is doing it again. Since when has she started it?"

"Oh, a few days ago, but I didn't say anything to you. It seems she wants to get into my room by herself, but she can't reach the doorknob, so she surrenders by lying down right on the spot and staying there for a long time — sort of thinking."

"Marie, you shouldn't allow her to do a thing like that," scolded the mother.

"But why, Mother? Is it wrong?"

"It shows a kind of defiant attitude. Why can't Therese seek help, by *asking* someone to let her in, instead of this obstinate continuing to try by herself. — And when she doesn't succeed, lying down as if in protest . . . ."

Marie wanted to add " . . . as if in sorry resignation," but refrained. She didn't realize then that the mother in one sentence meant to teach them a twofold lesson. The first was for Marie to learn how to lead others; the second, for Therese, was to check the beginnings of any attitude of rebellious protest which might tend to mar her young character.

Going up to the child still lying on the floor with her eyes forlornly pinned to the unattainable doorknob, Marie said, "Therese, get up from the floor at once! Don't you know that by behaving like this you are displeasing Jesus?"

Rising immediately, the little one began to cry. Nor was she consoled till Marie reassured her: "Of course, since you are sorry, Jesus forgives you everything. So don't cry any more." This was to remain an unchangeable trait of Therese's childhood, to recognize her faults and not excuse herself, but openly to confess and weep over them.

At three, she developed a new characteristic, one which would be a highlight in her spiritual career. Leonie, who was now ten, had entered the room where Celine and Therese were playing. On her arm was a basket filled with toys, games and other trifles. She felt that she was getting too old for such playthings and decided it was time to dispose of them. "My dears, here are my toys," she said. "You can choose whatever you like." Celine, who was six, looked over the collection and pulled out a ball. Therese thought for a moment, then without further hesitation, exclaimed: "I choose everything," and promptly set herself to carry off the whole basket of childish loot.

Not for Therese to be content with part if she could have the whole. Had she not been offered a choice? And if it was offered, wouldn't she honor the donor by accepting all? In later years, life offered other opportunities, but Therese who chose *all* at three would never be satisfied with less for the rest of her life. How she set about choosing *all* was soon to become such an amazing and edifying illustration that she blazed a trail to an entirely new kind of spiritual greatness.

A few days after choosing the "all" in Leonie's toy-basket, something happened which at first seemed to indicate that she had made a poor bargain. The two elder sisters were away at school. But Celine, who was six, was to study at home, under Marie's personal supervision. Therese alone was left out. "You've got all those toys from Leonie, so go and play with them while Celine comes up to my room for her lessons . . . ." said Marie.

The child looked up disappointed. Why couldn't she have lessons, too? With Celine. (She was longing for another kind of "all.") Unable to shake off the youngster, Marie offered a compromise: "Very well, Therese, you can come into the room while I'm giving Celine her lessons, but, mind you, you are not allowed to interrupt or you will be sent away at once . . . ."

Thus, knowing when to exchange one kind of "all" for another, began a phase of mental discipline at the early age of three. She proved to have such self-control that within a fortnight she learned the whole alphabet and was so obedient and quiet during the two-hour lesson period that when Christmas came, she, along with Celine, was given an award for her studious accomplishments. [2]

Among these was one prize that was to become a milestone in Therese's childhood. This had, at first, seemed unsuitable to Zelie.

"But, Marie, Therese is still too small for that yet," she remarked cautiously when Marie showed her the two prizes intended for the two children.

"But, Mother, you know how it is. If I give one to Celine, I must give one to Therese. She's been so quiet and attentive during the lessons that I wonder if we aren't underestimating her."

"Well, then, all right, Marie. Give Therese the same as Celine . . . . It can't do any harm."

---

2. *Autobiography,* p. 36.

THE WHOLE WORLD WILL LOVE ME

So, at three, she came into a possession that was destined to start her on a phase of intensified spiritual effort. She could not have guessed that, however, as she stood appraising the small object in her tiny hand. "What *is* it? Wosawy beads to pway on?"

"No, not rosary beads at all," Marie told her. "Come with me into the garden where we will take a walk. I will explain to you just what your present is," Marie said.

Once outdoors and by themselves, Marie began: "The beads I gave you are called 'Act Beads.' Now the purpose of these beads is not to *pray* on them but to *count* on them, each time you do something to please Jesus. For instance, you know how often you push Celine, or tease her, and sometimes even slap her, and then you run to Mama to tell her you were naughty? Of course, it's the only thing you can do after you are naughty — to go and tell Mama and be sorry. But these Act Beads — which you should carry in your pocket — are supposed to remind you to stop and think for a minute before you are naughty, so that you can make up your mind, for example, not to push Celine when you feel like doing it. This is called an 'act' or a 'sacrifice' which you offer to Jesus, and when you make such an act you are allowed to pull the first bead on your string over to the other side. That counts one good act for you. And every time you feel like being naughty, but you force yourself not to be, you can pull another bead, and still another, and at the end of the day you count up all the beads and show Mama how many acts you have made. Do you understand?"

Therese's face lighted up. She knew exactly what the program before her entailed. After you're naughty you must be sorry, of course, and tell Mama about it.

(That Therese did and so consistently that Zelie wrote, in a letter to Pauline: "Therese delights us all. She is extraordinarily outspoken and it is charming to see her run after me to confess her childish faults. 'Mama, I gave Celine a push; I slapped her once; but I will not do it again.' The moment she has done anything mischievous, everyone must know about it.") Therese's numberless little confessions indeed attested all too clearly that she had mastered the art of self-analysis, and knew well when she was to blame.

Now a new method was open to her. One *could* do and *ought* to do something about those faults *before* they were committed! From now on, she would think for a moment before she pushed Celine, and then, not pushing her, she would be allowed to move up one bead on the string, and count this an act of pleasing Jesus . . .! If Zelie had hesitated about letting Marie give Therese the Act Beads because of her extreme youth, she soon learned that there was no cause for worry. In a letter to Pauline she says: "Even Therese is anxious to practice mortification. Marie gave her little sisters a string of beads on purpose to count their acts of self-denial, and they have really spiritual, but very amusing, conversations together. The other day Celine asked: 'How can God be in such a tiny Host?' and Therese answered: 'That is not strange, because God is Almighty.' 'And what does Almighty mean?' continued Celine. 'It means,' said Therese, 'that He can do whatever He likes.' But it is still more amusing to see Therese continually putting her hand in her pocket and pulling a bead along the string for every little sacrifice."

If Therese was able to declare later in life that she had never refused God anything since the age of three, was it not because she was able to count her acts of self-denial — so forcibly brought to her consciousness by the Act Beads Marie had placed in her hands? One thing becomes evident: from this time forward Therese's Act Beads would take precedence, in importance, over her basket of toys, because making sacrifices for the Christ Child was to become her "all" — not in the manner of an adult, but according to the capacities of a growing child.

11

EXCITED CRIES of thrilling joy rang from the direction of the garden. Therese was enjoying her first ride on the new swing.

"Push harder, Papa, much harder . . . ." she commanded lustily.

"But, aren't you afraid?" he asked, complying with her urging somewhat cautiously.

"No, I'm not a bit afraid. I want to go higher, much higher!" she cried, and seeing herself soar upward she felt only a more bracing desire to scale the heights.

Proud of her daring spirit, Louis heaved her forward with all his might and sent her thrilling high up into the fresh spring air.

"There! You are now swinging as high as possible, my little queen," he said. He reflected how fitting, indeed, was the nickname he had selected for this child, his youngest. Many years ago when he nicknamed his first two children, he called Marie, the eldest, diamond, and Pauline, pearl. But then he was still a jeweler, and naturally compared his home treasures to the precious gems in his jewelry trays. But when his third, Leonie, was nicknamed Brave Lady, Louis showed that he had gone a long way indeed. Diamonds and rubies were lifeless objects. A nickname should suggest an ideal or a characteristic for which a soul should aspire. But his children were greater than jewels because they had souls and he felt his duty was to awaken a desire in them toward that ideal which would help them develop their personalities. When he saw the rewards the nickname Brave Lady yielded he was highly pleased. "Now, Brave Lady," he would say, "will you go on crying just because you lost your ball? Is that what a brave lady does?" On noticing with pride how quickly Leonie wiped her tears and struggled for composure, he felt the nickname had called forth a noble reaction.

Finally, when it was Celine's turn to be nicknamed, Louis was baffled.

"Zelie, I ran out of nicknames. I can't find anything better than Brave Lady. As there is no substitute for bravery, I don't know what to call Celine."

"Well, if there's no substitute for bravery, surely there is a synonym for it," Zelie answered, not looking up.

"But, of course! Why didn't I think of it? I'll call Celine, Valiant Lady, and the two girls can go on vying with each other to see what honors for bravery and valor each can win in the battle of life."

But when Therese came along, Louis, recognizing a spirit of unique excellence, unequivocally bestowed on her the title, Little Queen. This was prophetic, for Therese Martin was to maintain her lofty title of little queen in a way that would capture the admiration of the entire Catholic world.

Zelie was happy that Therese was so jubilant over her swing, for she sometimes worried that the child showed signs of a mental development far beyond her years, wondering if this might not have grave repercussions in her later life.

"It's good that Therese is so excited over the swing. She sometimes makes me anxious when she becomes so absorbed in her thoughts."

"What do you mean, Zelie? Does the child worry you?"

"No, but mind you, yesterday she came up and out of a clear sky exclaimed: 'Mama, you know what? I wish you would die.'"

"Did she say that?" Louis wondered what had induced her to say such a thing.

"Oh, don't worry, she had a good explanation from her point of view," Zelie smiled. "She said that she wished I would die because she loved me so much, and therefore wanted me to go

to Heaven, where it was so beautiful. Since it is not possible until after death, well, she wished I would die."

"The little queen is superb!" he replied, shaking his head.
"every inch a queen!"

But two days later the little queen was not so happy: she
was fretting. Without intending to be destructive, she had
pulled at a tiny bit of loose wallpaper in the dining room, when
lo, all of a sudden, the tiny strip was no longer on the wall but
in the palm of her hand. Oh, if she could only set the bit of
paper back on the wall again!

"Oh, look what Therese did! She tore the wallpaper!"
shrieked Celine.

All eyes turned on the culprit. She stood motionless with the
bit of faded paper in her hand. Marie came to her rescue. She
knew the paper at that spot on the wall had been loose for some
time. Yet, unwilling to exonerate Therese completely, Marie
said a few words, telling her not to handle what she was not
supposed to. Then Celine contributed:

"Oh, Therese, wait till Papa finds out! You know how angry
he got when Victoria broke the vase," she said, alluding to an
accident when the servant recently broke a gift of Wedgwood
Louis had given his wife.

When he heard that Victoria had dropped and broken it, he
was angry. "How is it you broke it? Don't you handle precious
objets d'art with any more care than you handle a wooden
bucket? Dropping a vase! Why, before you even touch an art
treasure you should wipe your hands and at least pause for a
moment to reflect that you are now about to hold something
precious. Breaking a Wedgwood vase that costs more than
your wages in two weeks! Such carelessness!" Louis was quite
angry: the children remembered it well. Particularly the two
youngest, Therese and Celine. Who knew how he was going
to take this incident of the torn wallpaper?

When, four hours later, Louis came home from his round of
business calls and the family gathered in the dining room for
the evening meal, Therese, at her usual place next to Marie,

tugged at her sister's sleeve and said, "Marie, tell Papa now how I tore the wallpaper."

At three Therese had already established sovereignty of her conscience over all other things. Her reason made the decisions, not her heart. She might have said, evasively, "The wallpaper tore," but, overruling this human prompting and unwilling to dislodge the truth from its place of sovereignty, she said, "I tore the wallpaper." By feeling that she had justly incurred her father's displeasure by this fault, she was not ready to face or to speak with him until, first, this barrier of guilt which separated them was removed by her sincerely taking the blame.

12

IT WAS a cold February day when Zelie received a letter from the Visitation Convent at Le Mans, a letter she was afraid to open because she was sure of the news it contained. Only a month before, though very sick herself, she had paid a visit to her sister in the convent, who was dying of tuberculosis. Slowly breaking the seal, Zelie read: "Our beloved Sister Dosithea has ended her saintly life early today by a most edifying death . . . ." Zelie could not make out the rest. Her eyes were too blurred with tears. This was her only sister. She had had the hope of entrusting the education of her younger children, especially Therese, to Sister Dosithea, in the event her own health became worse or she were called by God. And now her sister was dead.

"Mama, why are you crying?" Therese asked sympathetically, stopping suddenly very still as she watched her mother's grief.

"Mama is crying because your aunt, Sister Dosithea, just died," she answered. Then taking Therese by the hand, she went with her to Marie's room on the second floor to acquaint her with the news.

"Marie, I just got a letter. Your aunt is dead . . . ." For a while both wept. Finally Marie recovered and managed to say: "Sister Dosithea was such an inspiration, not only to me as her niece, but to all the girls at school."

"And to me, Marie, her letters held out a comfort beyond all description. I was able to bear up under every successive trial it pleased God to send, but this is true, He knows, because Sister Dosithea's letters were the sustaining force that braced me up.

She had such a way of writing that it lifted one . . . holding out promises of such rewards — that it made every sacrifice here below seem trivial."

"She meant that much to you, Mother?"

"Oh, yes, Marie. Particularly at the time we lost our five-year-old Helene, and it was Sister Dosithea, who hastened to console me . . . in one of her letters . . . . I never told anyone what she said to me on that occasion: it seemed too sacred to talk about."

Marie looked up inquiringly.

"But I will bring the letter from my chest and read it to you. Now that she is gone only her letters remain to give us courage to go on."

A few minutes later Marie listened as Zelie read the letter written years before: " ' . . . That faith and confidence of yours which never wavers will one day have their reward, a glorious one. Be quite sure that God will bless you and that the depth of your sufferings will be matched by the consolation reserved for you . . . .' "

"How comforting," ventured Marie.

"But wait, Marie. The most beautiful part of the letter is yet to come. Listen . . . 'For won't you be well recompensed if God, well pleased with you, gives you that great saint which for His glory you have desired so greatly?' "

Raising her eyes, Zelie now asked, "What do you think Sister Dosithea had in mind when she wrote this, Marie?"

"I don't know, Mother. Read the words again."

Zelie read again: " 'For won't you be well recompensed if God, well pleased with you, gives you that great saint which for His glory you have desired so greatly?' " Noting her daughter's gentle puzzlement, she added: "Now you must know, Marie, that I never spoke of such lofty hopes to Sister Dosithea. My great desire, of course, was that God might give me many children all of whom would be consecrated to His service . . . ."

Zelie did not realize that her sister had seen deeper into her heart than she did herself. Zelie did not fathom the depth of her own soul as deeply as did her sister in the convent. Mixed emotions of happiness, over the inspiring disclosure of the letter, on the one hand, and grief over her passing away brought fresh tears to their eyes.

"Mama, please don't cry! . . . Marie, please don't cry!" now came from little Therese who had stood by taking in the whole scene without, however, shedding a tear. And the two grownups, wiping their eyes, turned to look at the diminutive comforter holding her own in the face of death. They seemed surprised that Therese was not crying too. Yet she, who could send out waves of distressing cries when scolded for some fault, stood quite composed at the news of a death that caused her valiant mother and her big sister to weep so profusely. Did Therese understand, perhaps, that the death of her saintly aunt was her entrance into the unending joy of Heaven? Nobody knew why but Therese was not weeping. Zelie, with something more on her mind which she wished to confide to her eldest, Marie, told her to take the little one downstairs.

"Tell Victoria to look after Therese for a while. There is something else I want to tell you confidentially."

When Marie returned alone, Zelie began at once, as if anxious to unburden herself of something that had always been a mystery to her.

"Marie, I want to tell you about something that happened to me before Therese was born. It was kind of terrifying . . . . You won't be afraid if I tell you?"

"No, Mother, I'm never afraid of anything when you're with me." Marie reassured her.

"Well, about a week before she was born I went to my room in the late afternoon to read a spiritual book, as I always do for a while. It was winter, already quite dark, and so I lit a lamp. In the course of my reading I came upon a paragraph describing some of the awful terrors which the Saints and other great servants of God endured at the instigation of the Devil. I paused to reflect that I, for one, need never fear such diabolical persecution, because these things would never happen to ordinary people like me. 'It's only Saints who need to fear them,' said I to myself, when all of a sudden, right there and then, I felt an enormous weight on my shoulders bearing down on me. I was terrified. It seemed to me as if some savage beast was gripping me with his fierce claws. I have never experienced anything like that in all my life. I began to pray, calling on Our Blessed Lady to help me. Then, all of a sudden, I was freed. It lasted only a few seconds but it was real and horrible and I never forgot it."

"Oh, Mother, it must have been dreadful!"

"Well, I put it out of my mind, but when Therese was born I wondered if it had anything to do with her — maybe some sign that *she* was meant for something very special . . . ."

Zelie walked over to the window. This seemed to be a day destined for serious discussion; news of the death; the letter with the extraordinary allusion about things too high even to think about; and now the experience of that dreadful early evening before Therese was born. Zelie had one more thing to say, perhaps of greater consequence to her immediate family than all the other matters they had just mentioned in the tense atmosphere of Marie's room. She had to say it, and say it now!

"Marie, while we are talking about such serious things, I must tell you something else."

Marie looked up worried but somehow managed to steel herself for the worst. "Yes, Mother, what is it?" she asked, trembling.

"I am very unwell," Zelie answered.

Marie's face turned white.

"But, Mother, you will be all right. You've been having that trouble in your breast for about ten years. I think it's something chronic — and — and that you will be all right."

"No, Marie, you must listen to me. I am grievously ill. The swelling on my breast is now something serious. If I should die, promise, promise you will take my place with Therese, Celine and Leonie. I will be depending on you and Pauline, especially now that Sister Dosithea is dead . . . ."

"But, Mother, you won't die!" protested Marie, embracing her.

However, Zelie knew that no amount of protest could nullify the reality shaping up now in the form of a malignant tumor, which foreshadowed swift disaster for the household on St. Blaise's Street.

Louis, after talking it over quietly several times with Marie, wrote to his wife's brother, Isidore Guerin, at Lisieux. He was a druggist, an able man. Surely he would suggest some treatment — or perhaps a specialist who could help.

In the meantime, quite worn out and suffering, Zelie returned to her station by the window to work on her laces as always.

"But, Mother, you should rest. You don't need to keep working any longer," argued Marie.

"Well, my dear, I feel that I must go on as long as I am able."

"But why, Mother?" persisted her eldest.

"Because there are still orders to be attended to, and I feel it my duty to go on. Yet, believe me, I dream now more than ever of solitude and retirement. In fact, I only recently wrote Pauline how I long for the cloister. I wish I could live until I am very old, and then when my children are all settled, I could retire to a monastery where I could give myself over to silence, prayer and spiritual reading."

"Really, Mother?" asked Marie impressed.

"Honestly! But I quickly dismiss all such thoughts. That kind of life is not for me and to dream of it is vain . . . it will never come true. I realize it is better to keep busy at what God gave you to do than to go on wishing for the impossible. That's why I am still at my lacework. This has been my life's work and this is what I must continue doing. There are orders to fill and I want to satisfy everybody, and feel, also, that I am saving for the children so you will not want on my account. The worse I feel, the more I want to do — in the short time that might be left to me. Oh, no, it is not a fortune that I want to pile up for myself; only to provide for my children. After all, Therese, especially, is still such a mite. She's only four years old. So I must go on working as long as I am able!" Zelie finished. Then she brightened up. "But, Marie, let us not talk of these things any more. Pauline is going to be home in a few days for Easter, and I want you to help me make it as pleasant as you can. Do you promise?"

Marie only shook her head. There was nothing to do but enter into her mother's plans for the holidays. And so, when Pauline came home, she found only the customary peace and joy of the family's intimate life, so that she wrote to her friend Louise, who had remained at the boarding school:

"*Wednesday, April* 4, 1877. DARLING LOUISE . . . I profit by a lucky moment which, perhaps, won't come again for the whole vacation. Therese and Celine are in the garden, amusing themselves blowing bubbles. Mama is busy lecturing Leonie, Marie has just this moment gone to work downstairs, Papa is at the Pavilion; so I am in complete solitude . . . . I can therefore think at my ease of my dear Visitation and talk to my little Louise . . . .

"What do you do with your days? I hope you often see Sister Marie de Sales. I want you to tell her that in a few years she will have a future novice. Guess who? Marie? No. Leonie? No. You, then? . . . Nor you either . . . . Very well, the new postulant is Mademoiselle Therese Martin . . . . Listen to the motives which will bring her. Yesterday evening she gave me her whole confidence, and I could have died laughing: 'I shall be a nun in a convent because Celine wants to go, and then, too, people must be taught to read, don't you see? But I won't take the class; it would be too much of a nuisance. Celine will and I shall be the Mother. I shall walk around the convent all day and then I'll go with Celine and we'll play in the sand and with our dolls . . . . ' I hastily brought down her castles in Spain: 'Do you really think, my poor Therese, that you will be talking all day? Don't you know there has to be silence?'

[85]

'Has there? . . . Ah, well, in that case I won't say a word . . . .'
'What will you do, then?' 'That's no great trouble, for I shall
pray to the good Jesus; but then how can I pray to Him without
saying anything? I really don't know — and who will there be
to show me, as I'll be the Mother, huh?' I had a frightful desire
to laugh. But I kept serious. She looked at me thoughtfully. Her
little face had so candid an expression, and all that she said to
me came from so deep in her heart that it was impossible not to
be interested. At last, having reflected a few moments, she fixed
her big blue eyes on me and with a mischievous smile she made
gestures with her little arms like a grownup and said: 'After
all, Pauline, it isn't worth while tormenting ourselves now. I
am too little, don't you see, and when I'm big like you and
Marie, before I go into the convent, they will tell me what to
do . . . .' 'That's right, baby dearest,' I answered, covering her
with kisses, 'now it's late, let's go to sleep . . . . You can still
spend a few nights before calling yourself Sister Marie Aolysia
(that's the name she has chosen), you've still got time to think
about it.' Then we both went upstairs and I put her to bed . . . .
I love having my Therese with me. I feel that, with her, no
harm can touch me . . . . PAULINE." [3]

But after the Easter holidays, even Zelie realized the need
for rest and some medical relief, and she told Marie she intended consulting another doctor.

"I shall write you out a prescription," the physician said
evasively after making his examination.

But Zelie, whose brother was a pharmacist, was somewhat
acquainted with the kindlier aspects of the medical profession,
and knew of those deliberate falsifications intended to modify
the cruelty of an impending disaster, and so she asked the phy-

---

3. (*Lettres de Sainte Thérèse de L'Enfant-Jesus, Carmel de Lisieux*.) *Collected
Letters of St. Thérèse of Lisieux*, translated by Frank J. Sheed.
Hereafter this volume will be referred to as *Collected Letters*.

sician pointedly: "And of what good, kind sir, will the prescription be to me?"

The physician winced. He knew he was being asked for a clear verdict, so he answered, "The prescription will be of no good, Madame," and then slowly tore up the white scrap of paper, disliking for a moment this profession which thrust upon him the duty of handing down such a dreadful sentence to the gentle lady who sat calmly before him.

Back at the house, Zelie was careful not to disclose all she now knew, but she decided that the time had come for her to permanently wind up her career of lacemaking, and said to her husband, "Louis, I will not take any more orders for point lace . . . ."

"I am certainly glad to hear you say that. There is absolutely no reason why you *should* work any longer, especially since we can get along so well without it. We will sell the business and you can live more quietly. You will see, too, how much better you feel when you have no business worries on your mind."

Then the business was sold. Zelie now wrote to Isidore in Lisieux: "I am now going to live a retired life, and from every point of view, I think it is time . . . ."

On receiving this news, Isidore Guerin realized that his sister must be very ill. Finally, he succeeded in locating a specialist and another consultation, at the Martin's home, was shortly in progress.

"Tell us the truth, even if it be the worst possible news, doctor. We must know, because while there is life there is also hope. If your medical science cannot aid my wife, we know of another place where we *can* go for help," said Louis.

The physician surveyed the speaker dubiously. What was the retired jeweler speaking about? What help could there be for a woman dying of cancer, in perhaps less than two months? He had been asked to be frank. Therefore, without mincing words, he submitted his pathological findings, cruel though they were, and took his leave.

"My dear, when do you want to go to Lourdes, so that I can

make train reservations for you?" asked Louis affectionately.

"Then there is no hope?"

"Lourdes is the only hope," he answered tenderly, tears gathering in his eyes.

"In that case, since the school term for Pauline ends this week, and she should be home by Monday, you can make reservations for us for the week following. I want all three of the older girls to come with me. You can remain at home with the children, Celine and Therese."

So confident was Louis that at Lourdes his wife would be granted a miraculous cure that when the day and hour arrived to meet Zelie at the railroad depot on her return, he took Celine and Therese with him, full of anticipation. When he saw at last the sad faces of Marie and Pauline, who were supporting their suffering mother, he knew there had been no cure.

"Don't worry, Louis," she said consolingly. "I am wonderfully resigned. If Our Blessed Mother did not grant me a cure, she has given me something even greater. Although I did not hear her, yet it is as if she had spoken to me the same words she once said to Bernadette: 'I do not promise to make you happy in this world, but only in the next.'"

When July arrived and with it an intense heat wave, Zelie began to drink to the very dregs the bitterness that filled her cup of suffering.

Then came the month of August, which was to be her last on earth.

"Tomorrow is First Friday, and I want to go to Mass," she told her husband.

"As you wish, my dear," he answered softly.

With the help of Marie and Pauline, Zelie managed to get to church. Here she remained for the entire service and received Holy Communion, faithful to the very end in the practice of the First Friday Devotions to the Sacred Heart.

A few days later, Louis arranged with their neighbors to take Therese and Celine into their home during the daytime, so as to spare them from seeing their mother's sufferings. One morning, on their way to the neighbors, Celine whispered, "Therese, you know, we didn't have time this morning to say our prayers. Should we tell that we didn't say them?"

"Yes, of course," answered the tot. "When we arrive, you must tell."

When the kind neighbor heard Celine's timid admission of unsaid morning prayers, she said at once:

"Well, then you can say your prayers right now," and taking the little girls into a large room, she left them to their devotions, closed the door and left.

Therese and Celine looked at each other in surprise.

"This is not like Mama. She always knelt down with us, and we said our prayers together," said Therese.

But the children's mother was never to kneel down with them again. Her sufferings were intense now but her resignation was perfect. Though not denying that she was in pain, since it was all too obvious, yet she would not complain. On the contrary, she now told those who attended her that her present pains and sufferings had a place in her life, as equally as did her former joys and blessings. Furthermore, Zelie, now at the highest pitch of agony, gave expression to a statement singularly significant, exclaiming: "I must not lose a minute of the time that still remains. These days are days of grace which shall never return. I desire to profit by them . . . . "

Zelie was now proving, beyond the shadow of a doubt, as great an economist in matters spiritual as she had been in temporal affairs. Successful in business, proficient in rearing an incomparable family, she was now climaxing a spiritual bargain, accepting willingly the fearful sufferings of the last stages of cancer to turn them into profit for eternity.

When it was evident that Zelie could not possibly live another week, Louis informed her brother in Lisieux who, together with his wife, hastened to his sister's bedside. A few days later the priest came to administer Extreme Unction. Kneeling together with the other members of the family was tiny Therese, who although she watched her father sob bitterly, herself did not cry at all. Two days later Zelie Martin passed away, at the age of forty-six.

Therese looked for a long time at the coffin but even this time she hardly shed a tear. After the funeral the five mother-less girls sat huddled in the parlor, looking sadly at each other. Then Victoria, the governess, who had looked after the two smallest since their infancy, exclaimed: "Poor little things! You now have no mother."

Celine, who was eight, looked around and then going over to her eldest sister, Marie, now eighteen, threw herself into her arms saying: "Marie, you will be my mother!"

At that moment, Therese, the baby, too wanted to imitate Celine, but she suddenly paused. Perhaps Pauline, the second eldest, would be hurt if both girls chose Marie and left her out. So, wishing to forestall this possibility, Therese ran to Pauline and said: "And you, Pauline, will be *my* mother!"

13

IT WAS SETTLED, two weeks later, that the Martins were moving away from Alençon forever.

"We are going to live at Lisieux close to your Uncle Guerin, your aunt and your two cousins, Jeanne and Marie, who are just about the same age as you two," Louis was explaining to Celine and Therese.

The decision was as swift as it was far-reaching with its advantages to the Martin children, yet it had been prompted mostly by Zelie. When in her last agony, she had fixed a pleading gaze at her brother's wife, as if begging her to look after the orphans she was leaving behind. Herself a mother, Madame Guerin understood the anxiety which Zelie's pitiful look conveyed.

"Zelie," she said, "I promise you to look after all your five children and to be, as much as I can, a mother to them . . . ."

Louis saw wisdom in an arrangement that would bring his family to live close to the Guerins. A widower with five daughters needed some relatives, and Uncle Guerin and Aunt Guerin would be indispensable. His brother-in-law and wife were highly respected in Lisieux, so when on September 10 a letter came saying that a suitable house had been found by Mr. Guerin, the widowed Louis went there at once to look it over and after appraising it as adaptable for his family, decided to take it.

This became the famous home in Normandy, known as Les Buissonnets, so called because it was nestled in a thicket of tall trees and beautiful shrubbery against the remoter background of a private park, laid out with beds of flowers. The house was built of red brick, was trimmed in white, and had two stories with dormer windows above. Two entrance doors and four large French windows flanked the façade on the ground floor, while on the second floor were six attractive windows commanding a placid view in front. It was by every standard a residence of wealthier citizens, and into this house came to live the widower Louis Martin and his five daughters. Because it was only five blocks from the Church of St. Jacques in one direction, and the same distance, opposite, from the Guerins, Les Buissonnets was very conveniently located.

But if the villa had the superficial earmarks of a fine estate, there was no life of luxury nor any self-indulgence within its many rooms. If the Martins did have an eye for beauty and a taste for the more elegant surroundings, choosing a large, comfortable and strong house to live in, they possessed none of those propensities toward needless luxury which, like the little foxes of biblical tradition, destroy the vineyard.

Inside Les Buissonnets there was plenty of wholesome food, for example. But it was always plain food. Again, since coffee was expensive at the time in France, it became a delicacy at the Martin table to be enjoyed only at Christmas and Easter, and some few rare feasts. Money thus saved from unnecessary expenditures was not hoarded away, however, but, rather, set aside for the poor.

It soon became an unfailing custom at Les Buissonnets to parcel out on Thursday of each week a generous alms of food as well as money to the poor, who soon learned to form a regular line at the door of the Martin residence.

Louis, now retired altogether from active commercial work, busied himself with the garden chores and supervised the running of the new household. His wealth was estimated at about a hundred thousand dollars by present American standards,* and this assured him a comfortable degree of financial security. He turned, now, with added devotion to rearing his children and, as much as possible, taking the place of the incomparable mother they had lost.

*About $1,200,000 in 2005 dollars. —*Publisher*, 2005.

Marie now took over under his direction the running of **Les Buissonnets**, while Pauline, having finished school, busied herself with brush and easel, since she was an art student. It was no secret that she believed she had a religious vocation, and her father endorsed her wise choice of work as promising to one who was no doubt destined for the convent. Pauline also spent some hours each day with Therese, whom she instructed in reading, arithmetic and in religion.

But the best day of all for Therese was Sunday, the day in which she delighted and which she always awaited with eagerness. Not that Sundays held prospects of any frivolous entertainment, for that was unknown at Les Buissonnets. The reason for Therese's special attraction for Sunday — which remained with her all her life — was a rare understanding that the Lord's Day was a day set *apart* from other days, as one of joy and much gladness. Dressed in her best clothes, she would be seen joyfully on her way to High Mass, walking with her gray-haired father with her tiny hand in his and looking back occasionally to smile to her elder sisters following in pairs. This was a picture of family life scarcely to be excelled.

There was, moreover, a special reason why, for Therese, High Mass with a sermon had already become an event to which she looked forward with interest. One particular Sunday during Lent, when she was only five and a half years old, Therese listened attentively to the priest as he explained the sufferings and death of the Saviour. When he had finished, she became aware that she had understood every word and meaning of the sermon from beginning to end. From then on Mass with a sermon was to be her special intellectual treat, and one greatly increased when, from time to time, she'd glance up at her father and notice his fervent attention to the priest's words, his eyes filling with tears which he attempted to hide from her. At such times she became doubly attentive to what the priest was saying, since his words had produced so deep an effect on her father.

After Mass there was always special Sunday dinner, with

the added attraction of cake and pudding. Then, after a short rest, Therese might make some remark.

"It's my turn," she'd exclaim, "to go with Leonie to Uncle's house this afternoon." It had become customary with the Guerins, by special prearrangement, for two of the nieces to visit, alternately, their uncle and aunt every Sunday afternoon. On these occasions Uncle Guerin would take Therese on his lap and tell her some amusing tales, and sometimes, having a good voice, he would burst into a song with stanza after stanza relating all too graphically some tale of brigandry. Therese would smile condescendingly at this, for here was something at which she felt one ought to be horrified rather than amused. Her prudent uncle, noting her wariness, would promptly turn to some other pattern of entertainment. Overwhelmed by her precociousness, he would make remarks about statesmen, criticize some act of parliament to her, venture his opinions as to what the politicians ought to do for France if they wanted it to be great and prosperous; then he'd watch how these grown-up interests were being comprehendingly followed by the little girl sitting on his lap.

Promptly at five o'clock supper would be served, as only Aunt Guerin could serve it, Therese imagined. The novelty of a somewhat different dish always tasted to her exquisitely delicious. Immediately after supper there would be a game with her little cousins, Jeanne and Marie. Yet all of this seemed to pass too swiftly, bringing to an end that Sunday for which she had waited all week long. Still, no amount of regret could prolong her holiday and so when inevitably — at the stroke of eight — she saw her father, who had walked up the five blocks to the Guerins, come to escort his children back home, Therese was resigned, and would walk out with him into the night, her small hand firmly clutching his.

One night looking upward and marveling at the beauty of the starlit skies, Therese suddenly noticed something that impressed her.

"Papa, look," she exclaimed, "look up in the sky. My name is written in Heaven!"

"What do you mean, little queen?"

"Up there in the sky! Can't you see it, Papa? I mean the letter T. That's my initial. It stands for Therese. Sure, my name is written in Heaven."

At six Therese had rummaged through the vaults of Heaven, and discarding constellation after constellation, with their mathematical computations in millions of light-years, she placed her finger on Orion's Belt and, detecting in the planetary formation a resemblance to the letter T, very simply and irrevocably established for herself her position in the vast empyrean.

She no longer regretted that Sunday had ended. She had discovered something of ravishing promise; she had settled her place not only on earth but in the universe. Weekdays were to be less drab in the light of this amazing discovery that her name was indelibly written in Heaven.

14

PAULINE AND MARIE decided it was time to prepare Therese for her first Sacramental Confession. She was six years old and unusually intelligent, so they deemed it wise not to delay this important matter. Although the law of the Church then prescribed First Communion for children only after they had reached their tenth birthday, it was never the Church's mind to keep them from the Sacrament of Penance once they attained the use of reason.

If the world at large seemed to attach little or no responsibility to the deeds of children of six and seven, the Church held no such aloofness. Thrusting wide open thousands of confessional doors all through the Catholic world, the Church stood prepared, at the cost of great sacrifice, to serve the six- and seven-year-old child in the matter of conscience. Having only one purpose for her existence — the saving of immortal souls — the Church had always beckoned the sinner, of six or of sixty, to approach it for absolution.

So in accord with general custom, Therese, being duly instructed by Marie and Pauline, was ready and, as final instruction just before leaving the house to make her first Confession, Pauline admonished her.

"Now, remember, my little Therese, that it is not to a mere human person to whom you will tell your sins but to God himself, because the priest will take God's place."

"Yes," was the thoughtful answer. She knew how true that was and for the moment was concerned chiefly with the gravity of some of her sins. She had definitely decided which of these was her worst.

She remembered only too well that fateful day in May when she had acted so dreadfully. Pauline and Marie, who were not willing to take her with them to May devotions every evening because she was still so small, left her most of the time in Victoria's care. So one of these times, Therese decided to hold May devotions of her own and carry them out at home, together with Victoria. She decorated her small altar with miniature candlesticks and matching vases of flowers — in imitation of a larger altar in the Virgin's honor which her elder sisters kept in one of the second-floor rooms each year during May.

So as soon as the family left for evening services, she at once made ready to begin her May devotions with Victoria. She would have liked to have had a pair of real candle stubs to burn on her tiny altar but she had none. So she lighted her two paraffin vesta matches which she knew would last only a few brief moments, and would quickly leave her little altar without light. Anxious for the light to last at least for the length of the prayers, Therese called on Victoria to begin the devotions without delay.

"All right, Victoria, hurry and start the prayer: 'Remember, O Most Blessed Virgin . . . .' " advised Therese, and Victoria, obeying, did begin, but after a few words, seeing the child's anxiety, she burst out laughing.

"What's the matter with you, Victoria? Stop laughing and hurry on with the prayers before the vestas burn out," pleaded Therese. Victoria resumed, but after a few words she again burst out laughing. Kneeling, Therese looked imploringly at her nurse and dejectedly at the quickly consuming vestas. It was no use. They were nearly gone, and there was Victoria, not praying but giggling. The little one was angry, and, rising from her knees, she stamped her foot and cried indignantly: "Victoria, you old naughty thing, you . . . ."

Victoria, seeing Therese's reaction, at once stopped laughing: she was taken aback at what she saw. Fumbling under her apron, Victoria nervously produced two small wax candle ends and sheepishly handed them, not to her charge but, rather, to her youthful mistress.

The child blushed. She was suddenly as repentant as she had been tempestuous, especially on realizing what had happened. Poor Victoria had had real candle ends under her apron all along, intending to surprise her with them after the paraffin vestas had burned out. Unable to repress herself, on reflecting how pleased Therese would be at learning of the real wax candles in store for her, Victoria had given vent to laughing. If she had only waited a few moments all would have been pleasant for both; now she had ruined it all with her bad temper, scolding Victoria at a time when the poor servant really had planned to surprise her. And that awful way she had stamped her foot and the still more awful way she had scolded Victoria! Now she would confess this sin of anger together with other similar transgressions.

1   1

Her first Confession finished, Therese felt spiritual delight filling her heart, a sort of indescribable sense of relief that she could go out now and feel that her soul was as white as snow. But there was one other matter she wanted settled before leaving the confessional. She had received new rosary beads that needed to be blessed and Marie had instructed her to ask the priest to bless them. Reverently she said: "Father, will you please bless my rosary?" holding up the beads. All was now finished, and Therese returned to the pew where Marie and Pauline awaited her.

It was already dark when the three left church. When Therese reached the first street-lamp she paused, and taking out the rosary from her pocket looked at it intently, turning it over in the palm of her hand again and again.

"What are you doing, Therese darling?" asked Pauline who, with Marie, was wondering what caused this newly awakened interest. "Why are you examining your rosary so much?"

"Oh, I'm only looking to see what a *blessed* rosary looks like!"

After a rosary was blessed it became a sacramental, possessing a spiritual characteristic, she had learned from her catechism, and could hardly believe that the vital transformation from a mere string of beads to a sacramental would not be readily discernible to her eyes.

15

Two years swiftly sped by. The Guerins who used to spend several weeks each summer by the seaside at Trouville would invite the Martin girls to join them, and so Therese came to get her first glimpse of the deep blue sea. One evening as she sat looking out upon the ocean, with the setting sun dipping into its boundless depths, Pauline beside her began to draw gentle comparisons for her about the sea of life. The Commandments of God were like the sun showing men how to live so that they might reach the eternal shores safely and happily.

Responsive as always, Therese soon found herself "thinking" again as she listened, not realizing that she was deeply immersed in what is better known as "meditation." At her age, she could call it nothing loftier than "thinking." But the rare characteristics of her "thinking," which always came into evidence at the conclusion of her reverie, prove that in reality Therese was practicing discursive meditation, following all the rules laid down for this advanced spiritual exercise by writers whose tomes she could never have read at her tender age.

For example, on this occasion, having scanned the beauties of the vast rolling sea and the setting sun, Therese was imbued with the infinite power and majesty of God. Arriving at this conviction by some deeply subjective path, she was now ready to surrender all her affection to this Desirable Object of greatness and power, the Creator, and so make an inward act of love. This part of meditation, called "affective prayer," according to the explanations of spiritual writers, should come as a spontaneous reaction at the close of every meditation well performed.

Though Therese was ignorant of these rules, she nevertheless exhibited a remarkable adherence to them. At this point, surrendering to the desirable Object of Love, the God of Infinite Majesty, one might expect her to abruptly terminate her meditation. But no, her prayer, which she called mere "thinking," was by no means finished. There remained a final and most important phase of prayer to which Therese still had to attend before turning away her mental gaze, knowing the assurance that her "thinking" had come to a ripened conclusion and was to bear fruit in due season. The third and final part of her discursive prayer, her "thinking," had to do with forming a resolution, a something definite, before concluding the exercise of her prayer. This is, without doubt, a most important single factor in any meditation, without which prayer might often become a mere impractical pastime, a useless dreaming, and a meaningless retreat into non-being, and even an escape from the realities of life. Altogether unaware that spiritual masters like Father Olier and Thomas à Kempis all agree that prayer to be fruitful should end with a practical resolution, Therese, a mere child, on that day at the seashore, was drawing her resolution with striking adaptability. What of the fact that the vast sea was enchanting, and the setting sun beautiful beyond all power of words? What of it, even that God who made these out of nothing must perforce be the most desirable of objects? Yes, what of it, unless I do something about all this economy pressing down upon me from within and from without? Unless I can bring my will into play with this superb drama of reality, and, bringing my will into play, can perform some virtuous act, it is of little or no use to "think" merely about what is beyond and outside of me, even if it be God himself!

Not for Therese to dream of the lovely ocean, or even of the All-lovable God who created it out of nothing, unless, ascertaining her own comparative lack of loveliness or measuring the possibility of cultivating a greater loveliness within herself, she forges an act of will to achieve here and now something noble within herself. Convinced of the necessity of drawing a practical conclusion from her meditation on the sea, Therese thus climaxes her thinking: "Then I pictured my own soul as a tiny barque with graceful white sails floating in the midst of the golden stream and *I determined never to steer it out of the sight of Jesus*, so that it might make its way swiftly and tranquilly towards the heavenly shore."

In these words, Therese had drawn her resolution, applying it to herself in a solid, practical way. "*I determined never to steer it out of the sight of Jesus*," resolved Therese, as she looked at the sea with the setting sun, promising in these words never to commit a serious sin. Resolute thinker that she was, she concluded her meditation only when she drew for herself a practical resolution to be applied to daily life. And the powers of darkness watching her began to surmise that here indeed was one destined to give them a stiff battle. What chance would they have to trap one who had determined never to steer out of the sight of Jesus? And to draw such a resolution from the mere spectacle of a beautiful sea with its setting sun! What might she not dare to resolve some day were she to fasten her gaze on the surpassingly beautiful Countenance of the Saviour? The powers of darkness feared indeed to consider the possibility of reckoning, in their dark desperation, the losses they would incur from such commerce. Yet they connived to lay their snares nevertheless. They would watch shrewdly for an opening. Meanwhile they loathed themselves for fearing a little girl. But, then, their fears were not ungrounded, since they had a giant on their hands — in the form of a child with a "thinking cap" on her head. And before a genuine thinker who never gave up her mental deliberation until she had brought it to a ripened conclusion by forming a resolution that dictated a practical course of action, all the concerted powers of darkness were pitifully abashed.

But if, at the present time, they were repelled by Therese's flights of "thinking" which seemed to bar their every chance of assault against her at the age of seven, what indeed would be their plight should she live to seventeen? They must destroy her before then! True, they had no power over life or death but they had ways of making life more and more difficult.

16

IN THE FALL of the year 1881, Therese, being about eight and one half years old, joined Celine as a day pupil at the Benedictine school in town. Although she felt confident regarding her lessons, for she had consistently received high marks from Marie and Pauline who tutored her privately at home, she seemed uneasy about her chances of making good among strangers. In trying to make up to her the loss of her mother, her father and sisters showered on her a most tender affection. But how would this prepare her for the reception to be expected from strangers? She was known to be timid and felt happy only when with her own. How would she make out at the Abbey where she knew no one?

No one? Well, she had the consolation of knowing she would have Celine for company, which was something. Moreover, arrangements were made for the two girls to meet their cousins Jeanne and Marie at their uncle's drugstore and from there to set out together for the Benedictine school. It was encouraging therefore, at the beginning, to know she was to have a familiar bodyguard.

In class she found herself grouped with girls of eleven, and some even fourteen years of age. Yet she compared with them so well that when the general averages were read, she was the first in her class. She was then, for the first time in her life, to experience what envy would bring in consequence of her success. Good marks at home meant congratulations and rewards — her father expressing his surprise with profuse inimitable gestures at one so little doing so well, and with Therese, as always responsive, climbing on his lap to snuggle there a while without even stirring. But now, good grades at school only provoked jealousy in her older classmates, particularly one, a girl of nearly fourteen, who found a hundred ways to taunt Therese at recreation. Defenseless because of her size, and her sensitive nature which made her cry so easily, she was forced to do violence to herself — in the form of self-torturing discipline — to last out the day at the Abbey. Only the thought of returning to Les Buissonnets in the evening with Celine and her cousins, and the satisfaction that continued high marks at school would please her family, made life bearable.

Added to these trials, there now loomed in Therese's heart a new anxiety. Pauline, who had always given evidence of a religious vocation, was anxious to enter the Discalced Carmelite Monastery at Lisieux.

"Do the Sisters there teach children?" asked Therese, interested.

"No, they don't teach, nor do they nurse the sick as you saw the Sisters of Charity do," Pauline told her. "The Carmelite Sisters give their whole life to prayer and penance. They rise before five in the morning, and retire about eleven at night. They never eat meat, they fast eight months out of the year, they don't wear shoes, never leave the enclosure of their walls, nor admit anyone into it. The Sisters recite the long Divine Office which takes several hours each day, and then also they have hours of meditation and other prayers. They keep a continuous silence except during recreation periods, when they are allowed to speak to one another. For the rest, they must remain silent, keep their eyes lowered, look at no one and think only of God, of death and of the salvation of souls. In other words, they live like hermits in a desert . . . . "

Therese became intensely interested. "Pauline, will you wait for me until I grow up so we both will go off to be Carmelites and live like hermits?" she asked, and Pauline smilingly consented to wait.

Then, returning from school one day, Therese overheard a conversation between Marie and Pauline.

" . . . Six months will be over sooner than you think, and we may as well begin getting some of your things ready for the cloister," Marie was saying. She was two years older than Pauline, and now that Pauline had definitely chosen Carmel, Marie was anxious to give her all the sisterly attention which would make the final phase of her girlhood at home a cherished memory.

"What did you say, Marie?" asked Therese, visibly perturbed.

"We were speaking of Pauline's going off to the convent. You know she is going to be a Carmelite nun don't you, darling?"

"I know she is going, but not without me. She promised me she would wait until I am old enough to go with her."

"But, Therese, that is impossible. You are barely nine and Pauline is twenty."

Giving in to the logic of Marie's explanation, Therese now steeled herself for the worst, and asked pointedly:

"When are you going, Pauline?"

"I'm leaving in the fall, Therese, dear, if everything runs smoothly."

The weeks that followed were filled with grief for the youngest, who was so attached to Pauline that she could think of nothing but their separation: "Pauline is lost to me," she'd repeat, in the tone of an adult.

"When you grow up, Therese, I will be waiting for you in the convent, and we will both belong to Our Lord as we have planned. But you must first finish your school, dear, you know," Pauline would say, trying to assuage her grief.

"I suppose you're right, Pauline. I'll have to wait. But do tell me more about what the Sisters do in the Carmelite convent," she pressed. And Pauline would begin from the beginning and explain in detail the secluded and penitential life of a nun in the Order of the Discalced Carmelites. Then finishing off enthusiastically, she would add: "And what should make you happy is that the Mother Foundress of Discalced Carmelites is Santa Teresa, your own patron saint!"

"Her name is the same as mine?" Therese would ask, to make doubly sure, and then receiving an affirmative answer would appear somewhat consoled for her "loss" of Pauline.

One night, when Therese lay awake for a long time "thinking" again, she this time tried to fathom the *meaning* of a religious life in Carmel, as Pauline had described it to her. Its meaning soon loomed up to her: it held out a surprising number of promising ventures. Far from being inactive, to her it seemed crowded with possibilities and activities that appealed to her. One could "think" a great deal in the silence of the cloister, she reflected. (On more than one occasion she had disappeared, by hiding herself in the folds of the curtains and draperies at home, so as to gain that solitude she needed in order to "think" undisturbed.) . . . And reciting aloud all those long prayers each day was certainly important since those prayers were offered for souls who themselves did *not* pray, and who would undoubtedly be lost unless *someone* prayed for them. Inexorably Therese suddenly found herself confronted by the inevitable resolution: *She would become a Carmelite like Pauline and set out to save souls by praying and doing penance.*

That she was only nine no longer seemed to bother her. There had to be ways of surmounting such obstacles! In the seclusion of her room, that night Therese saw clearly, there and then, as one saw to whom a special divine call had been extended, that she would not rest until she had stormed the walls of the Carmelite cloister and entered its stronghold of uninterrupted prayer and penance — all for the saving of immortal souls.

The first thing the following morning Therese confided to Pauline, who had just returned from Mass, the desire and fruition of the previous night's "thinking" — and Pauline, listening, was impressed. The child described her *inward longing* for the monastic life so perfectly that Pauline knew it matched her own. God had ways beyond human norms of action, and He certainly *could* give Therese a vocation at nine; Pauline was sure of it!

"Very well, Therese, let me tell you what we shall do. Next Sunday I have an appointment with Mother Mary Gonzaga at the Carmelite monastery. Would you like to come with me and tell Reverend Mother everything exactly as you told me about your wish to become a Carmelite?"

"Oh, Pauline, yes! Will you take me?"

"Yes, I will. Provided you promise not to cry at anything that might happen, and be brave. Do you hear?"

At once Therese began rehearsing just how she would confide to the Reverend Mother her plan to become a Carmelite. When the appointed Sunday arrived, Pauline suddenly announced that Therese would have the company of her little cousin, Marie Guerin, who would go along with them to visit the Carmelites. This somewhat disappointed Therese who had planned on a strictly private interview with the Prioress. But, unwilling to hurt her cousin, and yet determined to have a successful confidential interview with the Prioress, Therese made the following suggestion:

"Look, Marie, since speaking personally with Reverend Mother is a great privilege, I think we should be on our best behavior. Out of politeness we should each tell her all our secrets, don't you think?"

Marie Guerin had no special secrets but then, since Therese wanted it that way, she saw no reason to disagree.

"Now," continued Therese, "since secrets must remain secrets, it will be necessary for you to go out of the parlor while I speak with Reverend Mother. When I finish I will leave and let you in. All right?"

Everything depended on cousin Marie's approval, which came rather hesitatingly, for she would have preferred Therese's company in the still and solemn atmosphere of the Carmelite parlor.

Mother Mary Gonzaga was visibly impressed with what Therese confided to her.

"Yes, child, it is possible that you have a real vocation to Carmel. To some, God makes His call known early in life and to others later," she said.

When she heard this encouraging response from the Prioress herself, she was nearly overcome by her apparently sweeping victory.

"Then, Reverend Mother, you think that although I am quite young, yet I can have a real vocation?"

"Yes, I do," answered the Prioress.

"In that case, may I enter the convent together with Pauline in October and make my First Communion in the Monastery the same day Pauline receives the holy habit?"

"But, my child!" the Prioress gasped, realizing that Therese had just made application for entrance into her convent. She had only intended giving the child encouragement, but, as it turned out, she found herself with a would-be postulant on her hands — one nine years of age. Recovering somewhat, the Prioress added: "You see, Therese, there are certain rules that absolutely prohibit one as young as you from entering. You will have to wait."

"How long, Reverend Mother?" pressed the child.

"Well, until you are at least sixteen, although some spiritual directors might prefer them to wait until they are twenty-one to enter our strict order."

Therese was bewildered. *Twenty-one!* She would have nothing to do with figures like that. Even waiting until sixteen seemed much too long. She would have to see how she could trim that sixteen down somehow, even if she had to ask for a special dispensation.

✦   ✦

Meanwhile Therese was watching Pauline's trunk being filled with the required clothing, linens and books which she was taking to the cloister. Finally, when her father was speaking of going to the bank to draw the money for Pauline's dowry to Carmel, Therese knew the inevitable separation was at hand.

"Aunt Guerin will call and take you to Mass at the Carmelite Chapel tomorrow morning with Leonie and Celine," said Marie, trying to sound casual.

"And what about you and Pauline and Papa?" said Therese.

"Papa and I, and also Uncle Guerin, are going along with Pauline to escort her to the convent."

"And can't I escort Pauline to the convent with you?"

"No, Therese, dear. You must go with Aunt Guerin to the chapel where we will meet you later."

The schedule outlined by Marie was carried out early the next morning, October 2, 1882, and Pauline, who was just past twenty, entered the impenetrable enclosure with its silences and penance. After Mass the family returned to Les Buissonnets, but, alas, without Pauline. Therese was consoled only by the thought that in the afternoon they would visit Carmel again and she would then be allowed to speak with Pauline, who was from now on to remain on the other side of the iron grating. The proposed visit was to last a half hour, the time prescribed by custom for these occasional parlor interviews, and Therese, who always had full access to Pauline at any time of the day or night, had to be content with a mere half hour. But when the visit was actually in progress, and the child stood in the parlor with her other three sisters, her father and her uncle and aunt, she soon began to abandon hope of ever recapturing the joy of uninterrupted talks with Pauline. Her father, of course, and Marie had the first place, and were conversing seriously at the grating with Pauline, exchanging those first few confidences that would assure them that all was well. Leonie, now seventeen, followed, for her share of the visit, as also her uncle and aunt, and then Celine, and finally Therese — who learned, bitterly, that only two or three minutes were left in which she could speak her few hurried words to Pauline, ere the black curtain was tightly drawn before them and the blissful visit ended.

⁊   ⁊

The following day Therese complained of a headache. This could be expected after such an exciting day as Pauline's entrance into the convent. When her headache persisted her uncle was informed; he gave her some medicine. She continued going to school but she seemed unwell. Then, a week before Easter, her father said that she and Celine would enjoy a week's stay with their uncle and aunt.

"I want you and Celine to be on your very best behavior while you are at your uncle's, especially as this is Holy Week. I am taking Leonie and Marie with me to Paris for a short trip, where we will attend all the Holy Week services in Notre Dame Cathedral," Louis informed his two youngest daughters, as he made ready for a vacation out of town.

When the visit to the capital was over, and they were on the train bound for home, a fortnight later, they all felt spiritually and physically invigorated by the change. They did not or could not realize how desperately they would need every ounce of this newly acquired strength to endure the ordeal awaiting them at home.

Therese had taken violently ill! She had shivering fits alternating with spasms of rigidity. Uncle Guerin looked worried as he described to his brother-in-law the details of the beginning at Therese's illness.

"I had her on my lap during Holy Week — as usual of an evening — and this time I was telling her all I could remember about her mother, what a remarkable person she was, recalling some of the memories of bygone days. Perhaps I should not have mentioned these things, but I had no idea . . . . Suddenly Therese burst into tears. I quickly changed the subject and tried to cheer her up, and so did her aunt, but she couldn't stop . . . . When it was time for her to go to bed, she was seized with a violent shaking. Her aunt stayed up with her all night long and we did all we could, believe me. Maybe you'll think I was to blame, but . . . ." he could not finish.

"Isidore, how can you think such a thing! You've been a father to the children since their mother died. Therese loves you dearly, as indeed she should, for all the affection you showered on her . . . ." Louis reassured his brother-in-law.

"Well, only that I spoke to her of her mother, and perhaps I should not have done it. I might have brought memories that upset her," Isidore said, still blaming himself.

". . . But we often mention her mother. It is our most delightful subject at home. If Therese is ill now, it is not your fault, Isidore, rest assured. We are grateful for everything you've done. And we're sorry you've had this trouble with her. We'll take her home, and maybe she'll recover in her own surroundings after a while."

Marie personally took over Therese's nursing during her strange illness, but Therese seemed no better. As the weeks rolled on she continued to endure sleepless nights and fretful days, suffering headaches and shaking fits. Medicines prescribed by physicians proved useless, and as Marie watched her withering patient she slowly realized that what Therese needed in her condition was not to be found in a medical prescription. Only unremitting love continually bestowed through a thousand and one acts of devotion and attention sustained Therese so that she could endure pitiful sickness, described by the physicians as a most unusual nervous condition for one so young. Louis, looking on, began to worry that she might never recover. But Marie, remembering her mother's dying plea that she take care of Therese, only redoubled her efforts to relieve the child's fearful sufferings. The more irritable and peevish Therese grew, the more patient and kind did Marie become.

"Darling Therese, drink this for Marie, won't you? It will do you so much good," she pleaded, but her patient felt quite unable to swallow.

"Papa bought beautiful white satin for Pauline's bridal dress which she will wear on her Clothing Day. Aren't you glad?"

"What's Clothing Day?" Therese fretfully asked.

"That's the day on which Pauline will be clothed with the Sister's habit and will forever after that be dressed as a Carmelite nun. You know that."

"When will Pauline have her Clothing Day?"

"Soon. Maybe next month. And on that day she will be allowed to come out of enclosure into the *outside* parlor and sit with all of us wearing her bridal gown and veil, looking just like a bride."

"Will I be able to go?"

"If you eat and drink what Marie gives you."

But from all indications it seemed that Therese would not be able to attend Pauline's Clothing ceremony, as the days that followed brought with them no improvement. Then, suddenly, Therese recovered so much strength, that Marie was amazed. She seemed completely out of danger.

And so, on Pauline's Clothing Day, Therese, along with the rest of the family, was dressed and driving in the carriage to attend the ceremony of investiture. For a while Pauline, in her bridal attire, sat in the outside parlor holding Therese lovingly on her lap, receiving her caresses and embraces. To Therese it seemed like old times again but it had ended all too quickly.

Then she found herself back in the carriage on the return trip to Les Buissonnets.

"You've been so well today that we must take care and get you to bed before you become too tired," urged Marie. But this precaution proved of no avail, for on the very next day Therese suffered a relapse. Weeks of intense misery now followed, sprinkled with severe hallucinations in which she imagined, in her delirium, that the bed was surrounded with gaping caverns into which at any moment she might be precipitated. A small nail in the wall took on the semblance of a thing of horror: a gruesome black finger pointing fearfully at her and paralyzing her into abject terror. When Louis entered the sickroom, the hat in his hand took on a horrible, frightening shape, and in panic frenzy she would cower under the bedclothes while the griefstricken father, sobbing, would retreat heartbrokenly. His little queen would surely die!

Marie was constantly at her bedside. Therese could not endure being left alone, and even when left for a while with Victoria, she would weep and scream for her sister.

"Marie, Marie," she would sob again and again and Marie, hurrying through her meal, would reappear hastily at her side, stroking her hair and whispering words of affection.

"She always frets for you," said Victoria one day, "except when you go to Mass in the morning, and when you pay a visit to Pauline at the convent. On those two occasions she remains quiet and waits patiently until you return. But otherwise she won't allow you any rest."

It was so. An unexplainable anxiety had taken possession of her entire being and even the daily visits from her aunt, who brought her some small gift on each visit, and Celine, consoling her after school, and Leonie's petting her, and the boundless love of her father reaching out with his affection left Therese unhappy, and daily advanced her further in her miserable state.

Finally Therese began uttering things she could not possibly have meant, feelings not like herself at all, and doing things as though forced to do them by some outside power in spite of herself. This new torture was manifested in her distorted facial expression and overpowered her so forcibly she seemed on the point of losing her reason. For hours at a time she remained in a swoon, incapable of making the slightest movement, yet hearing everything that went on and was said around her.

The physician shook his head. He had abandoned hope of any relief or cure. What began as a headache had developed into a disorder greater by far than any physical disturbance. What troubled Therese was beyond material science. Even a casual observer was compelled to admit this.

Marie and her father, as also Pauline — now Sister Agnes — at the convent, began to wonder whether the enemy of God and man had not injected his malice into Therese's destiny. This sickness was unearthly. It was inexplicable in a child of ten! Were the Powers of Darkness seeking vengeance against a family that was destined to do so much harm to his wicked empire? Was the Evil One aroused against Therese for her resoluteness to win souls? She who had determined at seven never to steer the ship of her soul out of the sight of Jesus, and asked admittance to Carmel at the age of nine, had to be halted in her unbridled will to reach out for the highest thing in life, spiritual perfection! Now that it was agreed that no physical science was able to counteract the dark obstacles flung into the path of Therese Martin, she seemed doomed, a victim of their daring assaults.

Her father was aware that to defeat the awful thing, the madness threatening his little queen's very life, would require supernatural help. Heaven alone could prevail against the foe and to Heaven alone would the father now appeal. And it was high time, for Therese had lost all power to recognize even members of her family.

Entering the sickroom, he came to Marie, and handing her some gold pieces, he told her to write to Paris and ask for a novena of Masses to be offered at the shrine of Our Lady of Victory for the purpose of obtaining a cure for his darling.

Marie sent to Paris at once for the Masses and received a swift reply that they were already in progress.

It was Sunday during this novena, and Therese was in the last extremities of desolation. Leonie entered the room to relieve Marie, suggesting that she take a walk in the garden while she sat watch with Therese. As Marie walked to the door about to leave, Therese began to call her in a low, moaning voice: "Marie, Marie! . . . Marie, Marie . . . !"

So Marie returned wearily to the bedside, but Therese, evidently unable to recognize her, continued sobbing: "Marie, Marie, Marie!"

"But I am right here, darling Therese. Why do you call Marie when you see that I am here?"

"Marie, Marie," continued the patient still, as if seeking beyond, somewhere in the garden, her Marie who seemingly did not want to return.

Looking on, Marie began to weep. This was indeed the end, it seemed. But she was unwilling to surrender and, walking up to Leonie, she whispered a plan: "I will go out into the garden and if our baby continues to call for me, carry her over to the window, and we will see if she can recognize me there . . . ."

Moments later, with Therese again calling for Marie, Leonie lifted her into her arms and carried her to the open window overlooking the garden.

"Marie, Marie," wailed Therese, and hearing her, Marie advanced and stretched out her arms invitingly.

"Therese, my darling, my little Therese. Here I am, my own dear . . . ." but from all indications she was a complete stranger. Therese did not know who she was.

Returning to the sickroom, Marie asked Celine and Leonie to join her in a fervent prayer to the Queen of Heaven to implore her help in this dread hour of need. In the corner of the room there now stood a large and beautiful statue of the Blessed Virgin, the one which Louis had bought many years before, before his marriage, and which had once stood in his Pavilion during his years of residence at Alençon.

As soon as the three sisters knelt down to pray, Therese herself felt a sudden lucid inclination to address a prayer to Mary on whose statue she now turned her fevered gaze. That she was even able to imagine praying in her condition, when she was incapable of recognizing her constant companion and sister, Marie herself, reveals the contradictory facets which came into play in this phenomenal tragedy. Yet Therese, unable to distinguish Marie, her sister, was evidently able to distinguish Marie, the Queen of Heaven and earth for, turning pleading eyes on Mary's statue, Therese asked her with all her heart to come forward with her Motherly assistance. And the Heavenly Queen, harkening to the prayers addressed to her in that haunted sickroom, was to reveal her power and put to flight the threatening forces that dared to establish their terrible reign in this sickroom at Les Buissonnets.

So, while the three elder sisters knelt praying, they were unaware that Therese, their patient, ardently regarding the statue of Mary, was being vouchsafed a signal favor. The truth was that at that moment the statue became animated with such radiant beauty that no words could describe. The sick girl beheld the Virgin's face take on an expression of unspeakable sweetness and compassion. What penetrated into the depths of Therese's soul, however, was Mary's ineffable smile, which was now bestowed on her. With this beaming smile the Blessed Virgin now advanced toward Therese who felt, simultaneously, all traces of pain and anxiety vanish. Herself restored to perfect tranquillity of heart and mind, Therese's eyes filled with tears of joy, and as they flooded her face she realized she was cured.

When she looked around she saw Marie standing at her bedside, visibly astonished. Therese was now completely restored. With her former remarkable alacrity she understood the cause of Marie's dazed expression. Therese was herself again! Guessing that a miracle had occurred, Marie paused a few seconds. Then she asked, "Tell me. What happened? Did Our Blessed Lady cure you?"

Therese seemed unwilling to speak to anyone of her experience, at first. Nevertheless she was besieged with many questions, and was obliged to tell her anxious and grateful sisters what took place. All would have been well save that Marie told their Pauline, Sister Agnes, at the convent, and she in turn told the Reverend Mother of the extraordinary visitation. On her first visit to the Carmelite parlor after her recovery, Therese found herself surrounded with inquirers.

"Tell us how the Blessed Lady looked."

"Did she hold the Infant Jesus in her arms?"

"Were there any angels around the Blessed Virgin?"

Therese's spirits fell. She had no amazing stories with intricate details to tell them, yet they all seemed to expect it.

"No, no, it was nothing like that," she confessed. "I only saw Our Lady looking most beautiful. She came toward me and smiled. After that I felt cured. Nothing more happened . . . ."

That, however, did not seem to satisfy the curious, who were disappointed not to hear descriptions of hovering angels and the other expected mystical phenomena. She was conscious, moreover, that certain individuals appraised her strangely, straining for a full view of her. (*Perhaps it was admiration because she said she had seen Our Lady smile?*) Therese shrank from this. Truly, she should have held to her first resolve and kept the secret to herself. Favors such as she had received seemed to lose all their fragrance when aired in the open. Was it not sufficient for them to see that she was cured? It was so unnecessary for them to know that she was also a recipient of Mary's smile! Too late now! Therese regarded herself with contempt, worried that others seemed to hold her in a certain kind of awe because of the extraordinary experience. She would have to undo that somehow. As long as she would live she would continue to feel repugnance at the mere recollection that, in an unguarded moment, she had unwittingly unveiled her soul.

17

THE FEARFUL and mysterious illness that nearly brought Therese to her death vanished completely and permanently and never again reappeared. But the remembrance of the ordeal left a lasting impression on her soul. Remembering her anguish, she would never underestimate the strength of the adversary of man. Remembering, moreover, the intercessory power of the Queen of Heaven, Therese was never again to fear defeat.

After a long vacation at the seashore that summer, Therese went back to her studies at the Abbey when school reopened in the fall. It was a particularly attractive school year for her because she was to be prepared for her First Holy Communion. By a happy coincidence, she was to receive her First Communion on May 8, which was also the date set for her sister's Profession of Vows at the convent. To help Therese prepare properly for the reception of the Eucharist, Sister Agnes wrote an outline of spiritual exercises to be followed during the two months preceding the date. Happy as the owner of a manuscript written for her express use, Therese carefully packed it neatly away in her bag when she left for a nine-day retreat at the Abbey, prior to making her Communion.

One night when the Sister came to look in on her just before turning off the lights, Therese addressed her: "Sister," she said, "I love you so much that I want you to see my secret." From under her pillow she then produced Sister Agnes' manuscript.

"You are very fortunate to have a sister in the Carmelite convent."

"I'm going there, too, that is, when I'm old enough," replied Therese.

May 8 dawned warm and sunny. Beautifully attired and well prepared, Therese made her First Communion. Returning to her pew, tears of joy flowed down her flushed cheeks. Her heart was flowing over with happiness.

"Did you see Therese Martin crying in church after Communion?" said one surprised little girl after Mass.

"Yes, I did, for she knelt right next to me. Why do you think she cried?"

"Maybe because of her sister in the convent. They say she is terribly fond of her and misses her dreadfully . . . ."

"Maybe she had something on her conscience," suggested a third, an older girl.

"Oh, go away," replied the first girl, rearranging her tulle veil, and then, left to themselves, the girls in white finally decided that Therese had cried because she was an orphan. "You know her mother is dead. Poor Therese, she must have felt it terribly!"

Later in the day, still wearing her white outfit, Therese went with the family to pay a visit to Sister Agnes at the convent.

"Were you very happy to receive Our Lord in Holy Communion this morning?" asked Sister Agnes.

"Yes, I was so happy that it made me cry. And some of the girls at school thought that I cried because I missed you or Mama."

"Why should you miss *us* when you had Jesus?" agreed Sister Agnes.

"That's what I thought, too. I only cried because I felt so happy," she said. "Besides, I had many favors to pray for."

"Did you pray for me?"

"Oh, yes, but then that was not hard to remember."

"Was anything particularly hard to remember?"

"In a way yes. For example, some people whom I did not know very well."

"And for whom did you pray this morning that you did not know very well?"

"It's rather a long story. But when I was quite little, about six, and Papa took me for a walk, we came across an old man on crutches, ragged and worn, whom I took for a beggar. So I ran over to him to give him a *sou* but he refused to take it and only smiled back at me. I always felt that maybe I hurt him by offering him money, so I decided that since God hears all prayers addressed to Him on the day of our First Communion, I would pray for this poor man when I made my Communion."

Therese was never at a loss to make up for any apparent misunderstanding so long as she knew she could repair a wrong, whether real or imagined, by prayer.

"Do you always keep the promises you make, Therese?" continued Sister Agnes, amazed that Therese should remember the old man whom she met casually on a side street about five years before, and for whom she resolved to pray on her First Communion day. Therese only nodded. She was so permeated with the spirit of truth that she seemed a complete stranger to the spirit of the world, to the destroyer of every good promise, and to the breaker of every solemn vow and high resolve.

But if, on the morning of her First Communion, she attended to a particular resolution she made years before regarding a ragged stranger, her First Communion day did not slip by until she had drawn up some new resolutions for herself. Running up to her bedroom, while guests awaited her in the dining room, Therese wrote in a notebook: "First, I resolve never to be discouraged. Second, I resolve to say a 'Memorare' every day. Third, I resolve to humiliate my pride."

This finished, the First Communicant was ready to sit down to a sumptuous dinner in her honor, with her uncle and aunt and cousins in attendance.

✦   ✦

Another year and then two slipped by and Therese was nearly thirteen, an age when the world begins to hold out its allurements and, not unconscious of her attractiveness, she was soon smiling at some of the compliments she received.

This was particularly so at Trouville, the summer resort, where her aunt invited her again, with Celine. Here, in the company of wealthy friends, and in an environment of beauty and comfort, Therese began to notice how attractive was that side of life. Conscious only of the swiftly passing vacation days, she played and rested, and enjoyed everything. One day her aunt gave her a pale-blue silk ribbon, which she at once twined around her long light-brown hair, and then stood admiring what she saw reflected in the mirror. It looked really grand. She was quite grown up. That pale-blue ribbon went well with the color of her luxurious hair, she thought. Then she walked out of her room and started waiting for the compliments which soon followed. Celine said she thought it was very pretty; her aunt said it was most becoming: and everybody else admired it. She found herself walking down the beach, being noticed, and she liked it, liked it so much, in fact, that when she knelt down to say her prayers that night, she was struck with remorse. "Why does a strip of ribbon make me so vain?" she asked herself. Then, "I'll never wear it again," she vowed.

The year following was to be one of decided readjustments for Therese. Marie, who for several years felt herself called to the religious life, decided to follow Pauline's example and also become a Carmelite. When she told her father this he not only approved her choice but encouraged her.

"There is nothing to hold you back, my dear."

"You won't be too lonesome, then? The thought of your getting old and my leaving you hurts me."

"But I still have the younger children with me. Besides, my family is not my property with which I can do as I please, for my comforts. If a daughter of mine wished to marry, I would certainly have to give her up. Shall I complain because you want to devote your life to God? My dear, this was ever your mother's fondest desire, that her children should be consecrated to

God's service. It was my desire too. Parting with you will cost something. And the thought that two of my girls are the brides of Our Lord in Carmel will be compensation enough for me to endure a spell of loneliness now and then. Life is so short!"

"You're right, Papa. I have a vocation, and I want to go, and I have no excuse for delaying except perhaps the thought of Therese's needing me . . . ." she trailed off.

"But Marie, you have done more than your share as regards Therese. You have brought her up, nursed her in illness, taught her and watched over her with more than a mother's devotion. You ought to have no worry about Therese."

"Then you think she will be quite all right without me?"

"Of course I do. True, she had to be taken away from the Abbey school last winter, but since I placed her under Madame Papineau's private tutorship, she's been doing very well."

"Oh, she's making remarkable strides in learning. Her lessons under Madame, as at the Abbey, leave nothing to be desired. But it is her scruples that cause me worry. Perhaps you don't know the whole story, Father, but really her every thought and every action, even the simplest, has been a source of trouble and anguish to her. Daily she comes running up to me to disclose some distressing symptom of scrupulousness. Every smallest triviality looms like a mountain of wrong and Therese is continually disturbed concerning the gravity of an offense she *thinks* she has committed."

"That is only part of her adolescence. She will get over it," replied the father.

But it was Sister Agnes who gave Marie the final assurance that Therese would be all right despite her scruples.

"Papa says it is due to her adolescence," Marie informed her.

"Partly, but mostly scruples are the portion of all souls striving for perfection. Marie, you must surely know by now that our Therese is no ordinary individual. You and I who have a religious vocation should be able to see that from earliest childhood she seemed called for something very special. I am not surprised, therefore, that our baby should be undergoing this trial now, for at one time or another nearly all the Saints endured it . . . ."

Marie needed no further assurance. Therese would be quite all right without her. Perhaps even better, for she could now help Therese reach her goal by praying for her inside Carmel.

"Father," Marie announced cheerfully, "I expect to enter Carmel on October 15."

"Fine. Since I know that you have all your things ready it only remains for me to go to the bank to draw the money for your dowry, as we did with Pauline."

On the day set, Marie joined her sister in the enclosure of the cloister, and, retaining her baptismal name, she was known in religion as Sister Marie of the Sacred Heart.

A month later, Therese, radiantly happy, ran in search of Celine to tell her the cause of her newly won happiness.

"I don't have scruples any more, Celine. I'm telling you, it's something marvelous . . .!"

"What happened?"

"Well, as you know, this whole month that Marie's been gone I was tortured to death with my usual worries and not having her to hear me out and console me, I knew I had to do something urgent. So I decided to pray to Mother and to our little brothers who died, saying that surely they are in Heaven and ought to help their relative on earth. I prayed just like that. Then I got up from my knees and I realized I no longer had any scruples. That was this morning, and since then I feel freed. I can't explain to you how relieved I am."

It was true. Therese's simple prayers had at one stroke gained her the much-coveted favor. Only later was she to learn that a trial such as she had undergone gives souls the advantage of a rare purification, like cleansing by fire.

18

IN HER newly won freedom Therese began to look optimistically to the future. She and Celine would often go to a room on the third floor after dark, and, seated near a dormer window, would look out on the starlit sky above. It always seemed the right atmosphere for exchanging confidences.

"You know, Celine, there is still one more thing that I should like to get rid of, and that's my over-sensitiveness, as Papa calls it. I realize it makes me unbearable at times."

"Oh, you'll get over that! You're not quite fourteen. When you're seventeen like I am, you'll be different."

"But why should I cry at the least thing? No one can hardly look at me when I find myself in tears. But maybe that will go some of these days, just like my scruples."

"Of course it will."

"It had better happen soon. You know, a thing like that sensitiveness, and tears, could keep me from entering Carmel."

"Oh, that's a long way off. You'll overcome that by then," Celine casually answered, not realizing how insistent the call to Carmel had been growing recently inside Therese's heart.

↗   ↗

The following month brought Christmas and, as usual in the Martin home, Therese's shoe was by the fireplace filled with gaily wrapped presents. The whole family, including Therese, had just returned from Midnight Mass, and it was the customary time to sit down by the chimney and unwrap the gifts. Mr. Martin, entering the dining room and noticing the shoe filled with presents, was vexed, and turning to Celine he said rather sharply, "All this is entirely too babyish for a big girl like Therese. I do hope it will be the last time!"

Celine's spirits fell. Turning around she scanned the room hastily to see if Therese was in hearing range, hoping strongly that her father's words had escaped her attention. But looking up, she noticed Therese at the top of the stairs, and knew instantly that she had heard every word. Celine darted upstairs wondering what to say to forestall a tragedy on Christmas, knowing how the baby sister reacted to the smallest reproof given by her father. To her utter astonishment she found her altogether composed.

"Celine, let's hurry downstairs to look at our presents — this will be the loveliest Christmas!" she said, taking off her gloves.

"Well, perhaps we had better wait a while. Papa seems a bit annoyed and I'm afraid that if we go downstairs now you might cry, and goodness knows I don't want you to cry on Christmas,"

"But, Celine, I have no intention of crying. Come on downstairs," she urged, holding her own, and Celine, bewildered at her sister's composure, even gaiety, trailed behind wondering what had happened. Meanwhile Louis Martin watched his little queen open present after present, thrilling with joy as she unwrapped her every gift. He had forgotten all about his protest of a few minutes before concerning the childishness of the custom of boots with gifts in them. It turned out to be one of the gayest of Christmas holidays.

In bed that night Therese knew she had been granted a generous boon: It was only three months since Marie had left for Carmel, and within those three months she, Therese, had scored a triple victory. She had learned to be resigned to the loss of Marie's companionship, she had triumphed over her scruples, and, tonight, over her sensitiveness which had made her weep so unnecessarily.

From now on she could rely on her self-composure. Not that

she had, at one stroke, gained a complete mastery over *every* emotion within the span of those three short months! Such a conquest over self would call for a lifetime of struggle. But she was to have from now on a more normal disposition. This was no miracle like her cure at the age of ten. Her newly won composure at this time came to her quite normally after she had got rid of her spiritual ordeal of scrupulousness and had, moreover, outgrown that stage of adolescence with its annoyances of a physical nature.

The holidays over, she resumed her lessons under the private tutor and continued to make her usual rapid progress in learning. Each morning found her at Mass with the rest — a family to whom daily Mass had always been a way of life. Having asked the priest in confession how often she was allowed to go to Communion she was told several times weekly, which she took advantage of.

In her newly acquired liberty of spirit she found more time than ever for her studies, to which she applied herself with tireless energy. She became so eager for more knowledge that besides the lessons outlined by her tutor, she took up certain subjects by herself. A few months later she was able to honestly say that she had learned more by herself at that time than she had ever learned at school. But, then, it was always appropriate to her caliber of genius to achieve through personal initiative, unhampered by antiquated systems, such stupendous and surprising success.

It now became increasingly clearer to her, however — in the light of her recent progress in learning — that, after all, the matter of pursuing science, lofty as it was, did not hold out the same promise of rewards such as attaining sanctity offered. Alone in her upstairs room, pursuing her studies, she realized she had to make a choice. Her logical mind, now remarkably developed, called out for consistency in thinking. Could she turn her back on the demands of logic? She had a vocation to be a Carmelite nun, and, thus, to strive for spiritual perfection, which is a complete perfection of the *entire* being — and not merely a high degree of mental accomplishment. So she soon realized, though she had tasted how sweet knowledge is and was convinced that wisdom is delectable and dilates the heart with unspeakable joys.

The studies to which she had given herself so enthusiastically were at this time a passion with her, but their pursuit, her prime obligation as a student, might too readily precipitate her into forgetting a far more important matter. Indeed it might have, had she not continued her prayers and spiritual reading along with her scholarly subjects. But the fact was that for years Therese had been known to carry with her in a convenient pocket a copy of the book *The Following of Christ* by Thomas à Kempis, which she read for some time each day. Often those at home, as did her aunt, uncle and cousins, would marvel that she never tired of it.

One day Aunt Guerin, coming upon her unexpectedly as she perused her favorite volume, said: "Therese, you must know that book by heart."

"She does," broke in Cousin Marie. "Take the book, Mother, and open it on any page, and begin reading a few words, and then ask Therese to finish, and you will see that she can go on from memory."

"Really?" marveled the aunt. Then deciding to put her niece to the test, she said, "Let me have your book, Therese."

Complying promptly and even cheerfully, Therese handed over the book, and Celine, looking on, was delighted with her sister's sunny smile, remembering that it was not always so. Only recently was she able to keep cheerful if someone teased her. In the meantime Madame Guerin, taking the small black-bound book, opened it slowly and after a few seconds began to read from it aloud:

He that would fully and with relish understand the words of Christ must study to conform his whole life to Him. For . . . .

. . . For what doth it profit thee to dispute deeply about the Trinity, went on Therese, quoting by heart, *if thou be wanting in humility and so be displeasing to the Trinity? In truth, sub-*

lime words make not a saint and a just man; but it is a virtuous life that makes one dear to God. I would rather feel compunction than know how to define it. If you did know the whole Bible outwardly, and the sayings of all the philosophers, what would it all profit you without charity and the grace of God?

The room became tense with a strange stillness. Nobody stirred. Aunt Guerin kept her eyes glued to the page in the book, and Therese, pausing to take a breath, continued to quote by heart:

. . . Vanity of vanities and all is vanity but to love God and to serve Him Alone. This is the highest wisdom, to despise the world and to make progress towards the kingdom of heaven. It is vanity therefore to seek perishing riches, and to trust in them. Vanity also it is to court favors and to lift up one's self on high. Vanity is it to follow the desire of the flesh, and to desire that for which hereafter there must be a heavy penalty. Vanity it is to wish a long life, and take little pains about a good one . . . .

Therese paused. Madame Guerin looked up from the page.

"You see, Mother, I told you Therese knew the *The Following of Christ* by heart."

"I see she really does," conceded her aunt, but Therese merely said: "Aunt, you chose a very easy chapter, for, you see, that's one practically at the beginning of the book. I wouldn't do as well further on."

"You did remarkably well," her aunt complimented.

"It's really nothing, Aunt, considering that Sister Agnes had me reading *The Following of Christ* even before I made my First Communion. That's about four or five years ago. I couldn't help memorizing."

Aunt Guerin shook her head in admiration. What other young girl would continue to read the same book of spiritual counsels by à Kempis for five years over and over again until she knew them by heart? What adult would have the strength of will to resist the novelty of the new books flooding the market in an era of accentuated publishing and continue to hold fast to à Kempis?

"If Therese wants to be a Sister she'll have to read *The Imitation*," again came from Cousin Marie. "Isn't that right, Therese?"

"*The Imitation?*" asked Madame Guerin.

"It's the same as *The Following of Christ* which also goes by the title *The Imitation of Christ*," Therese quickly announced. "As for Carmelites," she added, "they consider this the first among the best spiritual books ever written. They read it in refectory during the evening meal every day in Lent. Then, also, every nun has a copy in her cell and is expected to read a page a day." Therese seemed, indeed, well posted.

"Here's your cherished Thomas à Kempis," came admiringly from her aunt, reverently returning the worn volume to her niece.

19

"I KNOW you're older, Celine, by three years, and that you hope, too, to be a nun some day, but as for me I can't wait. I've just got to go to the convent soon . . . ."

"How soon?" asked Celine. The two girls were again by themselves in the attic room, their official headquarters for exchanging confidences.

"I'm hoping I could enter . . . at Christmas . . . ?"

"But that's only seven months away!" countered Celine, taken somewhat aback.

"I know, but by then I'll be fully fifteen. And that's only one year less than the age prescribed, which is sixteen. Is it too much to ask for a dispensation to enter only one year sooner?"

Unable to refute these logical computations, Celine was smitten with awe at this sister who seemed to bargain for *one* added year of self-immolation.

"When will you tell Papa?" was all Celine could say.

"I'll pray to know the right moment to speak with him. I'm worried somewhat because of the sick spell he had a couple of weeks ago."

"But Papa recovered from that easily. After all, it wasn't so serious since it did not even keep him from Mass that day," Celine explained.

"Yes, but you remember what he told us as we supported him on the way to Church? He said, 'We are as frail as the blossoms on the trees. Like them, we look splendid one evening, but in the morning after a frost we lie withered on the ground.' I only wish he were stronger," worried Therese.

"But that was two weeks ago. Believe me, Therese, there is

nothing to fret about. And I think that since you plan to enter at Christmas, you should tell Papa real soon."

A few days later, on Ascension Thursday, Therese began a novena to the Holy Ghost for counsel so that she could unerringly take those steps that would lead her into Carmel at the age of fifteen. On Pentecost Sunday, having finished her novena, she was flowing over with a desire to follow her vocation, even if she had to cast herself into flames, so she told Celine. In reality she had to resort to no such extremity, for, on returning from Vespers, she saw her father in the garden enjoying the cool air of the early evening, and decided that this was the propitious moment to tell him her decision. All that Sunday she had rehearsed her prepared speech and now she went to deliver it. However, when she sat on the bench next to her white-haired father, she found herself quite unable to speak. Her eyes were moist with tears.

Looking up, he put an arm around his child and pressed her to himself. "What is it, little queen, tell me!" Then, as if expecting to hear something of extraordinary significance to himself, he rose and, still holding his daughter close to him, he began walking slowly up and down the garden path, listening and wondering.

"Papa, I have something important to tell you. It is about my vocation. I want to go to Carmel, and it is useless for me to try to think of anything else. I belong in the monastery, as I always told you. I am fourteen and a half now. The Carmelite rules set the age of entrance at sixteen but I can ask for a special dispensation from this rule, and ask to be admitted at fifteen. That would be next Christmas, in about six months."

"Don't you think, Therese, that you are too young yet? Can't you wait?"

"I feel I can't wait. I feel I must offer myself now. To some, God can give a vocation early, even the Prioress admitted that . . . ." Therese grew ever more eloquent. She was not weeping any longer, only pleading with forceful logic to obtain her father's permission to seek entrance into the cloister at fifteen.

But most of her warm eloquence was unnecessary for her father needed no coaching, not even Therese's, to recognize the presence of the Paraclete at His wondrous works. Was this not Pentecost Sunday? Was not the Spirit of Love, the great Sanctifier, abiding in His Holy Church, moving hearts and recalling to them throughout the ages all the things whatsoever that Christ had taught on earth? *Come, follow me. He that leaveth father or mother for my sake shall receive a hundredfold, and life everlasting . . . .*

"Therese, how could I say no to you when you are asking me for permission to follow the Master? You can go, my little queen. You have my consent and also my blessing. I shall be the happiest of fathers to know that I will have three daughters at the Carmelite convent praying day and night."

Then noticing a small white flower growing on a low wall, he plucked it, root and all.

"God made that little flower," he said. "A thousand things could have occurred to destroy it, but it survived. You are like this little white flower. Now you want to be transplanted into the garden of Carmel and I will not hold you back."

For a while both walked in silence. Finally, when they were ready to turn into the house, the elderly parent seemed to have something on his mind.

"Therese, there is one thing I feel I ought to mention to you. Before you go to ask the Prioress to be received into the monastery, you must first go to your Uncle Guerin, lay your plan before him — as you did before me — telling him you have my permission to enter when you are fifteen, and ask him to give you his. He is the only relative you have on your mother's side, her only living brother. Since he has always interested himself in all you five children from the day of your mother's death, you must show yourself grateful for his truly exceptional loyalty and devotion to you. Besides, Aunt Guerin too has showered all of you with her attention. I want you to always remember this and to show your appreciation by consulting your uncle

before you take any important step, such as you are now about
to take."

"Yes, Papa, I understand, and I'll do just as you say."

In her room upstairs Celine was waiting to hear how Therese
had come out with their father, and seeing her sister's animated
face she knew all was well.

"Celine, Papa gave me his permission at once. You should
have heard him. He never attempted in the least to dissuade
me, nor did he say anything about himself, or his loss to see me
go."

"Then you're ready to ask the Prioress about entering at
Christmas?"

"Well, no, not just yet. Papa said I must first speak with
Uncle Guerin and get his permission."

"Oh, yes, Papa is right. Uncle would feel dreadfully hurt if
you forgot to take him into your confidence first. When will
you go to see Uncle?"

"Tomorrow or Tuesday," answered Therese.

"Well, it doesn't matter because he won't disagree with anything after Papa has given you permission."

On Wednesday Therese finally set out toward the Guerin
home to tell her uncle the pleasant news, to acquaint him with
the fact that she had her father's permission, and politely to
seek his.

"You say your Papa gave you his consent to enter the convent?" he asked her unsmilingly.

"Oh, yes, Uncle, he did," replied Therese, trying to break
down his sudden icy manner with her smile. When, without
even answering he turned from her and walked over glumly to
the other side of the room and stood staring silently through the
large French window, Therese began to feel numb. Suddenly a
streak of lightning flashed across the darkened sky. Isidore
Guerin, still at the window, realized that a storm was as fast,
gathering outdoors as it was in his heart. Then a loud thunder
clap shook the house. Turning away from the window, and advancing toward his fourteen-and-a-half-year-old niece, he faced

her squarely, looking more tempestuous than she had ever seen him. Isidore, always affable to his nieces, particularly to his youngest one, Therese — whom he called his sunbeam — now frowned and, setting his mouth with grim determination, said loudly:

"This is sheer folly! It is the most ridiculous thing I ever expected to hear from you. At fourteen and a half, you are only a child and nothing more, and therefore all this talk of becoming a nun must stop!"

"But, Uncle, I don't want to enter now."

"No?" he asked, brightening somewhat.

"No, not until Christmas, that is."

"Hm, but that's only six months away."

"But by then I'll be fifteen."

"And I suppose that should make up for everything."

"But, Uncle, I'm not asking for anything unreasonable. The Carmelite Rule *allows* a girl to enter at sixteen. I'm only asking to enter one year earlier."

Mr. Guerin only shrugged his shoulders and began looking out of the window again. Through a haze of conflicting emotions he was conscious that he was hearing his niece present argument after argument as to why, in her case, she must ask to enter at fifteen or fail in corresponding with the designs of God in regard to her. Once he actually conceded to himself that surely he would never have believed his niece capable of such eloquence, yet he chose not to heed it. At the end, Isidore Guerin was as unmoved as a stone.

"All I can tell you, young lady, is what I said before. This is folly. You should wait. The Carmelite Order is a strict order. You've been accustomed to a life entirely different from that lived in a monastery such as the one you speak of."

"Then am I to tell Papa that you refuse to give me your permission to go to Carmel at fifteen?"

"Yes, indeed. And what is more, you can be sure that I will not change my mind either. Young lady, mark this, I shall continue to oppose in every way possible your plan to enter the

Carmelites at fifteen, and only a miracle, do you hear me, Therese, only a miracle would induce me to change my mind!"

The rain was now pouring furiously, and the wind blowing the rain against the large French window seemed to be in tune with Therese whose profuse tears now flowed down her cheeks. Her dream of Carmel, like a castle made of sugar, had wantonly been melted away, in the deluge that poured down from the gray skies above. Her optimism on Pentecost Sunday now gave way to disappointment. As she made her way home in the drenching rain, she was unmindful of anything except her desolation, which continued for the next three days. To the end of her life she was never to forget it. It was not only that her uncle had refused the permission which she expected him to grant without protest. Something else had simultaneously happened to Therese that day as she walked back from his home to Les Buissonnets. There was suddenly cast upon her the devastating feeling that she was completely forsaken. It lasted fully three days . . . while the rain continued to pour as if in concert with her sorrow. On the fourth day, a Saturday, the would-be postulant decided to pay a visit to her uncle once more, not that it mattered what he would say regarding her vocation. Her unprecedented desolation of soul, now of three days' endurance, had made every other sorrow seem small. It was still raining when she reached the Guerins'.

"I want to speak with you in my private study," her uncle told her, and Therese was astonished to see him so interested and congenial.

"All right now, let us sit down and have a nice chat together," he said, offering her a chair. "Therese, surely you know how much I have your welfare at heart. If there is anything that hurts me it is to see you so distant and not confiding in me . . . ."

"But, Uncle . . . ." she began, when she was interrupted.

"Now, mind you, I'm not trying to say that you intentionally showed reserve toward me, keeping aloof. Yet the fact is you did hurt me. Therese, why did you stay away these three long days?"

So that was it. He, her uncle, had told her adamantly on Wednesday that he would oppose her every effort to enter Carmel . . . and yet he expected her to fly right back to him the following day . . . . But Therese saw through all this and recognized his devotion to her even as her father had told her. Uncle Guerin's was, indeed, a very exceptional affection for his dead sister's five children. If he stormed one day, he was most repentant on the next.

"Now, Therese, this matter of your vocation concerns me deeply. After you left on Wednesday I realized I ought to pray before handing down my judgment. So, believe me, I did pray very earnestly after you left, and asked God to direct me to do His will. And Therese child, believe me, I don't need a miracle any longer to understand that God is really calling you to Carmel at fifteen. I give you my full consent to go and also my blessing. I see clearly that you are a privileged flower which Our Lord wishes to gather to Himself. I want you to know," he finished, embracing her, "that I will not place the least obstacle in your way. I'll go further. Anything I can do to help you attain your desire, I shall be happy to do. Let me know, for you can count on me."

When Therese said good-bye to her uncle at last and walked out into the street she noticed that the clouds were scattering, and that the sun had begun to peer through. As she walked homeward she discovered, too, that the darkness had lifted from her heart. By the time she arrived home, there was no longer even a trace of clouds above as the sun beat down on Les Buissonnets in all its glory.

20

WHEN MOTHER Mary Gonzaga learned from Therese that she was eager to enter Carmel at Christmas, she lost no time making arrangements for an interview with Father Delatroette, the convent's Superior. But when he was approached by the Carmelites and consulted about securing a dispensation so that Therese Martin could enter before the required sixteen, he flatly refused even to consider it.

"I am altogther against it. She must wait until she is twenty-one," he told the Prioress. The nuns had not anticipated his opposition, but when he went so far as to set the age at twenty-one when the Carmelite Rule stipulated sixteen, they were utterly amazed. When Louis Martin was informed of these developments he took the matter into his hands.

"Therese, my child, I don't want you to think everything is over for you because of this. If you wish I will gladly take you to Father Delatroette personally so that *you* can lay the matter before him."

Though timid, Therese at once agreed to go with her father to see the Canon, but they were received very coldly, and he gave them a flat no for an answer. Walking toward the door, Mr. Martin paused to ask the priest a question.

"Since you give us no hope, Father, what are we to do now?"

"I'm sure I don't know," came the answer.

"I hope you will pardon my importunity, Father, but won't you promise to think it over and let us hear from you later?" Louis Martin pursued.

"I have thought it over, and I said no."

"But, Father, have you considered how many others who are

vitally involved disagree with your unbending attitude toward my daughter's vocation?"

"For example?"

"For example, I do. To be sure I considered my daughter's tender age as you have done, but I was obliged to conclude that God's ways are not always the same as men's ways. I therefore gave her my permission to enter at fifteen."

"You have a right to your opinion, sir, and I to mine."

"And, besides, her uncle also had considered her young age, but, after praying, was three days later enlightened to change his mind and now willingly endorses his niece's entrance."

"Lay people do not understand these things."

"But my daughter, Sister Agnes, who has been a nun for six years, is not a lay person, Father, and she discerns a real vocation in Therese. Besides, there is also the Prioress and the other nuns at the Carmelite convent who share the same opinion, namely, that Therese has a vocation and they are willing to receive her at fifteen."

Father Delatroette heaved a loud sigh.

"Mr. Martin, I am sorry, but I still say no," the Canon finished decisively. Then noticing Therese's fast falling tears and her father's unveiled disappointment, the priest felt too uncomfortable to end the interview with his unqualified negative. Besides, these Martins and Guerins were people one had to take into account for they knew their way around. Stinting every syllable that would go into his final semi-surrender, he said, "Of course, as you know, I am only a priest and as such in this case the Bishop's delegate merely. Should he, himself, allow your daughter to enter, I, of course, shall have nothing further to say."

Out in the street, later, Therese and her father started for home in another downpour of rain.

"Don't cry, my child. If you like, we can go to see the Bishop himself, and ask for the dispensation," he consoled his child.

"Could we?"

"Why, of course."

"But the Bishop lives in Bayeux," Therese said through her tears.

"And what of that? We can take a train to Bayeux, and be there in no time." He had a ready answer for any problem.

When Isidore Guerin was taken into their confidence regarding the advisability of approaching the Bishop himself, he proposed outlining a more detailed program. There was no sense at all in dashing off to Bayeux on a wild goose chase.

"Then you think it is useless?" asked Louis Martin, studying his brother-in-law.

"Not at all. But what I do say is this. First, let us try to secure a definite appointment with His Excellency. Leave this to me. I will call on Father Delatroette and ask him to write to Bayeux to arrange an interview between our Therese and the Bishop."

Confronted personally by Isidore Guerin, the Canon knew he was being gently constrained against every inclination of his unyielding attitude to contact the authorities in Bayeux to ask for an appointment that would have for its purpose the undoing of his veto. It was obvious that as far as the Martins were concerned, he had outlived his usefulness as an arbiter. He saw himself now being retained in the capacity of a secretary arranging the hours for the Martins' interview with a higher commission.

"Of course, an interview like the one you propose cannot be arranged at a week's notice. You understand, it will take some time."

"Reverend sir, we are prepared to wait our turn," politely came from the pharmacist Guerin who then took his leave.

Three weeks slipped by. During that time, even apart from the Martin-Guerin clan, someone was invariably approaching the Canon to raise the subject of Therese's entrance into Carmel. It seemed impossible for him to cross the threshold of the Carmelite convent where he was Superior without being interrogated on the score of Therese's vocation. When, for the third time, the Mother Foundress, Sister Genevieve herself, confined on account of her advanced age and weakness to the infirmary, began to plead with him to think it over and grant the Martin girl her coveted permission to enter as a postulant at fifteen, the priest threw up his arms.

"Reverend Mother Foundress," he exclaimed, "are you still talking about this child? I should think that by now you would forget it."

The aged foundress looked at him without saying anything and he went on, "Why do the nuns continue to press me about this? There is absolutely no harm done to anyone by making Therese Martin wait. Let her stay at home with her father until she is twenty-one."

Mother Genevieve winced. Here was Therese, deeply concerned in trimming one year off the prescribed sixteen, and the Canon continued to add five years to it, raising it to twenty-one. Then, making ready to leave, Father Delatroette concluded: "Judging from everyone's concern, one would think that the well-being of the whole Community depended on this single girl's entrance here!"

At that moment, unknowingly, the Canon had stumbled on a surprising discovery. He had only intended to emphasize what to him appeared as the one most far-stretched improbability in the world, that the well-being of the Community at Lisieux depended on Therese's entrance there.

But the one thing he had judged to be impossible was to come true. In a few short years history would prove that not only did the Lisieux Community depend on Therese's early entrance, but the well-being of millions, who would look up to Therese for every sort of solace and help, was to depend on her answering the call to religion as she did. But if the Canon's statement showed that he was the last person in the world to make such a concession for Therese, he was unwilling to leave until he had made one more protest. Pausing in the doorway, and turning to the Mother Foundress, he ended finally: "Mother Genevieve, I've had enough of this. And I want to make it clear that I don't want anyone to speak to me about this matter again!"

Returning to his rectory a few minutes later, the Canon was surprised to find a visitor, hat in hand, patiently waiting for him. It was none other than the pharmacist Isidore Guerin.

"As you might expect, Canon, I am here to speak to you on the matter of my niece's entrance to Carmel."

Father Delatroette struggled for composure. Had he not just finished announcing that he wanted no one to speak to him about this matter again? It must have been the Canon's unhappy hour for making assertions and predictions that were to have no effect.

"Yes, what is it, sir?" he asked, resigned.

"As it is now three weeks since I asked you about arranging an interview for my niece and her father to see the Bishop at Bayeux, I came to inquire whether you have succeeded in arranging an appointment . . . ."

"Not as yet. I hope it will not inconvenience you too much to wait . . . ."

Isidore Guerin, deferring courteously, bowed himself out, not without announcing, however, that he would be back.

21

"ANOTHER MONTH has passed without hearing from Bayeux," observed Celine on their way to Sunday Mass. "Aren't you beginning to feel discouraged?" she asked Therese.

"No, I made a resolution never to become discouraged. I'll continue to hope even if it should look absolutely futile."

"It looks so now, don't you think?"

"Not altogether! There are still five months to Christmas. In the meantime the suspense, I admit, is a source of suffering. But, then, everything worth while is bought that way. Don't you agree?"

Kneeling in her pew, Therese reflected. She had not always told all her thoughts — even to Celine. Prudence demanded this. The truth was, however, that recently she was inclined to feel somewhat resentful. She was being made to endure sufferings that seemed unnecessary. To endure pain at the hands of strangers and outsiders was understandable. But to endure this, and with opposition, from those who were of the household of the faith . . . . from those one felt entitled to cooperation, posed both a difficulty and a temptation. That was why she discreetly kept these thoughts to herself. Opening her missal, she began to prepare for the commencement of the Mass, unaware that before she was through her prayerbook would become a source of rare enlightenment for her. She was to learn the whys for those seemingly "unnecessary" sufferings.

It happened after Mass. Having finished reading her prayers, Therese was closing her prayerbook when suddenly a holy picture depicting the Crucifixion slipped partly out of the pages of her book revealing only one Sacred Hand of Christ, with its gaping wound, from which flowed a stream of blood. *With these have I been wounded in the house of them that loved Me!* said Holy Scripture describing the Saviour's passion. And looking at the wounded hand, Therese now, finally, understood. An indescribable thrill passed through her body. Grief such as she had never known before filled her heart at the sight of the Most Precious Blood dripping to the ground. Was there no one who cared about treasuring the Sacred Dew as it fell?

Whose suffering was less necessary than that of Christ? now suggested itself to the young Therese's mind. One tear shed by the Redeemer would have sufficed to pay the full debt of human sins, because of the infinite dignity of Him who shed it. But the picture of the Crucifixion, somehow partly slipping from the pages of her prayerbook, had revealed a Hand nailed to wood, and the cavity of which diffused a stream of Precious Blood. How extravagant was the Saviour in showing His love in order to win ours! As she meditated on these truths, an inspired resolution leaped swiftly to her mind. There and then Therese promised: "I resolve to remain continuously in spirit at the foot of the cross that I might receive the Divine Dew of Salvation and pour it out upon souls . . . ."

Drawing from her prayerbook the Crucifixion picture which had just fired her with a dart of love, she gazed at it with rapture. On that day, on Calvary, Jesus had exclaimed, *I thirst.* Yes, the Saviour thirsted for souls for whom He had died, Therese reflected. "And I," she resolved further, "imitating Him, must above all things in life also *thirst for souls.* For I do thirst for them in imitation of the Saviour. But I have nothing of my own with which to ransom sinners — nothing. But there is something the Saviour has which He does allow me to use as my own. The Precious Blood falling to the ground is mine, to gather and to treasure so that with it I can ransom sinners . . . ."

Therese walked out of church into the midsummer sunshine, not conscious of how intimately she was being drawn into the workings of the Mystical Body. Though recognizing the grace she had just received, and treasuring it all her life as the driving force that led her to heroic deeds, she was not at the moment aware of the suitability of the time element involved. For this was the month of July, especially dedicated to the mystery of the Most Precious Blood.

The Church, as the Mystical Body of Christ, had gradually, through the centuries, attained significant development through the institution of feasts destined to commemorate and glorify the mysteries of salvation. On the first Pentecost Sunday, it is true, the Church was born not as a child is born, but as a perfect *divine institution* reaching out with full powers of salvation to souls through the Seven Sacraments. But if the Church, representing the *abiding* of the Paraclete on earth, presaged a full perfection of being on the first Pentecost Sunday, the members of the Militant Church were meant to scale the heights only gradually, only progressively, in order to assimilate by degrees those deep and manifold aspects of Redemption which became their inheritance.

As mystics and Saints throughout the centuries gave themselves over to the contemplation of the various aspects of the Redemption, there developed, successively, a full calendar of Christian feasts, each to commemorate in a special manner some particular Divine Mystery.

As Therese knelt in church that July Sunday and became permeated with grief at the sight of the Precious Blood streaming from one Sacred Hand, she had been given the first sign that her destiny was to be indissolubly linked with the Mystery of the Most Precious Blood. It was inevitable that as a contemplative saint of the end of the nineteenth century, her preoccupation should be with that Mystery of Redemption which was reserved in a special manner for the needs of the present age. Keeping up with the times in things spiritual, Therese Martin was to keep abreast of ecclesiastical developments in a remarkably demonstrated way.

The week following she was to be brought face to face in a practical manner with a spiritual task that called for resourcefulness. The town of Lisieux was alive with news and gossip of the scheduled execution of a certain Pranzini who was convicted of some heinously brutal murders.

"His crimes are fearful. It is hard to conceive of such cruel and inhuman deeds!" said people everywhere.

"But most deplorable is his failure to repent," said Therese's father in her hearing. "Pranzini scornfully brushes off every priest who attempts to see him. Poor man!"

Therese showed keen interest in the remarks spread regarding the doomed criminal. Maybe she could do something. She would pray for Pranzini and obtain from God the grace of his conversion. Secretly, in her room, and on her knees in the church, Therese prayed, offering the Precious Blood for the conversion of her criminal. When his execution drew near, she made a final plea:

"My God, I am sure that You will pardon this unhappy Pranzini, and I shall still think so even if he does not confess his sins or give any sign of sorrow. Such is the confidence I have in Thy unbounded mercy. But because this is my first sinner, I beg for just one sign of repentance to reassure me." [4]

On the day of the execution, Therese avidly searched the Catholic daily, *La Croix,* for the report of how Pranzini died. Breathlessly she learned that the doomed man refused to go to Confession. Then, unabsolved, the convict mounted the scaffold — and the executioners were already dragging him toward the fatal block — when all at once, in apparent answer to a sudden inspiration, Pranzini turned around, seized the Crucifix the priest held toward him, and kissed the Saviour's Sacred Wounds, not once, not twice, but three times over! [5]

Therese folded the newspaper and dashed out of the parlor. She had had her sign — the one she had asked for as a special

---

4. *Autobiography,*
5. *Rose Unpetaled,* by Blanche Morteveille, p. 90, quoting *La Croix,* September 1, 1887.

favor. Unable to contain her joy, she ran to her room, where alone, and unseen, she poured out her thanks to God. She had now indeed commenced her life's work; pouring out on sinners the Precious Blood she saw streaming *as if wantonly* from the nailed hand of Christ that morning after Mass.

22

THE END of September saw the maples tinged with hues of orange and brown but the Martins still had no news to indicate that Father Delatroette had either changed his mind or that he had succeeded in arranging for the requested interview with the Bishop of Bayeux. The suspense of waiting four months began to tell on Therese. Each day the hoped-for news from Bayeux failed to come, and each day she went back disappointed to her room.

Looking at his niece, Isidore Guerin decided to take the initiative once more.

"You'll be prudent, Isidore, considering Therese's fate is in the balance. I — I mean, you'll handle the matter diplomatically, won't you?" came from Louis nervously.

"Of course I will . . . and don't worry. I have rehearsed my speech to Canon Delatroette and I am going to deliver it," answered Isidore, throwing an amused glance at Therese. After all it *was* a man's world, her expression seemed to say, returning his smile and grateful that they were standing by her.

"And what brings you, Mr. Guerin?" asked Father Delatroette.

"As you might guess, it is the unfinished business about my niece's interview with the Bishop," answered Isidore.

"Oh, that! Is the girl still serious about actually seeing His Excellency?"

"As a matter of fact, yes, she is," replied Isidore calmly.

"Well, I suppose it can be arranged," said the Canon leaning back.

"But we were under the impression that arrangements had

been in progress," answered Isidore, this time not too calmly.

"But, my dear Mr. Guerin, interviews with bishops can't be arranged in a week!"

"How true! We have waited four months!"

"Well, then wait just a little longer. After all, nothing was lost by a temporary delay," countered the priest.

"Nothing, did you say? Do you realize, Canon, what untold misery the suspense of the last four months has caused my niece?" There was rising warmth in Isidore's voice.

"Well, that's unfortunate," conceded Father Delatroette clearing his throat. "Now what is it that you would like me to do?"

"I request you to inform the chancery office that in view of certain contingencies and commitments on our time, we can't allow any further delays, but must see the Bishop this month."

"And what shall I tell the authorities is the urgent reason for pressing an interview this month? As I understand it, Therese is hoping to enter Carmel at Christmas. This is only October. There is time."

"But that's just it. There is no time. The Martins are going away on a pilgrimage."

The Canon looked up relieved. Traveling might help Therese see his point of view, he reflected.

"That's just fine. The distraction of a trip may convince the girl that she should wait until she is older to enter a convent," the Canon said enthusiastically. "In that case, I propose we wait before arranging an interview until Therese returns from the pilgrimage."

"But, Father Delatroette, you do *not* understand. You see, my niece must see the Bishop of Bayeux before going on the pilgrimage to Rome, because in the event that the Bishop should refuse her permission to enter the convent at fifteen, my niece intends to carry her request to a higher authority."

The Canon was unable to suppress an amused smile.

"And who may that higher authority be?" he said.

"The Pope," answered Isidore, and then suddenly realized

that the monosyllabic reply thundered through the room with a force that made all their previous conversation drift away into thin air. But if Isidore's faith did permeate him with reverential awe at the mere sound of the word *Pope,* his hearer was left unimpressed.

"Really, I have never in all my life heard of such a thing!" expostulated the distressed clergyman. Then, realizing that the case of fifteen-year-old Therese Martin was beginning to assume astounding proportions, and fearing difficulties in Rome, with repercussions that might prove embarrassing to his station, he decided to shift his approach.

"Mr. Guerin, when does the pilgrimage to Rome leave from here?" Making detailed notations of the answer on his desk pad, he looked up and finally announced, "You can tell your brother-in-law and Therese that they will hear presently from the Vicar General at Bayeux, Father Reverony himself."

A week before they were scheduled to leave on their pilgrimage to Rome, news at last reached Les Buissonnets that an appointment for Therese was arranged for October 30.

"That's the day after tomorrow," came from Louis. "Are you all ready, Therese, so that I can arrange for train tickets to Bayeux?"

"Yes, Papa, I'm ready," she answered bravely, and Celine, looking on, understood what it would cost Therese to stand up before any spiritual magistracies to personally plead her cause. Celine would have gone herself to the Canon to ask him to withdraw his objection, and, by allowing Therese to enter at fifteen, save her the needless anxiety. But Celine, as did the rest of the family and the Sisters at the Monastery, knew that further efforts to win over the Canon were futile. There was only the one course remaining. Therese was compelled to steel herself to the ordeal of facing the ecclesiastical dignitaries. They were of frightening magnitude at the tender age of fourteen and a half.

Two days later, in another downpour of rain, Therese and her white-haired father made their way to the episcopal palace, where they were introduced to Bishop Hugonin by the Vicar General, Father Reverony. Seated before a large fireplace in a magnificent room, Therese found herself in the center of the assembly. The aged Bishop peered at her from one side, the Vicar General scrutinized her from the other, and her father, looking for the moment uncomfortable in the solemn environment, motioned to her.

"Well, now, Therese, make known your request. Speak out . . . ." he said.

Except for the fire's encouraging crackle, the silence of doom permeated the vast hall with its tremendously high ceiling. Therese felt herself lost. She had hoped that her father would become the spokesman, as he generally did, and would make known the object of this visit. But now, in one sentence, he had placed the entire burden on her. Summoning all her courage, she managed to squeeze out that she was eager to enter Carmel at Christmas when she would be fifteen. But even as she voiced her request she sensed suspicion surrounding her from all sides. No doubt Father Delatroette had told these dignitaries well in advance that he was against her entrance to Carmel, and his word would undoubtedly count against hers. The Canon was a resident of Lisieux and the authorities would feel that his judgment should be given preference. The trip, the fear of facing the Bishop and the Vicar General, all now began to seem to Therese a waste of time.

"Tell me something, my child," now asked the Bishop, looking at her intently. "Is it long since you have wished to enter Carmel?"

"Oh, yes, Your Lordship, it is very long since I have wished to enter . . . ."

The room rang with a forced short laugh. It came from the direction of the Vicar General who now interrupted. "Come now, it cannot possibly be longer than fifteen years," he said, and Therese looking up colored at the caustic remark involving her age. But she was not at a loss for an answer.

"That is true, Father," she managed to tell him, "but then it is not so much less than fifteen years. You see, I have wished to give myself to God from the time I was three years old!"

The Vicar stirred uncomfortably. The statement he had ventured with such certitude, now flatly refuted, placed him in an awkward position before the Bishop as well as with Therese and her father. The Vicar could not possibly risk further disaster by attempting to disagree with the assertions of this straightforward girl who spoke of her soul's aspirations with such sureness. Meanwhile, the Bishop, who was in his eighties, and had heard many surprising remarks in his day, appeared stunned at Therese's frank reply. Could a child of three be conscious of having a vocation? But, unwilling to enter upon a topic that might involve debate, he now changed the subject to a higher one.

"My dear girl, you are still so young. Don't you think it right for you to remain with your father and be a consolation to him for a few years before you consider leaving him forever?"

Louis felt it was his turn to intervene: "Your Lordship, may I be allowed to say that I have given my daughter full permission to enter Carmel at fifteen. It is Your Excellency's consent that we came here to seek."

Therese sighed with relief, and Louis knew that he had warded off a possible calamity. Parrying, the Bishop now said that he would be obliged to consult with the convent's Superior, Father Delatroette, before he could render a definite decision.

"When you return from your pilgrimage to Rome, you will have my answer," Bishop Hugonin said with evident finality.

"But the whole case rests on receiving an answer from Your Lordship before we leave for Rome," said Louis, taking the matter into his hands. "Had not Your Excellency heard of my daughter's intention to present her request to the Holy Father in the event that you refuse to give her your consent?"

No, the Bishop had not heard of this. Turning, he looked

up to the Very Reverend Vicar General for an explanation. Father Reverony, stepping forward, began to stammer something to the effect that the Reverend Delatroette had mentioned that the Martins were planning to address Therese's petition to the Holy Father while on their pilgrimage in Rome, but he felt there was no occasion to bring up the matter. The Bishop stared at him in frank amazement. He had come to know Rome well and certainly did not relish having his name linked with that of Therese Martin's, as refusing her a spiritual favor. As matters stood, it seemed that it was high time for the Bishop to make what concessions would place him in some safe position in the background. The Martins already had two daughters in the Carmelite Convent, and wanted now to offer a third. If their own Ordinary denied them his permission, the Martin girl was ready to appeal to Leo XIII for a dispensation, the Bishop reflected, and he knew even from this short interview with the girl, that she would do it. Smiling more genially than he had thus far, he offered her a compromise.

"Although I cannot give you any answer," he said, "yet you will not have to wait for it until you return from your trip. My plan is to speak with Father Delatroette when I am in Lisieux on business next week. My answer will be sent to you while you are in Italy. Wait for it there."

Three days later, Therese and Celine left with their father on their pilgrimage, especially organized to commemorate the Pope's Golden Jubilee, for it was fifty years since Leo XIII had been ordained a priest. Father Reverony, whom Therese had met at the interview at Bayeux, was in charge of the pilgrims from their diocese, about one hundred in number.

While, for Therese, the pilgrimage suggested natural enjoyment as she marveled at the picturesque countryside, mountainous regions and wooded lowlands, her heart was really concerned with only one thing; entering Carmel at Christmas when she would be fifteen. So it was with anxiety that she often glanced in Father Reverony's direction hoping for news of the Bishop's decision. But the day for the scheduled papal audience arrived and still there was no news from Bayeux.

Then Therese turned to Celine: "I love this day, yet I dread it for I know I will be obliged to seek permission from the Pope. I tremble at the thought of daring to address the Holy Father in the presence of bishops, archbishops and perhaps even cardinals. But I have no choice. Papa has heard nothing from the chancery back home . . . ."

"I just can't understand it," Celine sympathized.

After attending the Pope's Mass at eight o'clock, the Martins and other pilgrims assembled for the great audience with Pope Leo. Here the Vicar General, Father Reverony, of course, presided, and after tendering the Pope the homage of the diocese of Bayeux, the pilgrims began to fall in line. One after another they came before the Holy Father, sitting on an elevated throne surrounded by dignitaries of the Church. The pilgrims knelt before him, kissed his slipper and his ring and then received the Papal blessing. Two noble guards, meanwhile, stood at attention and placed their hands on each pilgrim's shoulder to indicate when he should rise and make room for the person next in line. Father Reverony, in the meantime, stood at the Holy Father's side, to make introductions, adding some remark which he deemed a propos. When the Martin family came into view and Father Reverony noticed the reverential Louis Martin kneeling before Pope Leo, he said:

"Your Holiness, this is the father of two Discalced Carmelite nuns in Lisieux . . . ."

The Pope rested his hand affectionately on the white head of the pilgrim kneeling before him. Next came Celine, and behind her Father Reverony spied Therese, the cause of so much recent stir at Bayeux. He scrutinized her intently for any sign that would show her resolve to address the Holy Father. Everybody knew, of course, that silence in the Hall of Audience was to be observed, but noting a quiet resoluteness accentuated by a suffused blush in the white fair face of Therese, the Vicar General could not trust her to remain silent unless, of course, he now bound her with a special command. Appearing to address in general all the pilgrims assembled, Father Reverony now said in a clear and loud voice:

"I absolutely forbid anyone to address the Holy Father."

At that precise moment, Therese was replacing Celine at the foot of the Papal throne, ready to kiss the slipper and the fisherman's ring. The unlooked-for command descended on her and on Celine like a sentence of doom. What was she to do now? She had only a fraction of a moment in which to make up her mind. She used it to look up at Celine in the hope of obtaining direction. Celine did not fail her. In one earnest effort to help her distressed younger sister, Celine now said in a whisper: "Speak!"

Somehow there was a power in the hushed tone of that one word spoken by Celine, greater by far than the loud command of the Reverend Reverony. Turning imploring eyes to the Supreme Pontiff, Therese said: "Holy Father, I have a great favor to ask of you," two large tears blinding her eyes.

The Pontiff bent forward as if eager to hear the petition, and Therese went on: "Holy Father, in honor of your Golden Jubilee, I beg you to allow me to enter Carmel at the age of fifteen . . . ."

History was in the making. But if the pages of history were to resound with joy at recalling the incident, the Vicar General for the time being seemed to share none of this enthusiasm. Amazed and visibly displeased, he now turned to the Pope, trying to explain:

"Your Holiness, this is a child who desires to become a Carmelite. But the Superiors of Carmel are looking into the matter!"

"Well, my child, do whatever the Superiors may decide," the Pope said to Therese kindly.

"But Holy Father," replied Therese, resting her folded hands on the Pontiff's knee, "if only you were to say 'Yes,' everyone else would be willing . . . ."

"Well, child, you will enter if it be God's will . . . ." the Pope replied, slowly emphasizing each word with such sympathy that Therese seemed to have lost all her self-consciousness, and was about to press her request further when two of the noble guards told her to rise. Seeing, however that she continued to kneel, the guards took her by the arms, and with Reverony's help, lifted her to her feet, forcing her gently to move. The Holy Father then placed his hand on Therese's lips for a moment, then raised it in blessing over her head, his eyes following her as she walked away. The historic audience was over.

Outdoors a slow drizzle began falling over the city of Rome and for the rest of the day no sunlight shone on the Vatican gardens, as Therese observed once more how nature seemed always to sympathize with her disappointments.

23

ON THE two days following, the pilgrims went to Pompeii and Naples. All except Louis, who begged off: "Celine, you go along with Therese and the rest. I will stay behind." And so the two sisters joined the other pilgrims in their sightseeing while Louis, not too strong, his white hair adding years to his appearance at sixty-five, began a private tour of his own. He made inquiries, finding his way through Rome's strange streets, searching for addresses; he entered buildings that seemed prohibited to laymen, and finally he had knocked at many doors that opened and closed. Judging from his expression, one could see that Louis was evidently pleased at the progress he was making. Finally it was beaming with positive triumph for, indeed, in his notebook he now had one special name and address that indicated hopeful prospects. It was that of Brother Simeon, the founder and director of St. Joseph's College, an important institution of learning.

Louis had been duly assured that if anyone could help him to obtain permission of the kind he wanted for his young Therese, then Brother Simeon was the man to see.

For, apart from his vast work in the field of science and learning thrust upon him by his directorship of the college he had founded, Brother Simeon was distinguished in Vatican circles for even greater services to his neighbor than that of imparting the light of wisdom. This outstanding religious, with his important store of knowledge of Canon Law, had earned an enviable reputation for using this knowledge of ecclesiastical jurisprudence to help those who needed the protection of the Sacred Canons. He was never too occupied to listen to unhappy individuals who came to him with their sad reports of unfair treatment, or unjustified demotions.

There were specific laws to safeguard workers in the Church, as it were, against possible infringements by those in more elevated positions who occasionally overlooked the tenets of the Gospels. Brother Simeon, who knew these laws well, became a spokesman and champion for those members of lesser rank who suffered from violations of such laws, which were enacted and upheld in Vatican Courts for their protection. In short, Brother Simeon knew his way around in Rome, and he chose to use this well-rounded wisdom to bring back the tranquillity of order by applying the justice of the law in cases where it had been disregarded. It was his great desire to do whatever he could to help others: to amend wrongs; to repair injuries inflicted on reputations that deserved, instead, respectful mention; and to restore to a place of rightful honor the good names of toilers in the vineyard who through slander and detraction had their names smeared with blame, blotted with suspicion, or, perhaps, even eradicated altogether from the lists of the militant followers of Christ, where by their profession and vocation they so strikingly belonged.

Advanced in years, Brother Simeon knew from experience how essential it was for the growth and expansion of the Church to have her Code of Canon Law. But what he realized even more was that unless the justice of those wise laws were invoked against those who disregarded them, unless the benefits of those Sacred Canons were enforced in particular cases where violation of them had been sadly exhibited — bringing loss, shame and mental suffering to the innocent — the priceless value of Church Legislation was destined to fail in rendering its noblest service. For that reason Brother Simeon had for a long time made himself his brother's keeper in Vatican circles, where his services were sought and his remarkable deeds began to reap their store of benefits — bringing solace and justice in a practical way to those who deserved it.

It was, therefore, no secret in Rome that Brother Simeon stood ever ready to perform what so many otherwise apparently zealous men invariably shrink away from, bowing out apologetically from any slightest effort in using their position to favor those who had evidently been mistreated. And the more he saw how others drew away, into shelter, becoming unavailable when they should have emerged to intercede, the more Brother Simeon came forward to render those services of charity that others found distasteful. No problem was too great or too small for his attention. He was interested in listening to any who approached him whether for a service small or great, ready to exert himself to perform that act of charity that would lift a burden, or which would restore serenity to a face scarred with shame and embarrassment despite what evidence existed that within that brow there dwelt a blameless conscience and a record of a spotless life.

Anyone deserving to be heard was certain to be welcomed by Brother Simeon, so Louis learned on his tour of seeking information. Keenly disappointed that his daughter, in spite of every exertion for a dispensation to enter Carmel at the age of fifteen, was still left in suspense, her father decided to take the matter into his own hands and to plead her case in Vatican circles before those who were disposed to take on such a duty. That is why he was now on his way to see Brother Simeon who, he learned, was an indefatigable champion of those who wanted something good and noble for the Church but were deprived of a hearing or cooperation.

Seated at last across the table from him, Louis said: "Brother Simeon, although I am quite a stranger in your Holy City, for

I am here merely on a pilgrimage, my first to Rome, yet it was not difficult for me to learn from every available source that if I needed help, I would certainly receive it from Brother Simeon, the director and founder of St. Joseph's College. For that reason I am here . . . ."

"As one white-haired man to another," replied the Director, "let me tell you, Mr. Martin, my worthless services have been greatly overestimated."

"Obviously, I am facing not only a famous educator and college founder, but also a prodigiously humble man," said Louis smilingly, and Brother Simeon returned the smile and was about to make a witty reply. But Louis prevented him, saying: "But, then, only a very humble man could be expected to take on so distasteful an occupation as begging favors for third parties, and taking the side of the underling, when it is much more enjoyable to agree with the influential."

"Some people think I am nothing more than a meddler in other people's affairs," laughed Brother Simeon at this.

"Undoubtedly you are, in the way the good Samaritan was once a meddler," replied Louis with a twinkle in his eye, "except that your meddling has a far nobler end. And whereas the Samaritan gave charitable help to a neighbor physically wounded, you proffer charitable help to a neighbor spiritually in need of your services."

When Brother Simeon saw himself increasingly more entangled in a network of praise from which he hoped to escape only to find himself the more drawn into it by his exceedingly kind, but, in his mind, opinionated visitor, he sought retreat by coming to the point: "Mr. Martin, if you will take me into your confidence and tell me your story, I shall do what I can to help . . . ." he said.

In his own judgment, Brother Simeon never appeared to be in any way extraordinary. If during his long years of experience he continued to bring to the attention of proper authorities in the Vatican certain cases that deserved consideration, it was only that he did that which his conscience required of him, and no more. Now, leaning over in a gesture of friendly confidence, Brother Simeon was ready to listen to another story of disappointed aspirations.

"It is about my daughter Therese who six months ago asked for a dispensation to enter Carmel at the age of fifteen," he began. Then he explained the whole story of the successive thwartings and disappointments and misery which they brought to the aspirant, who was his youngest and most cherished daughter.

"Did you say you were made to wait five months for an appointment with the Ordinary on such an important matter as a Carmelite vocation?" asked Brother Simeon amazed.

"Yes. And, as my brother-in-law said, it seemed a cruel thing to inflict this suspense on my daughter. You see, he had also interested himself in her case, and did what he could to help, but in the end said that he thought the whole case was mishandled."

Brother Simeon now took out a notebook and began making lengthy notations of the whole case, while Louis went on to explain each difficulty: "Now, Brother Simeon, understand me, it is not that we wish to complain about anyone. It is only that we feel we must do what is right. Since my daughter feels herself called to the convent at fifteen, we feel obliged to help her achieve this spiritual end. God knows that the parting will be no easy matter for us, but we can't refuse to do God's will."

Brother Simeon began genuinely to admire the courageous white-haired visitor before him.

"Now, this Father Delatroette, who is the Superior over the nuns at the Carmelite Convent, staunchly refuses even to consider allowing my daughter to enter . . . . He has persisted in his objections for nearly six months. But the worst of it all is this: that he continues to assert that he prefers to delay her entrance until she is twenty-one. The Carmelite Rule places the age at sixteen. So you see that instead of working toward admitting my daughter one year *before* the scheduled sixteen — as set by the Rule — this Father Delatroette is pressing for an extra five-year delay, even *beyond* what the Carmelite Rule stipulates. Naturally, this attitude frightens my daughter. And I don't see how the Canon can inject his own opinion when it is contrary to the Rule."

"He cannot do it. If the Rule says sixteen, the Superior cannot stretch it to twenty-one. There are weighty canons which regulate all these matters . . ." Brother Simeon said resolutely.

"Did you say there are laws to safeguard my daughter against waiting until she is twenty-one?" asked Mr. Martin in amazement.

"Indeed there are," replied the Director assuringly.

"Thank God! Now I know I have come to the right place for help. You see, Brother Simeon, I am getting on in years, and I suffered a stroke a few months ago. While I am able I feel I must exert all my strength to do what I can to settle my daughter in her vocation. Now, if she must wait six years more, as Father Delatroette demands, that's a long time, and who knows what can happen by then? Perhaps I shall not even live that long. Besides, what can happen to my daughter's vocation during those years? She has no mother. I am greatly distressed about her future. And all this is so needless, since she wants to choose her state of life *now*! . . . And to join her two other sisters in the cloister. Moreover, as the Carmelite nuns are willing, nothing holds her back, except this opposition by Father Delatroette which the diocesan authorities seem to be upholding . . . ."

Brother Simeon continued to write in his notebook, promising to interest himself in every way possible to see that Therese would be accorded the attention her case deserved and, of course, the dispensation she so much desired. Looking up from his notes and shaking his head, he now declared: "Mr. Martin, I am in full accord with you and your brother-in-law that the case of your daughter deserved better handling. I am amazed that they can get away with things like that in France. Believe me, they would think twice before they would dare to attempt such mishandling here in Italy. It would not be tolerated!"

Those were strong words, indeed, coming from one whose judgment had to be taken at its face value, thought Louis. But when he now indicated that his story about Therese was as yet unfinished, and then began to relate to the Director the episode in the Audience Hall, right before the Holy Father, Brother Simeon laid down his pencil and listened breathlessly to every word.

"Did you say that your daughter actually addressed the Holy Father yesterday?" he asked almost incredulously.

"Yes, she did. Before the whole assembly she spoke up and asked Pope Leo for permission to enter Carmel at fifteen . . . ."

"And what did the Holy Father answer?" Brother Simeon asked excitedly.

"Ah, Brother, that precisely is what I want to take up with you and explain at large," replied Louis.

"Tell me everything!"

"Well, you see, while my daughter was addressing her request to the Holy Father, the Vicar General of the diocese stood at the Pope's side . . . ." began Mr. Martin, but was interrupted.

"You mean, Father Reverony?" asked Brother Simeon.

"Why, yes! Do you know him?"

"I know him well," replied the Director.

"Ah," sighed Louis, "then in that case it will be difficult to tell you, for I have a grievance against him. However, since his unsympathetic gesture was no private matter — for he made it openly and publicly in the Pope's presence yesterday — I feel at liberty to discuss it."

"What did Father Reverony do?"

"Well, when my daughter finished her plea to the Pope, asking his permission to enter Carmel in honor of his Golden Jubilee, Pope Leo seemed most sympathetic. However, Father Reverony interrupted. 'Your Holiness' he said, 'the Superiors of Carmel are looking into the matter . . . .' "

"Ah, that's too bad! That's really too bad!" lamented Brother Simeon.

"That is how I felt too. To say that the Superiors of Carmel were looking into the matter was indeed an understatement considering they had done nothing about it in six months. Now, had Father Reverony taken my daughter's part there before the Holy Father, or, at least, at least kept his silence, who knows, perhaps the matter might now be settled in her favor," grieved Louis.

"Yes, it is too bad. And I'm surprised Father Reverony would take that stand . . . ." came thoughtfully from Brother Simeon.

"You would be even more surprised were you in my place. You see, Father Reverony had promised us to do all he could to help Therese secure permission. Then, when the moment came for him to raise a finger in her defense, he disappointed us, and openly took the side of the Superior of Carmel, Father Delatroette, whose opposition has opened us to all this trouble from the beginning."

There was a knock at the door and Brother Simeon, making some final addition to his notes on the case of Therese Martin, for whom he intended to plead in Vatican circles, looked up and said in a flat tone: "Come in!"

The door opened and, to their surprise, the visitor was none other than the much-discussed Vicar General himself, Father Reverony. Louis was the first to say, "We were just speaking of you, Father . . . ."

Something in his voice made the Vicar wince. Brother Simeon meanwhile dropped his eyes but Louis, holding the floor, went on: "As this is the first opportunity I have of speaking freely with you, Father, I want you to know, of course, that we were all deeply disappointed at your conduct toward my daughter in the Pope's Audience Hall yesterday."

"But what could I do under the circumstances?" asked the Vicar rather embarrassedly.

"You could have showed a more cooperative spirit. However, it is too late to speak of that now. I have come here to tell Brother Simeon the whole story of my daughter's vocation and to appeal to him for advice since we had nobody left to whom we could turn."

The straightforward sentences cut like steel and the Vicar began to feel uneasy, only to hear now the reproachful voice of Brother Simeon, entering the conversation as intermediary.

"Frankly speaking, Father Reverony, I just finished telling Mr. Martin that his daughter has undoubtedly a most unusual vocation."

"You think so?" asked the Vicar, surprised that a complete stranger, drawn into confidence, should arrive at such certitude.

"Indeed! That she should not hesitate to address a Canon, at fourteen, and then a Vicar General, and an Ordinary in another city, indicates a high resolve. But that she should not shrink from personally addressing her petition to Pope Leo XIII, as she did yesterday, proves a rare, very rare vocation."

"I suppose you may be right," conceded Father Reverony.

"Well, then, why all this opposition and needless delay?"

"The Carmelite's Superior, Father Delatroette, seems to think she should wait."

"How long?" pointedly asked Brother Simeon.

The Vicar shrugged his shoulders to indicate he could not tell exactly how long.

"I understand that the Canon has made it quite apparent to everybody that he wants Therese to wait six years."

Father Reverony looked up, but said nothing. Brother Simeon went on:

"Well, that's the fact in the matter, isn't it? Let's face it. Therese asked to be received when she becomes fifteen, and the Canon, objecting, sets the age at twenty-one. And, if you please, directly in opposition to the clearly defined Rule that sixteen is the prescribed entrance age. Really, this is preposterous! And, all along, the chancery office condones the Canon's unreasonable demands."

Brother Simeon was now the canonist fighting for those priceless ecclesiastical statutes that were to set the Church on her triumphant phase of expansion and glory.

"Why does the Church here in Rome exhaust her energies," he continued, "burning the night oil to make a Code of Laws, if we are to disregard them and order our affairs according to our personal likes? Let us look at this Rule which stipulates that at sixteen the Church allows a young woman to enter Carmel. Is it a wise law? And, if so, why do we challenge its wisdom? Let us take the case of Mr. Martin's daughter who wants to enter at an earlier age. Who are we to deny her this permission and, in spite of the law that sets the age at sixteen, go on record to appoint an arbitrary age of our own liking, and tell her she must wait until she is twenty-one? What can happen to a girl in six years' time, did we ever ask ourselves? If she is called now and is forced to wait six years, how do we know she may not lose her religious vocation by then? Furthermore, how do we know she will even be alive six years from now? Hers may be a short life." Brother Simeon paused for a moment before resuming.

"Believe me, Father, I am going to do something about this if you won't. Do you churchmen in France realize the strides of progress that are on the march here at the Vatican? Do you know that Leo XIII is discarding all the worn-out notions of bygone days as regards administration, and that up-to-date efficiency is being inculcated into every department here? We are living in an era of advanced civilization with undreamed-of progress in science, and the Pope is exerting every ounce of energy to increase efficiency at the Vatican. Aloofness from the problems of men is not tolerated! Do you know, for example, that Leo XIII is blazing a new trail in the field of social justice? Right now he is making a historic move to lift the workingman to a place of dignity and security to which he is entitled."

"Yes, we have heard about the Pope's concern for the welfare of the working class, but what has that to do with the present matter?" came from the Vicar in a subdued tone.

"It has everything to do with it! Do you think that Leo XIII, who is making a historic effort to promote the welfare and security of the millions working in shops and factories, is likely to close his eyes to what is detrimental to the security and welfare of those offering their lives to work exclusively for the Church? Do you realize that religious vocations are the prime concern of our Holy Father, as they were of Christ himself, who before He did anything else in public, first attended to the matter of religious vocations? Allow me to inform you that Leo XIII has been tirelessly engaged in conferences for years with the best juridical minds on the important matter of codifying an entirely new and improved legislation, the New Code of Canon Law. One of its chief aims will be to promote religious vocations to the priesthood and the sisterhood, as well as to safeguard those vocations which God has manifestly conferred. In short, explicit Canon Laws are being added to those that have already existed, in order to guarantee ever more and more a place of honor, security and welfare to all those who have dedicated their lives to labor for the Church. For, indeed, it would be a sorry program of social justice that would promise rewards to the factory worker, the business man and the teacher, and then slam a door of unconcern and aloofness in the face of the most sacrificial worker, the worker in the vineyard of Christ! You may be sure of it, the Vatican under Pope Leo stands ready to champion the rights of all those who wish to labor for the Church, and who have labored for it . . . ."

There followed a strange stillness for a few minutes. Somehow it dragged on like an age. Then Brother Simeon began again:

"But social justice for the industrial worker and the Church worker is only part of the Vatican program. Leo XIII does not move in one sphere only. He is determined that the Church forge ahead in every way. He has even opened the Vatican archives and made them available publicly, to the whole world. Unafraid of the truth, he bids historians and scholars to approach and examine every record heretofore kept sealed. The Church, you see, is fighting her battles out in the open because the Holy Father wants it that way. On the occasion of opening the archives to the public, he declared: 'The first law of history is not to dare to utter a falsehood; and the second law of history is not to fear to speak the truth!' "

"Ahem," came from the direction of the Vicar.

"So you can see for yourself that a Pope who takes up for the underling on the one hand, and unseals to open view the Vatican's archives, is a Pope who wants progress. That is why there is an ever greater efficiency here at the Vatican. One thing is sure, as I have told Mr. Martin, the way his daughter's case has been handled was anything but praiseworthy. With two members of her immediate family already in Carmel, and she requesting to give her life to work for the Church, why, I ask, why is no attention paid to her?"

"But, but, we are working on it . . . ." apologized the Vicar.

"Perhaps you are, but certainly not the way the Vatican would like it."

"In what way do you mean?"

"I mean that Rome would certainly frown on learning that Mr. Martin's daughter, who aspires to enter Carmel, is made to wait in suspense for six months before even getting an interview with the diocesan authorities . . . ."

"Oh, that!" came meekly from the Vicar.

"Yes, that for one! And then the matter of stretching the entrance age to twenty-one when the rule places it at sixteen. Believe me — as I just finished telling Mr. Martin — perhaps at Lisieux they can do things like that and get away with them. It would certainly not be tolerated here in Rome!" [6]

The Brother's words did not lack directness. The Reverend Reverony began perspiring profusely though it was a normally cool November day. He was in no position even to attempt to justify the incidents of which Brother Simeon knew and which he attacked. The Vicar General prudently decided to rectify his stand. Turning to Mr. Martin, he promised him that he would do all he could to remedy the situation, while Brother

---

6. Regulation has been changed since her entrance.

Simeon meekly withdrew to a window. He had won a case for Therese Martin though he was unwilling to own that his intervention was responsible.

At the other end of the room, Father Reverony continued his overtures of amendment, but Louis, although cordial, remained quite hesitant about taking too much for granted. He had been too frequently and too recently disappointed with the Vicar, and begging his leave he began walking to the door.

"Before you go, Mr. Martin, I want to assure you that although I cannot undo yesterday's deed, I will make up for it. As soon as I return to Bayeux I will leave nothing undone to help your daughter secure the dispensation she desires. And, Mr. Martin, even if your daughter should not invite me to her Clothing, I shall invite myself, and be there when she receives the Holy Habit," the Vicar promised earnestly.

Three days later, when Therese, having missed her carriage while on a sightseeing trip, was obliged to share another in which rode the redoubtable personage, the Vicar General, the Reverend Reverony himself, she looked at him with apprehension. But, leaning over, he managed to say several kind words and again later, at table, he bent forward to listen to her conversation, making those amenable gestures toward reconciliation that bespoke his complete change of heart and full desire for amendment. Finally, before the pilgrimage had ended, Father Reverony told Therese openly that he would leave nothing undone to help her enter Carmel at fifteen. Unlike Father Delatroette, who would continue voicing his protest even when his overruled objections ceased to carry any weight, Father Reverony was the symbol of spontaneous repentance, recognizing a mistake and setting himself to its undoing.

Before they boarded the train homeward, Louis offered Therese to extend the pilgrimage by taking her to the Holy Land, but this she refused. "I've had enough of traveling. It is to close myself within Carmel that I desire, in order to save souls," she told him.

Home from the pilgrimage, Therese waited eagerly for news

from the diocesan office. But ten days later, nothing having been heard, her Uncle Guerin helped her write a letter to the Bishop of Bayeux, reminding him that it was already December, and that she was awaiting his permission to enter on her fifteenth birthday, which would be on January 2.

Came January 1, her birthday eve, and with it the surprise of her life. A letter from Mother Mary Gonzaga, the Prioress of the Carmelite Convent, informed her that the permission for her to enter at once had been received by her from the Bishop.

The Vicar General had kept his word.

There was only one small drawback. Despite the Bishop's consent, Father Delatroette still continued to object, so that, to appease him partially, the Prioress decided that Therese should wait until after Lent when the rigorous Carmelite fast would be over. She was to remain at home another three months. It was a wise arrangement, and as such it met with everyone's accord.

On April 9, 1888, escorted by her family, Therese stood at the door of the enclosure, ready to be received. Everyone wept save Therese. As she was about to go inside, Father Delatroette, who was also present, made a final observation in a loud voice: "Well, my Reverend Sisters, you can sing a *Te Deum*. As the delegate of His Excellency, Bishop Hugonin, I present you this child of fifteen whose entrance you have desired. I only trust that she will not disappoint your hopes; but let me remind you that if it turns out otherwise, you, and not I, will bear the responsibility!"

And Louis coming home, wrote a letter to a friend: "Only God could require of me so great a sacrifice!"

24

"Now that you've been welcomed by all the nuns, the Mistress of Novices and I will show you to your cell," said Mother Mary Gonzaga.

Leading the way, the two nuns escorted Therese to a small bare room about nine feet square. The bed at one end, covered with black woolen serge, was in reality nothing more than two unpainted planks resting on narrow wooden trestles, with a straw mattress, a pillow and common blankets. At the other end of the room was a small table, a bench, and, finally, a water jug and wash basin.

"I want you to notice that the cross which hangs in your cell has no figure of the Saviour on it," the prioress now said, pointing to the unadorned black wooden cross on the wall. "You are to consider yourself nailed to that cross in His stead."

"Yes, Reverend Mother," Therese answered seriously. She had been told of the cross without the figure of the Saviour, which hangs in every Carmelite cell throughout the world, wherever there is a Monastery of Discalced Carmelites of the Primitive Rule. Now, however, that she actually saw it in this, her own, cell, it took on a new and deeper meaning. Surely all these particulars planned by the great foundress, Saint Teresa of Avila, were bound to make a Carmelite nun reach her goal.

"We will leave you here for a while so that you may change your blue dress and put on your nice black postulant uniform which you will wear until the day you receive the Holy Habit. And, by the way, pin up your hair, child. You have your little black cap?" she asked.

"Yes, I have, Reverend Mother."

"Very well, then, let us see how neatly you can tuck that mass of hair into it. When you are ready, come out. We will be close by."

There was, of course, no mirror for Therese to see whether she had pinned her thick brown braids neatly into the net cap with its small ribbon tied under the chin. There would never again be a mirror for her into which she would look. A few minutes later, Therese, looking solemn in her black dress with its cape falling over her shoulders and reaching to the elbows, joined the Prioress. She was next conducted to a room called the novitiate, where stood a small altar before which she and the other novices knelt while the Mistress recited prayers especially prescribed for the occasion of receiving a new postulant.

"This room is a sort of classroom," the Prioress now told Therese, "where your Mistress assembles you daily to instruct you in the use of the breviaries, how to perform the rubrics in choir, and in all other matters. And, last but not least, you will learn here also what will be your share of monastic duties during the hours appointed for daily manual labor."

Having finished, the Prioress left Therese in charge of the Novice Mistress and walked away, wondering how the new, fifteen-year-old postulant would make out.

Dismissing her other novices, the Mistress, Mother Mary of the Angels, kept Therese behind for a first get-together talk. It would ultimately be her burden to initiate the fledgling into all the rigors of Carmel, but that would come gradually. Since it would be her chief obligation to help the new postulant attain perfection, it was necessary for her first to observe her in order to determine what were her talents and inclinations. For it is the keynote of all Carmelite spirituality not only to allow, but to encourage, each individual soul to develop her powers for good, according to her own particular attractions, as God indicates. Not reserved to the Mistress is any privilege of imposing on all alike her own preferred system or method, no matter how well-intentioned this may be. Hers is the duty to strive to learn what *God* desires of each individual nun, and then to help her advance along that special way indicated by Providence.

For example, if the rarest mysticism with its accompanying phenomena of ecstasies and visions be the path by which God chooses to lead a particular nun, then certainly the environs of Carmel are made to shelter that mystical state and to develop it as no other Order in the Church can do. For, indeed, the legacy of Carmel is in the direction of this mysticism — the very deepest! Again, if a nun be drawn to perfection by ordinary means, daily perseverance to the Rule, with no trace of the mystical surrounding her, in the walls of Carmel she, too, has a secure haven. For indeed, the Teresian Rule, prescribing a specific duty for every moment of the daily life, leaves nothing to whim or hazard! And, finally, if a nun is a combination of these two states, called to partial contemplation and partial routine duties, here in Carmel there is full scope for both her alternating attractions.

By what path would God lead her new charge? wondered Mother Mary of the Angels. It was possible, of course, that one so young as Therese — who was only just fifteen — could have a strong *desire* to be a nun; but on the other hand, she might find herself inside a cloister with *no* particular religious attractions . . . .

Smiling pleasantly, the Mistress now asked, "Are you happy that your name in religion is to be Sister Therese of the Child Jesus?" She did not realize that the sentence would serve as a direct avenue by which she was to discover her young postulant's chief spiritual attraction.

"Oh, yes, I am very happy over it because, you see, I have for some time resolved to be a toy for the Christ Child," Therese answered. Then she stopped suddenly: she had always found it difficult to speak of herself.

"Oh, you did? In what way did you resolve to be His toy?" the Mistress asked, trying to help her overcome her self-consciousness.

"Well, I used to think that He would be pleased to have a

toy with which to play in any way that He felt inclined. So I told Him not to treat me like one of the precious toys which children only look at and dare not touch, but to consider me as a little ball of no value that could be thrown on the ground, tossed about, pierced, left in a corner or pressed to His heart, just as it might please His fancy. In short, I wanted to amuse Him."

"And did the Holy Child throw His ball on the ground sometimes, or leave her in a corner?" the Mistress asked, trying to fathom the depths of her new postulant's outlook.

"Yes, He did, especially during the last nine months when I had so many trying difficulties in order to enter Carmel," Therese confessed. Then, hearing the sound of a bell, she looked up.

"That's the bell for the noonday meal, which is taken at eleven o'clock during the summertime. Come with me and I will show you your place in the refectory," said the Mistress, rising.

On entering the large room, with a small table at the front and two long tables along opposite walls, the Mistress whispered:

"That small table at the head is where the Prioress and the sub-Prioress sit. The long table to your right and this one to your left is for the other Sisters, who sit according to seniority, that is according to the number of years they are in religion. Your place is here at the end. Now that you know where you will sit, come with me to the choir."

"The choir?" asked Therese.

"Yes, you know, that is the cloistered part of the chapel," she explained. "You see, when the dinner-bell rings, the Sisters never go directly to the refectory to eat. They first go to the choir where they kneel for five minutes to think over how they spent the morning. It is called Examen."

Therese was being slowly initiated into the routine of a Carmelite day. Five minutes later, as she sat in the refectory, she noticed the earthenware plate and still coarser-looking enameled cup that stood at each Sister's place. (This was not Les Buissonnets with its good porcelain.) The nun whose turn it was to serve the dinner during the current week approached each Sister at the table with a tray. On it were two pans, one filled with boiled potatoes and the other with hard-boiled eggs.

Each Sister took one egg and as many potatoes as she desired. Then came another tray with boiled carrots and, finally, a last portion — a bread pudding sweetened with a few raisins, and tea. There would never be anything different. The vegetables would vary to include cabbage, or peas, or beans, and instead of the egg, there would be sardines or salted mackerel, or fresh fish on occasion, but there would never be a slice of meat, not even at Easter or Christmas, for all flesh meat was forbidden.

As Therese ate her first dinner in the cloister, she listened attentively to a Sister who, seated on a raised platform at the other end of the refectory, began reading a spiritual book, *The Liturgical Year* by Dom Gueranger. As it was the Feast of the Annunciation, a chapter explaining this Mystery was chosen as suitable for the day's reading. This was an exquisite work, as are all the volumes explaining the feasts of the year written by Gueranger.

Listening to the reading in the quiet atmosphere of the refectory, Therese already realized that this literary treat readily made up for some privation in the menu. It was to be one of her main delights all through her life in Carmel to know that every day during dinner and the evening meal there was to be reading to which she could listen and be inspired.

Dinner finished, there was an hour's recreation, and Therese found herself in the garden surrounded by all the nuns, including her own two sisters, who pressed her for information. "Did she like the cloister? What did she think of it?" Since the nuns retain a perpetual silence except during one hour following the noon meal, and one hour following supper — when they are allowed to converse together — these recreations become for them occasions of real merriment. From the first day Therese was to excel in making these recreations as joyous as possible, thinking in advance what she might say or do to give a pleasant touch to them. The Sisters lived a life of great penance, and she felt she wanted to do her utmost to bring some cheer into their midst.

In her cell that afternoon, Therese began to reflect. So this was Carmel. And this was the holy atmosphere where she would live. She was beginning to realize its possibilities, concluding that from what she already saw these were enormous. In this environment of silence, restraint, detachment and prayer, she would, perforce, learn everything about the Saints and, imitating them, would reach her goal.

Following the evening recreation, Therese was instructed to return to her cell and retire.

"We have prayers that will continue until quite late, but you are to go to bed now. You will have time enough to be initiated gradually into the full Carmelite exercises," the Mistress said.

Therese was very grateful, since at this point she could not distinguish one exercise from another for her heart was too full — this was inaccessible Carmel, now her home forever! When, finally, Therese lay down on her cot, and felt for the first time the pinching discomfort of the two boards, and reflected that such was to be the holy monotony of her entire life, she found it difficult to fall asleep. The following week she had a backache and was worried lest she might become ill. This was not a malady, however — only the result of sleeping in a bed without springs and an adequate mattress. She would get accustomed to it as one got accustomed to all penance, when through habit it would become sweet.

Yet, not in the way indulgence in comfort and pleasure is sweet; but in a far different way, which only those know who have slept on boards through deliberate choice. As only those know who have abstained from meat, eating their unsavory meatless meals year after year. As only those know who have gazed upon a black cross in their cells with no figure of the Saviour upon it, and knew that it was their turn to hang there until the end of their earthly lives.

25

Six weeks later Sister Therese was well initiated into the routine sublimity of a Carmelite day. She rose with the others at 4:45 A.M., and retired with them about 11 at night.

One morning Sister Therese asked the Mistress: "Do you still wish me to go to weed the garden for a half hour every afternoon?"

"Yes, Sister, of course I do."

Therese walked away and said no more. The reason she was worried about going to the garden each afternoon was that one day the Prioress coming upon her outdoors said to her in a quite harsh tone: "What is this? The postulant taking a walk in the garden? Really, this child does absolutely nothing. What are we to think of a postulant who must be sent out for a walk every day!"

Sister Therese colored but said nothing. This was not the new postulant's first moral victory in which the Prioress featured prominently. Outstanding among these was her resolve never to go to the Prioress' cell to speak with her unless required to do so. Nobody had told her to bind herself with such a resolve. To some it might even appear as an act of virtue for a postulant to frequently visit the cell of the Superioress in a gesture of humility.

Sister Therese had known Mother Mary Gonzaga for years, visiting with her in the parlor, and had become attached to her, naturally. One day, longing for another chat with the Prioress, and on the way to her cell, she was struck with remorse. She had no problem to discuss with her. Well, then maybe she could beg leave for one of a number of trifles or seek some small permission which Carmelites never take for granted, but for which they beg the Superioress personally, on bended knee. But no, she needed nothing, not even permission for a straight pin. Silence was one of the chief penances imposed on Carmelites, she admonished herself. Examining her motives, Sister Therese turned back to her own cell, resolving there and then that although she would be compelled to hold on to the banisters, which she did again and again, to prevent herself from yielding, she would not knock on the Prioress' door except for a valid reason.

In the meantime the Prioress did not suspect why, recently, she had had so few visits from the postulant. Perhaps, too, this estrangement made it easier for her to administer frequent reprimands.

A couple of weeks passed. Then the Mistress said to Sister Therese: "Reverend Mother wants you to have extra manual labor. In addition to sewing in the linen room, and helping in the laundry on washday, you are also to sweep and dust two of the corridors."

Donning an apron, the novice was off with broom and dustpan to clean the corridors, but more out of simple obedience than any conviction that a duty such as sweeping held out promising possibilities toward sainthood. She had practiced many virtues, but of the value of common domestic chores as a means of sanctification she knew little. She had not been accustomed to wait on herself, nor ever expected to do any housework whatsoever. This phase of endeavor was foreign to her because it had never entered into her life at Les Buissonnets. So, unskilled in the manifold movements of wielding a broom or brush effectively, Sister Therese went through the corridors, apparently without setting too much store on thoroughness as a major virtue.

An hour later, on the way to recreation, the Prioress, glancing down the corridor, noticed a cobweb. "Sister Therese, did you sweep that cloister this morning?" she asked.

"Yes, Reverend Mother," she replied.

"It is disgraceful. It is easy to see that our corridors are swept by a child of fifteen. Go, get your broom, and sweep away that cobweb at once. And, in the future, be more thorough in your manual labor," added the Prioress, while the other Sisters, already gathered for recreation, stood by.

Sister Therese, embarrassed, took the harsh reprimand to heart. She realized that not only lofty prayers and high moral virtue, but the performance of ordinary household chores well done, also entered into a career of building toward perfection. Carrying her meditation further she realized, moreover, that the very exigencies of living were such that every individual contributed his share of deteriorative elements; his clean clothes became grimy; his polished bedroom floor took on a coating of soot; his daily food intake made for a world of untidiness that someone, somewhere, must forever cope with and continue to amend, else the world would fall apart, in complete disorder.

Therefore each person who is sincere must realize, ultimately, that he must willingly assume his portion of menial tasks and so contribute toward a maintenance of order in a life scheme continually calling for trying sacrifices of manual labor, to combat disorder; or, shirking it, become a burden to those around him. And Sister Therese, now meticulously sweeping her corridors, began the resolution to give herself to manual labor with the same application she exercised in her quest for high moral virtues, realizing that it is of the essence of charity to reduce the burden of work for one's neighbor — by assuming as great a share as possible of its annoyances — and thus abide by the spirit of Paul who said, *Carry ye one another's burdens, for thus shall you fulfill the Law of Christ.*

Moreover, in the near future, she would make a vow of poverty, reflected Therese further, and by this means incur the responsibility of living like the poor — which was mainly by ordinary labor. Now Sister Therese bound herself with the resolve to be heroic in her menial work, bent on not losing a moment but remaining diligently occupied during the hours prescribed for labor . . . particularly in her cell, where she was unnoticed — sewing, mending, embroidering, and in doing art work.

The Prioress was unaware of this, and took occasion to lecture her on the necessity of correcting her ways. The postulant listened attentively, respectfully, but when the hour was finally over, she honestly told herself she did not even know what the Mother was referring to. Not concerning themselves to find out whether their charge was doing her utmost as she worked in her cell unseen, Sister Therese's superiors failed to take into account hidden virtue, the essence of the interior life. And it was not to be restored to its true perspective until it was too late!

Misunderstood, Sister Therese began to learn the price for desiring to become a Saint — solitariness. She would have to depend on God alone. The following week brought a glimmer of hope. Father Pichon, a very enlightened Jesuit priest, came to the Convent to preach a nine-day Retreat. In his sermons Therese recognized a challenge to continue on her way: striving to become a Saint. Approaching the priest in confession, she managed to explain, though with difficulty, some of her aspirations; and, although so young, Therese succeeded in impressing the Jesuit to such an extent that he was astonished at the workings of grace in her soul. This priest, combining knowledge with virtue, recognized that the postulant already sought horizons beyond those which her superiors in Carmel envisioned. "Sister, may Our Lord himself always be your Superior and your Novice Master," he told her.

Sister Therese was overjoyed, feeling sure that she now had a promising director under whose guidance she would advance safely. But he was to prove more of a prophet than a director. For, suddenly, without notice, he was called away from France altogether and assigned to work in Canada. As the month of June slipped by and July unfolded, Therese again found herself alone — *May Our Lord himself always be your Superior and your Novice Master . . . .*

Pauline, known during her eight years of religious life at Carmel as Sister Agnes, began to glance sympathetically at her youngest sister in the cloister, and recognized from her expression that she was in urgent need of a helping hand. Once, during her childhood, it had been her task to instruct and uplift her. Perhaps she should try to reach out to the postulant with a bit of aid? Though the Carmelite Rule did not permit unscheduled friendly conversations, yet it prudently ordains that occasional permission to speak on spiritual subjects was not only to be given, but encouraged, as a means of advancing in perfection. Sister Agnes now approached the Prioress for such permission in order to speak to her sister.

"By all means, Sister Agnes," the Prioress agreed pleasantly. "Arrange for a nice talk with Sister Therese on Sunday . . . in the garden. Is there anything else?"

"Yes, I would like to give Sister Therese our copy of Father Janvier's latest, *Life of Sister Marie Pierre,* and to instruct her in the Devotion to the Holy Face. It would be a splendid book for her to study as a preparation for receiving the Holy Habit."

"Yes, I am glad you suggest it. It is time for Sister Therese to become acquainted with the mission of our own dear French Carmelite at Tours. Better still, keep your copy, Sister Agnes, for I know how often you refer to it. I will give you a fresh one for Sister Therese, one of five I just received from the Carmel at Tours a few days ago. The Reverend Mother also wrote me quite at length and said that the demand for the book on the life and revelations of Sister Marie Pierre was growing by leaps and bounds."

Sister Agnes felt a thrill of joy that she belonged to an Order that placed such high importance on literature. For it is one of the inflexible points of Teresian monasticism to emphasize spiritual reading, and a binding obligation for a Superior to secure for a Sister, regardless of the trouble and cost involved, such books as might inspire her to attain perfection, and aid her to live her secluded and penitential life in greater peace and fruitfulness.

And there was cause to rejoice as she left the cell of the Prioress, for the book she now held in her hand was soon to be avidly read and reread by Sister Therese, who, assimilating its worth, was to establish herself not only in Church history, but in world history as well. Sister Agnes, of course, could not have known the results of the mission on which she now embarked, but she had an inkling that anyone as logical and as earnest as her sister Therese would surrender to the treasured volume whose spiritual significance defied comparison.

On the appointed Sunday afternoon the two sisters met in the garden: "You like Carmel, don't you, Sister Therese?"

"Yes, everything here delights me," came the answer reassuringly.

"Then, you found everything here just as you expected?"

"Yes, in every way."

"Even the share of bitters?" pursued Sister Agnes.

"Even that."

"I do hope you don't mind too much," said the older nun.

"But why should I, since I expected it? God in His mercy has always preserved me from illusions," answered Therese smiling.

"Tell me, how did you like the Retreat Master, Father Pichon?"

"I thought he was splendid. I certainly was sorry to learn that he had been called away to Canada."

"You miss him?"

"Yes, I do, because he seemed to understand me from the very first. I felt with him a little as I did with you at home. I naturally began to plan a rosy future under his guidance."

"And now, I suppose, you are lost without him?"

"Not quite. He left me a very consoling lesson. Would you like to know what he told me?"

"You know I would. I am interested in everything that concerns you."

"Well, Father Pichon told me, 'Sister, may Our Lord himself

always be your Superior and Your Novice Master . . . .' Now that he is gone, I realize I'll have to do just that, look up to Our Lord himself for guidance, even as Father told me."

Sister Agnes recognized that this was the moment for her to introduce the *great subject*.

"Sister Therese, I think that Our Lord wants to lead you himself, as He not so long ago led another Carmelite who lived only a short distance from here."

"Whom do you mean?" asked the postulant with interest.

"I mean Sister Marie Pierre of Tours, the nun who had all those exalted revelations about the Holy Face of Our Saviour. Here, take this book, for I have permission from the Prioress to give it to you. Once you penetrate the depth of wisdom contained in this volume, you will, like Sister Marie Pierre, surrender your whole being to Our Suffering Lord. You and she have so much in common, Therese . . . ."

"What do you mean, Sister Agnes? Do you realize that whereas this Sister Marie Pierre was one of the rarest of mystics — from the few things I've heard mentioned about her — I am almost continually steeped in aridity?" It was out, and although she did not mean to trouble her sister with more of her trials, she could not recall the words, so she went on: "I am the last sort of person in the world to be compared with a soul like Sister Marie Pierre, who I understand, spoke with Our Lord, as it were, face to face . . . ."

"But Sister Therese, did you ever read her whole life?"

"No, I did not, it is true, though I heard it mentioned that Our Lord spoke to her intimately as in the case of Blessed Margaret Mary. Isn't that so?"

"Yes, precisely so. And, similarly, as Our Lord asked Saint Margaret Mary for the inauguration of Devotion to His Sacred Heart, as a means for Catholics to rise from tepidity, and to approach the Holy Table frequently, so the Saviour asked Sister Marie Pierre for a devotion — that of the Holy Face — as a means of combatting blasphemy.

"There is a militant move on the march," continued Sister

Agnes, "to establish atheism in government. Wicked men are spreading grave dangers. Unless they are stopped, men all over the world will lose their liberty to worship God as their consciences dictate.* Through the prayers offered to God in reparation, disaster can be averted. That is the message of Christ to Sister Marie Pierre. Nothing could be more timely. You see, dear, we all don't have to be mystics like either Margaret Mary or Sister Marie Pierre to benefit by their life histories. Our Lord does not have to repeat himself. It should suffice that He speaks to one, and through that one transmits to us His message. You, yourself, said that Father Pichon told you he hoped that Our Lord himself would be your Novice Master. Very well, then, if you want to know what He desires of you, read the story of Sister Marie Pierre, our own contemporary, and make the words He spoke to her your own. You will find out what He wants of you . . . ."

Therese took the new book from her sister's hands and read the title page aloud: *The Life of Sister Marie Pierre, a Carmelite of Tours, France, written by herself,** and further collated and completed by means of her letters and the annals of her monastery. Edited by The Reverend Peter Janvier.*

Therese looked up at her sister thoughtfully. "How long is it since Sister Marie Pierre died?"

"Only about thirty years. She belongs to us. She's modern!"

"Hm, thirty years is a short time in which to become so famous as to have your life published abroad, don't you think?"

"And translated into English, Spanish, Polish, German, and a number of other languages."

Therese shook her head. "And, my dear sister, do you now suggest that a soul like this prodigious mystic, Sister Marie Pierre, resembles poor little me, and that I can hope to become like her?"

"Yes, I say she does because there are such striking similarities between you two. She was, for example, greatly devoted to the Christ Child. Even that's your title, isn't it?"

---

[184] *That is, their consciences formed by the Catholic Church's teaching. —*Publisher,* 2005.

**Her autobiography and revelations are available in English as *The Golden Arrow* (TAN, 1990). —*Publisher,* 2005.

Therese smiled and answered with a tinge of melancholy, "Yes, that's my title."

"And it fits you. Since you were ever so little you always wanted to please the Holy Child and never have you once disobeyed me, to please Him. Sister Marie Pierre also had this great attraction to the Infancy of the Saviour. And just as you wanted to be a mere toy for the Holy Child, to amuse Him, so did Sister Marie Pierre long to be a little donkey, at His service."

"Did Sister Marie Pierre really say that?" asked Therese, surprised that so exalted a mystic should have made such a pronouncement.

"She did. And in her simplicity she humbled herself as a little child, on and on for years, until Our Lord, pleased with her littleness of disposition, chose her as a special instrument to launch a lofty Devotion in the Church!"

"The Devotion to the Holy Face?" Therese said solemnly.

"Yes, Devotion to the Holy Face as a means of Reparation for the unspeakable crimes of our age, atheism in government. Now here is the book that will tell you all about it. Read it, and study it, for it is a book that should make you a Saint. You loved Christ's Childhood. Now study His Manhood and follow Him right up to Calvary. You have it in you, Therese, and don't be afraid that you are too ordinary to reach the same holiness which belonged to Sister Marie Pierre," finished Sister Agnes, the eldest Carmelite of the Martin family, as she initiated the youngest, Therese, into the secret of the Holy Face.

"I will read and study the book," she promised.

"One more thing," said Agnes as an afterthought. "I want to show you one other resemblance that exists between you and Sister Marie Pierre."

"What is that?"

"Your special attraction to the Precious Blood. You remember the occasion when you looked at the picture of the Nailed Hand and were filled with grief at the sight of the Sacred Blood spilling to the ground as if unheeded? You resolved then to spend your life in spirit at the foot of the cross to gather the Precious Blood and offer it for sinners . . . ."

"I remember that," said Sister Therese quietly.

"Sister Marie Pierre had a similar attraction to gather the Precious Blood and to offer it for sinners."

"She did?"

"She did! But you must go to the book itself to find that out, for it is a long but most beautiful story. I can't explain it in one afternoon. July, Sister, is the month especially dedicated to honoring the Mystery of the Precious Blood, the fountainhead of which resides in the brow of Our Saviour, His Holy Face."

Suddenly the bell rang. There was no time to say more. But before the sun of that fateful Sunday in July had crimsoned the sky, Sister Therese began to understand that if a year ago a mere picture of one isolated nailed hand of Jesus streaming with blood could awaken in her such grief that she resolved ever after to treasure the Sacred Dew and apply it to souls, what indeed would a picture of Christ's Holy Face, isolated from the rest of His Sacred Body, and painted miraculously on Veronica's Veil, be able to effect in her now that she was shielded from every distraction inside a cloister. Clasping the autobiography of Sister Marie Pierre, Therese was indeed on the verge of a supreme discovery. She was still far from believing, however, that any similarity existed between the Carmelite of Tours, whose book was published a scant thirty years after her death, and herself, the Carmelite of Lisieux, whom the Prioress scolded almost every time they met.

26

"I HOPE they are not too small, Sister Therese," solicitously came from Sister Angela, the lay Sister in charge of the nuns' footwear. She was trying on a brand-new pair of sandals, called "alpargates," intended for Therese, for whose Clothing Ceremony the nuns were now preparing, since it is ordinarily scheduled after six months of postulancy.

"Oh, no, they aren't too small," was the answer. "I think they fit perfectly."

The footwear for a future Discalced Carmelite always seemed of pressing importance to Sister Angela who was never happier than when she was getting a postulant ready for her Clothing Day. Now, since the very word "discalced" meant "without shoes," it is only reasonable to expect that alpargates, used by Carmelite nuns in place of shoes, were of necessity bound to possess characteristics all their own. To begin with, they were entirely made by hand inside the cloister, which, in itself, sufficiently explained their lack of resemblance to any finished product in a shoemaker's shop.

Moreover, as nothing even distantly related to any kind of leather, real or simulated, went into their assembly, this explains further why alpargates pass for that entity which enables a Carmelite of the Primitive Rule who wears them to call herself "barefooted" or "discalced." For, in reality, this footgear is made entirely of common brown rope, the kind designed for heavy duty in a shipping room, where cartons required solid tying. This ordinary rope is ingeniously plaited into braids and otherwise assembled. The credit for the originality of alpargates must go to the sixteenth century reformer of Carmel,

Saint Teresa of Avila herself. Intent on restoring primitive rigor into the convents of her nuns, and unwilling to allow the Sisters to go without some covering for their ankles, the foundress arrived at this modest compromise, which for four hundred years had carried on its venerable tradition of restraint with remarkable effect. For, indeed, the gentle lady who in the world was even moderately inclined to heed the dictates of fashion in the realm of attractive footwear learned that Carmelite alpargates, in one solitary stroke, destroyed every initial stirring toward vanity.

Still concerned over the proper fitting of Sister Therese's alpargates, Sister Angela continued to bend studiously over her feet, examining the product.

"You see, I would not for the world want you to suffer with alpargates that did not fit," protested Sister Angela with a tinge of professional pride.

"Oh, but they fit just fine, I assure you," replied Therese, who wondered the while whether there was any real difference between alpargates size 4 or size 9, for to her they all seemed very huge, and quite unsightly.

"Walk up and down a few steps, now," further counseled Sister Angela, observing the postulant as she walked with grace in that even, measured way, neither fast nor slow, but with a sure, very sure step which they all soon came to recognize as belonging to her exclusively. So much so, that even when, with her veil over her face, she would enter the parlor, all would at once know her by her gait.

"How quietly one steps wearing alpar- - - alpargates," she managed to remark.

"That is one of the reasons why Saint Teresa wanted her nuns to wear them. A Carmelite should pass through this life unheard," answered Sister Angela.

"Oh, yes," agreed Sister Therese, inwardly resolving to so pass through life: unheard, unnoticed — even as Sister Angela had suggested.

With the alpargates finished and tucked away together with

her new Holy Habit, all was in readiness for the forthcoming Clothing Ceremony and the Prioress now approached the convent's Superior to talk over with him the matter of arrangements for services.

"Father Delatroette, since next month, on October 8, to be exact, it will be six months since Sister Therese's entrance here, we are quite ready to go on with the Clothing."

"What? Do you actually propose to give the Holy Habit to a fifteen-year-old girl?" retorted Father Delatroette.

"But, but I don't understand," remarked the Prioress, who seemed bewildered at this unexpected turn.

"Reverend Mother, I am opposed to it. In fact, I don't care even to discuss it. A Clothing Ceremony at this time is simply out of the question."

"Well, Father, if you want us to postpone it, of course, we can. But in order to know where we stand, how long, do you think, our postulant must wait?"

"I don't know! But you can ask me again three months from now," the Canon replied arbitrarily.

Therese seemed less disappointed on hearing the news of her postponed Clothing than did some of the other Sisters. An alteration in exterior arrangements did not trouble her too much. Inside the Carmel, she was pursuing an altogether interior life, and external accidentals could not disturb her serenity.

In December the Prioress again pressed the Canon for setting a definite date for Sister Therese's Clothing. Further delays were unjustified, she said, in the light of their Rule and Constitution. — The date was finally set for January 10, 1889.

Overjoyed with the news, Louis Martin hurried to the Monastery.

"But, as if Therese's scheduled Clothing Ceremony were not in itself enough, I have yet another surprise," he told his three daughters in the small Carmelite parlor. "Celine has told me for certain that she will also later become a Carmelite nun. And I can see that she will carry out her resolve. Therefore, my children, on our very next visit to the Blessed Sacrament, let us thank God for the graces He has bestowed on our family, especially for the great honor He has done me in choosing his spouses from my household. Truly, were I possessed of anything better, I would hasten to offer it to Him . . . ." Then, becoming jovial, he invited his daughters to help him determine the choice of materials that were to go into Therese's bridal outfit.

"Oh, it won't matter, Papa," at once came from the direction where sat the postulant.

"But it matters to me. You will wear a coarse brown woolen habit for the rest of your life. For your wedding day, therefore, with the mystical spouse, you shall have the very best. I will see to it."

Since they knew that it would give their father pleasure to outfit his youngest daughter in the very best taste, they encouraged him. He was an artist by nature and profession, a connoisseur of fabrics and of jewels.

"Since the occasion falls in midwinter, I have decided on white, shimmering chiffon velvet, trimmed in Alençon point lace . . . ." He went on with the details.

"But you are going to too much trouble, Papa," politely remonstrated Therese. "I will wear the bridal outfit only for about one hour during Mass in the outside chapel."

"An hour, yes, but, little queen, what an hour! The best the world has is not too good for such an hour of triumph and of grace. You are giving your life to God, and the hour shall be a memorable one. So I am planning to leave for Alençon, to get the point lace there."

The following week Louis returned, his shopping tour a complete success. The materials he went out to seek were found, after due and relentless searching for quality, texture, and just the right shade of white tending slightly toward cream as if a ray of sunlight were upon it. The price? He was not interested in a bargain, he told the merchants whom he knew so well from years as agent for his wife's laces. The fabrics he was now buying were intended for his youngest daughter's bridal day.

"Oh, so she's to be married?" they'd begin to congratulate.

"Hold on, my friend. The bridal day I speak of is not the ordinary kind. You see, my daughter, Therese, is to have a mystical bridal day. It is not to promise to marry someone but to promise never to marry anyone, which constitutes the essence of her bridal day . . . ." he explained.

"We know now. Your daughter is to be a nun, right?"

"Yes, my friends, that is right."

Now, in the Carmelite parlor, Louis had, of course, to tell his three daughters all the details, and he knew that he had to hurry. For only a half hour is allowed in the parlor for a visit, and, since Therese was always watching the hour glass so keenly, he knew she attached much importance to the matter of not prolonging the visit even an added two minutes.

"Before I go, I want to tell you of a wonderful grace I received. While in Alençon I was kneeling in the Church of Notre Dame when, suddenly, I was so filled with untold consolations and such fervor that I felt obliged to offer myself to God as I had never done before. So, praying, I said: 'My God, it is too much. I am altogether too happy. It is impossible to reach Heaven in this way. I must suffer something for Thee. Therefore I offer myself to you as a ——' "

He was unwilling to finish the sentence by saying that he offered himself as a "victim," for he knew they understood all too well what he meant. He was sixty-six. His religious fervor was no mere adolescent inclination. It was the fruit of a life well lived, of duties strictly performed, of prayers faithfully said, and, recognizing that God had rewarded him even here below, granting him prosperity and the devotion of his entire family, he wanted to give God something in return. Nobody forced Louis Martin to ask or seek the sorrows he implored: to offer himself as a victim. He could have gone to Heaven for being the exquisitely just man that his spotless record of life showed him to be. But Louis Martin wanted more. He wanted to imitate the Victim of Calvary, through an act of willful self-sacrifice. He closed this heavenly bargain there in the Church of Notre Dame, just prior to his youngest daughter's Clothing, and God was to take him at his word!

27

IT WAS January 10, 1889, the day of Sister Therese's investiture, and, according to Carmelite custom, the ceremonies were scheduled for the outside chapel. During these services Sister Therese would be seen publicly for the last time as she knelt before the altar, wearing white bridal attire.

A few minutes before the ceremony Louis was standing in front of the large enclosure door of the Carmelite parlor awaiting breathlessly the sound of a heavy key that would turn the lock and bring him face to face with his youngest daughter, Therese. Finally, the enclosure door opened, revealing a lovely creature in dazzling white raiment.

"Ah, look, here is my little queen!" he exclaimed through tear-filled eyes, embracing her tenderly. "You have grown, my dear. I can't believe my eyes. Little Therese is a tall young lady," he said, his appreciative eyes beginning to drink in the picture of beauty before him. The bridal gown for which no expense had been spared showed off to rare advantage the youthful beauty of Therese at sixteen. Her light-brown hair could be seen under the veil of tulle as it fell in long curls over her shoulders. Her fair complexion added luster to her large dark eyes expressive of wisdom far beyond her years. But perhaps the most arresting was the quiet virginal purity that beamed from her brow on that day and was ever to hold it upon an uncontested throne.

The sheaf of lilies she carried on her left arm now had Celine's attention, for it was high time to make the last touches since the Bishop and clergy were already in the Sanctuary.

"Take my arm, little queen," said Louis, strikingly handsome in his black suit. Father and daughter, followed by members of the family, walked down the aisle of the Chapel where many people were gathered, curiously straining for a glimpse of the girl who entered, at fifteen, the strictest Order in the Church. All through Mass, as she knelt in the Sanctuary, the congregation admired the lovely sight she made, but from her father and uncle she held the greatest attraction. Both men, looking longingly at her gentle charm, dazzling in white velvet and lace, silently wished that one other person were there — Therese's mother. For, though ten years had elapsed since she had passed away, her memory could never fade from their minds.

The religious service finished, Louis escorted his daughter back to the enclosure door, from which she had emerged for one hour's public ceremony. Inside the Prioress and sub-Prioress awaited her anxiously, for it was now their chance to turn their services into action. This was the Clothing Ceremony, the end of which was to transform a person of the world into a religious of the Primitive Rule of Mount Carmel. The glimmering attire of velvet and lace was now to be removed; the flowing brown hair waited to be hastily cut off.

As swiftly as possible, therefore, once she was inside the enclosure, Therese was ushered into a side room where with all dispatch the Prioress and assistant went to work on her. For, at a *prie-dieu* in the choir, directly in front of an opened grill for the occasion, Sister Therese, now clothed as a nun, was expected to reappear, in order that the final ceremonies could there be concluded by the clergy still waiting in the Sanctuary.

With almost reckless abandon, therefore, the sub-Prioress now began abruptly to pull off the soft white kidskin shoes, replacing them with the coarse alpargates. At the same time, the Prioress herself was busy snatching at the bits of tulle veiling so as to get at the mass of soft brown hair destined for the hapless scissors that lay before her ready for the appointed task. Therese, surrendering to the competent hands of her superiors, soon saw the costly white raiment of velvet and lace gathered in a heap on a chair. They were, indeed, abandoned expendables. In rapid succession another type of apparel began to replace the worldly one. A few moments later, Sister Therese stood up to her full five feet six inches in her flat alpargates, a white toque over her head, and a tunic of coarse brown wool covering her figure from shoulder to toes.

To the inexperienced eye, she perhaps now appeared to be one wearing the Holy Habit of Carmel, but this was not true in the least. For, to a Carmelite of the Primitive Rule, the Holy Habit is one, and only one, small garment, whose singular excellence seven hundred years of Church history have endeavored to extol. That garment is called the Holy Scapular and consists of two straight panels of brown wool held together by two shoulder straps of the same material. This Scapular is worn by a Carmelite [7] as her outward garment, over the basic brown costume with its long sleeves and flowing skirts which is gathered at the waist with a girdle.

For this garment of singular importance — the Scapular — Sister Therese had next to present herself at the open grill of the choir, where she would receive it at the hands of the priest celebrant. Modestly advancing forward to the appointed place at the front, Sister Therese now paused, standing erect in full view of the assembled congregation, among which were the members of her family; as also before the nuns of her community who knelt in their places a few feet behind.

"Sister, what is it that you desire?" the celebrant now asked her.

"I desire the mercy of God, the poverty of the Order, and the society of the Sisters," answered Sister Therese according to formula. In these words the Carmelite Novice gives formal voice to the same desires which King David nourished when he declared, "One thing have I asked of the Lord, this will I seek after, that I may dwell in the house of the Lord, all the days of my life." [8]

---

7. Today, as for centuries past, this Scapular in abbreviated form is also worn by millions of the Faithful all over the world.
8. Psalms 26 : 4.

A deep hush fell on all present as Therese now breathlessly awaited the supreme moment: investiture with the Scapular of Our Lady of Mount Carmel.

And as the narrow panels of brown wool were reverently slipped over her head, falling in graceful lines until they reached the hem of her wide brown skirts, Sister Therese of the Child Jesus at last realized that she had been dressed with the clothing of the Mother of God.

✦ ✦

But why was a vestment called the Scapular, which now draped Sister Therese with its straight panels falling loosely at the front and at the back, referred to as the Clothing of the Mother of God? The truth is that the Immaculate Virgin called it her livery when, more than seven hundred years before, she came down from Heaven and personally entrusted into the hands of one of her servants this excellent garment composed of two panels held together with two straps of matching material. The recipient, tradition has it, was none other than Saint Simon Stock, an English hermit, a member of the Carmelite Order which claimed the Prophet Elias as its founder nine hundred years before Christ.

Surrendering her vesture of purity to Saint Simon Stock, the Mother of God told him to wear it and to have others wear it as her special badge. Furthermore, she gave the Carmelite hermit a promise, saying that anyone who would die wearing her Scapular with piety would be saved from eternal perdition.

With Therese's investiture, the ceremonies came to an end. The celestial hosts descending from the heights of Heaven now returned to their celestial realms. The church, too, grew suddenly still as the congregation dispersed, and there remained only the flicker from the Sanctuary lamp to give the sign that Someone was still there.

✦ ✦

When Therese retired that night she wondered that only so

few noticed that in addition to her altered appearance in dress, there was a corresponding alteration in her name. For on that day Sister Therese of the Child Jesus became Sister Therese of the Child Jesus and of the *Holy Face*. And, similarly, as the celestial clothing she now wore surpassed in its spiritual excellence any garment hitherto known to the world — for the Scapular is the livery of the Mother of God, — so, now, the sublime alteration in her title, and of the *Holy Face* was to distinguish her in a singular manner from all other Saints in the annals of the Church. With her sublime uniform of brown wool, and a yet more exalted banner of white silk on which was imprinted the Countenance of the Sorrowful Saviour, Sister Therese was ready for further spiritual conquests: the capture of souls for God!

28

DURING THOSE FIRST DAYS following the solemn Clothing, there was little occasion for anyone to attach any great importance to Sister Therese's seemingly slight alteration in her religious name. Moreover, since she was always on guard to escape being singled out for any special notice, there was no reason to expect that she would emphasize her rearrangement of title. But her eldest sister in religion, Sister Agnes of Jesus, learning that her newly clothed sister had added to her title the words "and of the Holy Face," knelt just a little longer in choir to thank God that she had so unhesitatingly surrendered to the Noble Seal of the Divinity, the Sacred Countenance of Christ.

She had maintained from the first that Sister Therese and Sister Marie Pierre had much in common. When Sister Therese, as early as nine months after entering the Convent, used the occasion of her solemn investiture to announce an alteration in her name, Sister Agnes was certain that, in very deed, Sisters Marie Pierre of Tours and Therese of Lisieux began to have everything in common with each other.

Meanwhile, to everyone else in the community, Therese seemed to be the same amiable person she had ever been — but certainly no mystic. On the contrary, her inclination to be the first in offering her services in the laundry, or the kitchen, or, in general, wherever there was scope for any common labor, made their verdict quite unanimous that the newly clothed novice was definitely the "active" type. This classification was intended to carry with it, at least, a mild innuendo of inferiority, always associated with the word *active* when used in purportedly contemplative circles. Obviously, this novice was not likely to distinguish herself for anything extraordinary in the realm of mental prayer, the overwhelming preoccupation of Carmelite monasticism which had earned it world fame. Surely no Teresa of Avila — this Therese of the Child Jesus — they concluded, not even bothering to add the rest of her title. Yet in that very title lay the astonishing hidden clue that their own contemporary, Therese was to surpass the one of ancient glory.

But while they were disregarding the most evident sign, their Sister Therese's newly altered name, she herself had become intensely occupied in pursuing her new goal. As once in childhood she had found her name written in the stars on a darkened night sky, so, now, as a nun, she had found her place in the sun! That enviable place was none other than before the humiliated and suffering Face of her God — and Sister Therese was determined never to exchange this place for any other.

Carrying her meditations on the Holy Face with her to the choir, in the long recitation of the Divine Office at which the Carmelite spends three or four hours daily, Therese soon noticed with surprise and gratitude that it was the very Face of God which the ancient Prophets had sought above all else. She saw allusions to the Countenance of the Saviour scattered on practically every page of the Psalms of David.

Augmenting the words of the ancient text with the recent Revelations on the surpassing excellence and merit of adoring the Face of Christ, as unfolded in the life of Sister Marie Pierre of Tours, Therese resolved never to shift her devotion. Recognizing that the Face of Christ on the Veil of Veronica was the closest spiritual Image of the Blessed Trinity itself, which those Prophets had incessantly besought and the Carmelite of Tours had emphasized, Therese was convinced there was nothing loftier to seek. As a child, having resolved never to steer from Jesus' sight, as a nun she could now carry out her resolve in a practical way — by living continually before the Image of the Holy Face. From this vantage point she was to emerge with an entirely new method of arriving at perfection. Her method was destined to reanimate, rather than revolutionize Church history. With no aim to upsetting the existing order whatsoever, her purpose was to perfect it, by making sanctity accessible to all rather than only to the privileged few.

It would have amazed the Community of Sisters who classified her as the active type to realize how completely they had underestimated her "activity." In fact, in seeking jobs which others normally shirked, Therese had done the one and only thing she could have done as a consistent thinker. The important thing to remember is that she never asked to be exempt from the spiritual exercises prescribed by the Rule in order to give herself to the various menial tasks. Moreover, since prayer duties in the choir absorbed some eight or nine hours of each day, what could be more reasonable or desirable than to apply herself diligently to menial work during those three or four hours which the Rule appoints for manual labor?

Therese, in studying the Countenance of Him who was *truth itself*, was to be preserved from any bias, and a one-track mind. Manual labor was calculated to complete and not counteract her prayerfulness. She never forgot the constructive criticism of Mother Mary Gonzaga who so relentlessly criticized her for the cobweb which had remained unswept in the corridor. To one as young and as new as herself in the convent, the correction might have been administered with greater gentleness, but, aside from that, Therese knew it was deserved. Those slow ways she had, therefore, and that lack of thoroughness in her work would have to give way to improvement, she counseled herself. But Sister Therese was to learn that the *will* to handle a broom or brush or needle was not of itself sufficient to produce success at one stroke.

The hands unaccustomed to the tools of manual labor were, hence, unable, at one effort, to perform with ease — or to produce satisfactory results. Her initial awkwardness, her slow and unsure movements, had to be overcome slowly. Moreover, thoroughness in work could only become a reality when ample experience with work would make that happy result possible.

Coming from Les Buissonnets at fifteen, she could have absolutely no idea about such a complex thing as thoroughness in work. Now, as an apprentice, determined to learn to work with her hands, and to produce not only quality but quantity — as an essential part of her religious life at Carmel — Therese was grappling with basic problems indeed. But to those looking on, she became merely the "active type."

Finally, when at recreation Therese found ways to entertain her companions and even amuse them with her mimicry (at which she was quite good), to most of the older nuns she appeared indeed a congenial person, but certainly no saint! Themselves forgetting that the great Teresa of Avila had explicitly urged her wittier daughters to contribute a measure of fun for the others at recreation, Therese's companions were very slow to acknowledge any trace of greatness in the tall nun who made them laugh. Meanwhile, the French nun, secure in her stand, was just as unwilling to take on any of the ways of the others as they were unwilling to submit to hers. She was to go on, quite alone . . . .

It was fortunate for Therese that she had managed, even in the strict environs of a rigorous convent, to preserve her sense of merriment, despite the great odds. To her were reserved several grave trials that the others never had to face. And without a gentle and well-balanced humor she could never have triumphed as she did.

One such trial now awaited her. Mother Mary Gonzaga had just received dreadful news. "I do not want to alarm you, but something has happened to your father," she announced gravely.

"Is he ill?" asked the daughter anxiously.

"Worse by far . . . . He seems to have lost the use of his reason . . . ."

"Oh God, have mercy . . . ." was all Therese could bring forth.

"Celine came to tell me that your Uncle has arranged for the best doctors, but it appears that his symptoms point to a permanent injury to his mind . . . . In a few days he will have to be taken away . . . to an insane asylum." Mother Mary Gonzaga felt that it was her duty to declare the unvarnished truth to the three Martin sisters in her convent.

Sister Therese was deeply smitten. Nothing worse could possibly have happened. Nothing more humiliating could have befallen the Martin family, and the three Sisters left the cell of the Prioress with downcast eyes, feeling they could never raise their heads again . . . . The stigma of insanity in their family, and their dearest and most devoted father now consigned to imprisonment for life in an asylum, this was the one unpredictable and unexpected trial.

To the impressionable nature of Therese at sixteen, the cross seemed almost too heavy for her shoulders. Only a little more than a year ago her father had taken her with him on a pilgrimage to Rome, and he had pleaded with the Vatican authorities to grant her permission to enter Carmel. Now he was reduced to the state of an irrational being, and instead of Les Buissonnets he was to have an insane asylum for his home; yes, in place of Celine and Leonie and Uncle and Aunt Guerin, and his three Carmelite daughters, he was to have the company of raving lunatics, yelling unconsciously their curses and blasphemies.

"Leonie and I," said Celine to her one day, "together with Uncle and Aunt are going to accompany Papa to Caen. He will be placed there in the Asylum of Bon Sauveur . . . ."

Therese felt a paralyzing numbness taking hold of her. No matter what would ever happen after this, it would be nothing, she brooded, compared to the fearful humiliation and inexpressible agony she now endured.

"It won't be too bad, since Leonie and I are going to live at Caen, at the Sisters' Orphanage there, and we'll be able to visit Papa every day," Celine explained.

But even this consolation was to be denied them. For hardly

had a month passed when Celine and Leonie were back at Lisieux.

"The Sisters at the asylum, who at first allowed us frequent visits with Papa, told us that we had to line up with the others and we'd be allowed just one visit a month . . . . So, under the circumstances, there was no point in staying at Caen . . . so we are now living with Uncle at his house . . . ." explained Celine to her sisters at Carmel.

"And how *is* Papa?" insisted her sister Therese.

"No better . . . . He's lost his memory . . . . He'd look at Leonie and me as if we were strangers . . . indifferent to everything . . . even when we mentioned his cherished Therese . . . ."

"God have pity!"

"Is the Asylum of Bon Sauveur anything of a decent place?" asked Sister Agnes bravely.

"It is managed by the nuns . . . and . . . well . . . ." began Leonie; but Celine interrupted.

"Oh, why hide the truth? No, it is not decent. How can it be? Have you ever seen an insane asylum, or been through one? It is worse than a prison. Papa is isolated. They put chains on his feet, and lock these to an old iron bed. A dog is allowed on the street, but Papa is locked up behind barred doors and windows. Besides, it is a dreadfully huge institution, like a town. There are seventeen hundred inmates in the various buildings scattered around the grounds, and Papa is only one of these seventeen hundred who don't count. He is referred to as a lunatic, merely, just like the others. But by some weird accident of his condition — would you believe it? — he occasionally lapses into a few moments of perfect mental balance."

"Tell us about it," urged Therese eagerly.

"Well . . . suddenly his mind will become as clear as it always was, as for example when we first arrived at Bon Sauveur. Looking around, he recognized the place as an asylum for the insane, and he knew that he was to be locked up there. The Sister in charge, noticing this quiet, normal attitude, said to him: 'Mr. Martin, you will be able to do a great deal of good here by speaking to the patients, many of whom do not believe in God.' Papa reflected for a minute, then answered her: 'That is true, but I would prefer to be an apostle in some other place rather than this one. Still, since such is the will of God, let it be. I think it is done to break my pride . . . .' "

"Celine, our time is up, and we must go," said Sister Agnes, who, seeing how pale Therese had grown, realized it would be best to end this painful ordeal.

During the days following, even Mother Mary Gonzaga knew she ought to make some effort to allay the suffering of Sister Therese.

"Sister Agnes," she said, "since it is such a lovely spring day, I want you to have a talk with Sister Therese in the garden this afternoon. Let her open her heart to you. She looks pale . . . ."

"It is on account of our father. You see, she had only so recently lived together with him at home. Now the thought of his humiliating isolation at the asylum weighs her down more than it does any of the rest of us," explained Sister Agnes logically.

Alone in the garden, Sister Agnes spoke with her youngest sister, encouraging her to accept the trial.

"But, Sister, I am perfectly resigned; surely you must know that. Even more, I have come to consider this trial as a Great Treasure."

"A great treasure?" repeated Sister Agnes.

"Oh, yes, for when suffering becomes so acute that we feel we cannot bear more, then we fold it to our heart as a Great Treasure. As I see Papa humiliated and abased through this loss of his reason, I know he is enduring the cross for which he asked when he prayed at Alençon, before my Clothing, to become a victim. He wanted to give God something in return for all the blessings God had given him. And God heard his prayer. The sacrifice asked was the forfeiture of Papa's rare mind. And I know better than anyone what a beautiful intellect Papa had. How I used to revel, listening to him discuss those deep subjects with Uncle Guerin! And how I marveled! Of course, they did not even know that I was paying attention, but I was!"

"You remember all that, Therese?"

"I do, just as if it happened yesterday. For example, let me tell you what happened when I was about ten. Papa seemed to notice that I preferred grown-up talk, so one day he really leveled a barrage of serious conversation . . . speaking to me as if I were an adult, expounding his ideas about our country, how it should be managed, and what the statesmen ought to do so that France might be great. When he finished I said to him: 'Papa, it is positive that if you spoke like that to the great men who govern our country, they would make *you* the King, and then France would surely be better off than she has ever been. But in that case, you would be unhappy, because such is the lot of a good king, and, besides, I would no longer have you to myself, so I am glad, very glad that they do not know of you . . . .' "

"I remember Papa telling me all about the incident and how proud he was that you thought he was so brilliant. Anyhow, to Papa it mattered more to be esteemed highly by his own family than to be hailed by the whole world," said Sister Agnes pensively.

"Oh, yes, he lived for us. Our names were always on his lips, and Mama's. He loved our home, and the rest of the world could never tempt him . . . . Yet, even though I know he offered himself as a victim, and is reaping great spiritual benefits from it, still I don't suffer less on that account although I accept it."

"Yes, I understand. Accepting the trial brings peace, but it does not take away the reality of pain."

"The reality remains, of course," agreed Sister Therese. "Sister Agnes, I can't help, during these days, going back in my mind to recall that day when I was about six. You remember it . . . . Papa had gone to Alençon and was not expected until late. The rest of us were all at home — at Les Buissonnets. It was about two in the afternoon of a bright sunny day. I was alone at a window looking out on the kitchen garden and my mind was full of pleasant thoughts, when I saw in front of the wash-house, opposite, a man dressed exactly like Papa, and with the same height and appearance, though more bent and aged. I say aged to give you an idea of his general appearance, for, the head being covered with a thick veil, I did not see his face .... Slowly, and with measured steps, he advanced, and passed by my own little garden. Overcome by a feeling of preternatural fear, I called out loudly and frightened, 'Papa, Papa!' The mysterious person didn't seem to hear and, continuing on his way without even turning around, he went toward a clump of fir trees which divided the garden walk in two. I expected to see him appear again beyond the tall firs, but the vision had vanished. Though it was all over in a minute, it impressed me so deeply that even now I can recall every tiny detail. You and Marie, hearing my cry of 'Papa,' were also frightened. Hiding her feelings, Marie ran up to me and said, 'Why do you call Papa like that when you know he is at Alençon?' Then I described to her what I had just then seen and, to reassure me, she told me that the maid must have covered her head with her apron so as to frighten me. But when I questioned her, Victoria declared that she had never left the kitchen, and, besides, the truth was that it *was* a man I saw, and the man *was* exactly like Papa. Then we went out to look behind the fir trees but we found nothing. I always knew this experience was some sort of sign. And now that Papa's face is hidden from sight in an asylum, I realize that the thick veil I saw over his head symbolized the nature of the trial he was to endure. Just how much he suffers only God knows. Since his mind is clouded it is difficult to know what he endures. But for me to know that his fine intellect is forever impaired is a fearful loss. Believe me, Sister, only my meditations before the Holy Face — shamefully humiliated — make it possible for me to keep my peace. I could not endure the trial, let alone benefit by it, if you had not opened to me the Secrets of His Holy Face.

"As it is, I can clasp the cross and call it the Greatest Treasure. Now when I look at the Holy Face I see a resemblance. We can't always smile with the Infant Jesus. We must also suffer with the Man Christ. There will be a time of trial for all of us: for some a death, for others different losses. But they will most certainly arrive whether we will it or not. When they come, if we can look up into the Sorrowful Face and detect a resemblance, we will be lifted. Oh, I would wish to tell everybody to study and venerate an Image of the Holy Face as He left it on Veronica's Veil. When sorrow strikes, it will be the only consolation. No matter what our grief, surely it will never be as fearful as was His!"

When Sister Agnes left her sister, she was convinced that no matter what happened, Sister Therese would know how to take care of herself. She had become an adorer of the Bruised Countenance of the Saviour, in truth. She was bound to become a dazzling Saint!

It was July again, and irrepressibly Sister Therese was again drawn in a special way to the adoration of the Precious Blood. In this, the month dedicated to commemorate the Mystery of the Holy Face bespattered with Blood, Therese wrote a letter to her sister Celine. It was dated July 14, 1889.

"My darling Sister," it read, "I am ever with you in spirit . . . . It seems to me that God has no need of years to perfect His labor of love in a soul. Celine, during the fleeting moments that remain to us, let us save souls. There is but one thing to be done here below: to love Jesus and to save souls for Him. We are His chosen lilies, and He dwells as a King in our midst. He lets us share the honors of His royalty — His Divine Blood . . . ."

Permeated ever more and more with the surpassing worth of concentrating her efforts on plumbing the depths of the Mysteries contained in the Head of Christ, she was anxious for others to benefit from this devotion. Three months later she was writing to Celine again: "My dearest Celine; I send you a picture of the Holy Face. The contemplation of this Adorable Countenance seems to belong in a special manner to my little sister who is truly the sister of my soul. May she be another Veronica and wipe away all the blood and tears of Jesus, her only Love! May she give Him souls. May she force her way through the soldiers, that is, the world, to come close to His side . . . . Happy will she be when she sees in Heaven His lips, once parched with burning thirst, speaking to her the one eternal word, Love! Good-bye, dear little Veronica. 'Let us go and die with Him.' "

The following month the Prioress approached Father Delatroette to speak about arrangements for Therese's Profession of Vows. In January it would be one year since she had received the holy habit, and, therefore, according to the Rule, she was ready to pronounce her vows of poverty, chastity and obedience.

"Am I to understand that you actually intend to admit Sister Therese to Profession of Vows in January?" he asked.

"Well, yes, Father. It is the rule to admit a novice to vows one year after Clothing," she answered sheepishly as if apologizing. It had become an ordeal for her to mention this Sister to Father Delatroette, who, up to that time, persistently adhered to vetoes whenever there was question of further establishing Sister Therese in her religious vocation.

"I object to it . . . . Sister Therese must wait . . . . I *refuse* to allow her to make her Profession in January . . . ."

"Well, of course, Father, if you say so, we will wait."

"Indeed! Why, she is still only sixteen!"

"But in January she will be seventeen!"

"I dont care to discuss it further. The Profession must be delayed."

"How long, Father?"

"I don't know. But it will be a good long time before I can bring myself to admit so young a girl to Profession of Vows!"

Father Delatroette still was of the opinion that Therese was a very dubious aspirant for Carmel's standards. When news of the delay was brought to her, she again found in it no special cause for anxiety. She would make her vows sooner or later, and just so long as it was not her fault they were delayed, it did not concern her very much. She was at Carmel; she wore the Holy Scapular, and she had a sublime routine of prayer and good works to fill every waking hour from 4:45 in the morning until 11 at night — and that was sufficient for her.

It took an additional eight months for Father Delatroette finally to consent to the Profession of Vows. The solemn day was set for September 8, 1890.

As is the custom, the Sister making the vows must go into a ten-day retreat, immediately preceding her Profession. During this retreat she wears a special veil over her regular one, which she draws down over the eyes as she goes through the cloisters or even in choir. It is to help keep her from observing anything that would serve as a distraction. During these ten days, more than ever, she is to withdraw within herself. Although she joins the nuns in the choir for the Divine Office, she does not perform her mental prayer with them, but retires into a separate oratory by herself. Nor does she, during these days, attend recreation, but spends the period in spiritual reading or prayer, in her cell.

What the topic was of Therese's prayer in those ten most important days preceding the vow-taking is revealed in a short note written to her elder sister, the beloved Pauline of her childhood, now Sister Agnes of Jesus:

"Your little hermit must give you an account of her journey. I told my Beloved that I had only one desire, that of reaching the summit of the Mountain of Love. And Our Lord took me by the hand and led me through an underground passage where it is neither hot nor cold — a place where I see nothing but a half-veiled light. This is the light that gleams from the downcast eyes of the Face of Jesus . . . ."

Sister Agnes paused. The words were actually there, in the retreatant's own handwriting, and allowing no misunder-standing. Sister Therese was spending the most solemn Retreat of her life before the Holy Face of Christ! *Our Lord led me to a place where I see nothing but a half-veiled light. This is the light that gleams from the downcast eyes of the Face of Jesus!* Reading the note again, Sister Agnes realized that pondering the humiliated aspect of the Saviour, exploring the mental phase of His Passion, had become the consuming preoccupation of her sister. Nor was Sister Agnes ever to lose sight of this most essential reality in her sister's spiritual career! Therefore, when nearly everybody else forgot that the Bruised Counte-nance of the Beloved was for Therese the only pivot for her prayer and heroic deeds, Sister Agnes was not among them.[9]

After all, this Devotion to the Holy Face was the pre-dominant devotion of Sister Agnes herself, and of the Mother Foundress, Sister Genevieve, who, now infirm and aged, was for the most part kept to her bed. Having imbibed it from the Foundress directly, Sister Agnes accepted contemplation of the humiliated Face of Christ as *her* life's occupation. So, convinced herself, Sister Agnes had hastened to transmit, at the begin-ning of Therese's conventual life, the exalted lessons of ascetic love contained therein, that which she had herself received from the venerated Foundress. Thus, Sister Therese chose her ten-day retreat before the Image of the Holy Face, surrendering to its beauty, writing about it in her own hand to Sister Agnes; there could never be any more doubt or misunderstanding as to the driving force behind Sister Therese's heroism.

Moreover, since Therese took occasion in her life's most solemn retreat to write that she chose the Bruised Countenance of her Redeemer above any other portion of the Sacred Hu-

---

9. Testifying at the Process of Sister Therese's Canonization, Sister Agnes sub-mitted this evidence: "However tender was her devotion to the Child Jesus, it cannot be compared to that which Sister Therese felt for the Holy Face."

manity, as the Supreme Object of her Adoration, it is important to remember certain relevant facts: What, actually, was the position of the Carmel of Lisieux regarding this rather new Devotion in the year 1890, when Sister Therese made her retreat? To trace its history is to come away inspired and assured that at Lisieux the Devotion had, indeed, taken deep roots.

To begin with, the Foundress of the Carmel of Lisieux, Mother Genevieve, as early as in 1847, while Sister Marie Pierre still lived in her Tours cloister, had already accepted the Revelations concerning *Reparation* through Devotion to the *Holy Face*. The records prove that, having become acquainted with a few facts concerning Sister Marie Pierre, Mother Genevieve was at once completely won over to the new Work, exclaiming with emotion: "When I think that the good God chose Carmel to ask *that*! . . . ."[10]

Without delay she had got the picture of the Holy Face, as imprinted on the Veil of Veronica, and had exposed it in the public chapel of the convent, and another in the enclosure. These were the years, when Sister Marie Pierre received only partial approval for her glorious work from the local authorities. There was as yet no Archconfraternity of Reparation to the Holy Face. Only the slightest public mention was even allowed that God had demanded this Reparation, and, yet, news of it had trickled into the Carmel of Lisieux and Mother Genevieve, learning of it, had at once embraced it for herself and her convent both privately and publicly.

There was, likewise, the Bishop of Langres who heard of these Revelations, and he, also, was at once won over to them. Since the local Ordinary of the Diocese of Tours had done nothing to promote the Work, Bishop Parisis of Langres then made a gesture in this direction. While he did not ask for a Confraternity to the Holy Face, yet he did petition Rome for the erection of a Confraternity to repair for sins of blasphemy,

---

10. *Life of Sister Marie de St. Pierre of the Holy Family,* by Sister M. Emmanuel, p. 7.

THE WHOLE WORLD WILL LOVE ME

which was at once accorded and at least partly set in motion *the program which Sister Marie Pierre* begged for. [11]

Mother Genevieve of Lisieux, learning of this Confraternity of Reparation now existing in France, hastened to appeal to the Archbishop to erect a similar Confraternity of Reparation in their diocese. She succeeded in winning the Prelate to the cause whose aim was reparation for blasphemy — although this was not the full program demanded by Our Lord as He revealed Himself to Sister Marie Pierre. Elated with the gradual progress, nonetheless, the Foundress looked to the future with hope. For, indeed, having canonically established a Society of Reparation at Lisieux, the Archbishop gladly endorsed and formed similar societies in nearly all the cities of his diocese.

Then, at the end of a glorious year of progress, came news that Sister Marie Pierre was dead. Mother Genevieve, mourning her early passing, yet felt that the cause of Reparation would be hastened now that the Saint of the Holy Face had gone to her reward.

Customarily, when a Discalced Carmelite dies, a short biography, called a Circular Letter, is written by the Carmelite convent where she lived and died, and this is sent to all the Carmels of the country. And for this Circular Letter, disclosing the life and revelations of the great mystic of Tours, Sister Marie Pierre, many waited hopefully and prayerfully. Among them was Mother Genevieve. Writing to Tours, she asked the nuns to send her relics of the dead sister, saying that veneration for this pious nun could not be greater than at Lisieux, and adding further, "You will be consoled to learn that the Association of Reparation is established in nearly all the towns of our diocese." A few months later Mother Genevieve wrote again: "Our worthy Prelate has just published a decree which will spread in our diocese the Work for which Sister Marie Pierre did and suffered so much."

But a prophet is ever without honor in his own country!

---

11. *God Demands Reparation: The Life of Leo Dupont,* by Rev. Emeric B. Scallan, p. 136. This book has been reprinted as *The Holy Man of Tours— The Life of Leo Dupont* (TAN, 1990). —*Publisher,* 2005.

[212]

If, at Lisieux, the Archbishop and the parishes were accepting Sister Marie Pierre and her mission of Reparation, and forming societies and carrying on the Devotion, there was no such endorsement of the Sister in her own diocese of Tours. If, in distant Lisieux, all were eager for a full life story of Sister Marie Pierre and had reread with interest all the pamphlets treating briefly with her mission which had been published during her life, in the city of Tours, where she had lived, had sanctified herself and had died in the odor of sanctity, there was no such enthusiasm. Mother Genevieve now learned there would be no Circular Letter depicting Sister Marie Pierre's life and works. Furthermore, the Archbishop of Tours had ordered complete silence and secrecy in everything that concerned the dead Sister.

In view of this action, not only were Sister Marie Pierre's revelations suppressed, but the Carmel of Tours was forbidden to even mention her name. The Work of Reparation to the Holy Face had been frozen at the roots. Therefore, during the years 1850 to 1876, there was no longer the merest mention of the name of Sister Marie Pierre in the letters exchanged between Mother Genevieve and the Prioress of the Tours Carmel.

Then, finally, came the year 1876, when a fourth, new Bishop took over the Diocese of Tours. His name was Bishop Colet. On entering office, he at once threw open the diocesan archives with the intention of publishing the life and the mission of Sister Marie Pierre. Bishop Colet was to go down in history as an Apostle of the Holy Face.

And it was high time, indeed, that Reparation was to have an advocate such as Bishop Colet. For, during this long span of some twenty-six years of imposed silence on the Carmelite Community of Tours, the Devotion to the Holy Face had been kept alive only through the efforts of one layman. This was Leo Dupont, a wealthy retired lawyer and widower, resident of Tours, and a devoted personal friend of Sister Marie Pierre. Believing in her mission from the first, Dupont procured a picture of the Holy Face, the Vera Effigies, after the Sister's death, and hung it in the drawing room of his home, honoring it with a light perpetually burning before it. Miracles and cures soon followed. Leo Dupont was to be, for a quarter of a century, acclaimed a thaumaturgist, and, through the spreading of the Devotion to the Holy Face, to become known as the Holy Man of Tours. And now, as Bishop Colet arrived at Tours to become its new Superior, Leo Dupont, at seventy-nine, lay dying of paralysis. With his passing there would probably end the semi-public cult of the Holy Face which he had carried on as a layman in his home at Tours. But Divine Providence decreed otherwise. Before he expired, Dupont learned that the new Bishop not only approved the works and revelations of Sister Marie Pierre in his own diocese, but was determined to exert every effort to make her name and mission known to the whole world.

A short time later, under the new Bishop, a full-size biography was written, published and translated into several languages. Simultaneously there was also published an extensive biography of the venerable Leo Dupont, her personal friend and collaborator, who, single-handed, had kept the Devotion alive for twenty-five long years.

With the help of the press the Work of the Holy Face received the stimulus it needed. Nine short years later, Pope Leo XIII endorsed the Cult of the Holy Face by establishing an Archconfraternity of the Holy Face, stating that the devotion was not only for France but, indeed, for the whole world, as a singular cure for the evils that had begun to engulf civilization.

Now that the dread night of doubt, suspicion and secrecy was over, at Lisieux Mother Genevieve, on learning of the great triumph of the Sister in whom she believed from the first, realized that she could do but little to advance the work.

She was now old and very infirm. Once, when she was young and strong, she had given herself eagerly to promoting the Work of Reparation, when it received only a semi-approval. Under her there was Worship of the Divine Countenance inside the enclosure and regularly scheduled devotions in the outside chapel which the faithful could attend. Now that Leo XIII had officially endorsed the Work and conferred on it the honors of an Archconfraternity, what, indeed, was not possible toward making the Order of Carmel glorious throughout the world by wresting from Heaven its choicest blessings through this most exalted Devotion in the Church?

But Mother Genevieve, confined in the infirmary, aged and suffering, knew that her days of working for God's kingdom on earth were almost spent. However, there was that novice, Sister Agnes, who showed promise of rare spiritual discernment. Mother Genevieve now encouraged her to pin her gaze on the Face of Jesus and keep it there in a spirit of Reparation, and so fulfill the destiny of a Carmelite to whom this Great Work was entrusted. Young Sister Agnes obeyed, and she discovered a world of new meaning in her vocation. When her youngest sister, Therese, entered Carmel a few short years later, she enjoined her to embrace it.

*   *

Indeed, the time was truly ripe for Sister Therese to discover the secrets of the Divine Wisdom contained in the Head of Christ, for the Archconfraternity of the Holy Face had just then been established (since this was the year 1885), and Therese, joining the Order in 1888, was to become the first fruit of the excellence of that Divine Worship. Embracing it, she was soon to add world fame to her monastery.

But it was the Foundress' zeal that had first prepared the way for Sister Therese, destined to become one of the world's greatest Saints. Now a novice in retreat, the future Saint was preparing for her vows of poverty, chastity and obedience, having spent some two and a half years at Carmel already, and with sufficient time to decide where her chief attraction lay. When her elder sister first introduced her to Worship of the Divine Countenance two years earlier, Therese had embraced it, saying at the time that she was progressing gradually in her vocation "under the shadow of His cross, having for refreshing dew His tears and His Blood, and for its radiant sun His adorable Face.

"Until then I had not appreciated the beauties of the Holy Face, and it was you, my little Mother [Sister Agnes], who unveiled them to me. Just as you had been the first to leave our home for Carmel, so, too, were you the first to penetrate the mysteries of love hidden in the Face of our Divine Spouse. Having discovered them, you showed them to me — and I understood . . . . More than ever did it come home to me in what true glory consists. He whose 'kingdom is not of this world' taught me that the only kingdom worth coveting is the grace of being *unknown and esteemed* as naught, and the joy that comes of self-contempt. I wished that, like the Face of Jesus, mine 'should be as it were hidden and despised' so that no one on earth should esteem me; I thirsted to suffer and to be forgotten . . . . And He never left unsatisfied any wish He has inspired in me . . . ."

Two years had passed since Sister Therese had made this resolve to so dedicate her life. Now, on the eve of her final vows, that would forever seal her destiny inside the cloister, Therese, during her Retreat, in a written note to her sister, proves conclusively that she had not shifted a single hair's breadth from her position before the Adorable Face. She could not resist the logic that told her clearly that here was no picture painted by hand in oils. Here was a picture of Christ's Face traced in His Own Blood on the Veil of Veronica, who had wiped His Face when he was worn out and condemned to death, walking the road to Calvary. The Sister could not help marveling at the sacrificial love of her Spouse. For, indeed, who would ever consent to have his picture taken at the height of his degradation and abasement? Who would do it but God, bent on appealing to the nobler sentiments of His creatures, whose redemption He bought, but whose following and affection He had hoped to secure by showing them the fearful sufferings He had endured willingly in their behalf?

For Therese, at the time of her Profession, the Sublime Drawing painted in Blood became her solitary treasure. The case being such, was the Retreat *before* her Profession one of ecstasy or pleasant rapture and consolation? No! Not at all! She says explicitly the light she had was but a *half-veiled* light. From such a half-veiled light she could not expect any glimpses of Beatific Vision, nor did she desire them. That joy was to be reserved for Heaven. For Sister Therese it sufficed to have only a glimmer of light, as much as could be expected from the downcast eyes of Jesus, as they looked down at her from the picture of Veronica's Veil. Then, studying the lowered eyes, Sister Therese began to discover things that escaped others.

True, the iron nails caused the gaping wounds and the streams of Blood, but the lowered lashes and the bloody sweat on Christ's brow were caused by a deeper agony, that of the mind. He had just now, arrived at the climax of His evangelical career, with many public works attesting to His wisdom, His zeal, and His goodness. These works should justly have won Him the first place among His people. But He now learned from His judges that even the least place was too good for Him. Officially branding His works as undesirable and unnecessary, He was now told openly, to His Face, that he could no longer hope even to be integrated with his fellow men. As a result, He was arbitrarily ordered removed from sight and contact. — Even the least place was deemed too good for one such as He! That statistics then showed a prevailing scarcity of religious men who offered, themselves, to teach the poor, was not enough to induce the authorities to tolerate His presence. Shame, confusion and disgrace now cover His Face, and He lowers His eyes — never to raise them again!

Studying the personality of Christ from the revealing portrait He had left to the world on Veronica's Veil, Therese became inspired to seek further enlightenment by consulting the Sacred Text. She now became wholeheartedly engrossed in the Holy Bible. For a full word description explaining the tragedy of the Man-God, whose Face on the Veil indicated such frightening endurance of disgrace, the Sister turned to the Prophets, David and Isaias:

I am a worm and no man . . . . Who is this that comes with dyed garments, this beautiful one is His robe, walking in the greatness of His strength? Why is your apparel red and your garments like theirs that tread in the winepress? Answering his self-asked question, Isaias says: *I have trodden the winepress alone and there is not a man with Me. I have looked about and there was none to help; I sought for someone, but there was none to give aid.*

But Isaias was not yet finished, for, he continues: *There is no beauty in Him, nor comeliness; and we have seen Him, and there was no sightliness that we should be desirous of Him. Despised and the most abject of men, He was a man of sorrows and acquainted with infirmity; His look was as though it were hidden and despised, therefore we esteemed Him not. We had thought Him as it were a Leper, and as one struck by God and afflicted . . . .*

Still, the Prophet Isaias had not told all he knew, for it was most necessary to explain whether these sufferings became His lot justly, as a malefactor and a disobedient man, or whether they came to Him unjustly. Now Isaias concludes:

But He was wounded for our iniquities; He was bruised for our sins; the chastisement of our peace was upon Him and by His bruises we are healed. All we like sheep have gone astray, every one of us had turned aside into his own way, and the Lord had laid on Him the iniquity of us all. He was offered, because it was His own Will, and He opened not His mouth; for the wickedness of My people have I struck Him; He had done no iniquity, neither was there deceit in His mouth; and the Lord was pleased to bruise Him in infirmity. If He shall lay down His life for sin, He shall see a long-lived seed. Since He had delivered His soul unto death, and was reputed with the wicked, while He prayed for the transgressors, I will distribute to Him very many [souls] . . . .

From this Retreat before the Holy Face to which Therese had given herself wholeheartedly before taking vows, she was to emerge with a thirst for Scripture that was never to leave her. From the light that shone from the downcast eyes of the Saviour, and by that light, she would set out on a study of Sacred Writ, not for the sake of earning a great name, but, that learning more of Him she could strive to become ever more like Him. Before finishing her missive to her sister that day, the retreatant made one more direct allusion to the Holy Face:

"Therese," she wrote, "the spouse of Jesus, loves Him for himself; she looks on the Face of her beloved only to catch a glimpse of the tears which delight her with their secret charm. She longs to wipe away those tears or to gather them up like priceless diamonds with which to adorn her bridal dress. O Jesus, I would so love Him as He has never yet been loved!"

It remained now for her to arrive at a method by which she would perform this service. On another sheet of note paper she began to write another letter, addressed to the Divine Master himself, which she intended wearing on her breast when two days later she would pronounce her vows to Him:

"O Jesus, take me from this world rather than allow me to stain my soul by committing the least willful fault. May all creatures be as nothing to me and I as nothing to them. May no earthly thing disturb my peace. O Jesus, I ask for peace and, above all, for love without limit. Grant that no one may think of me; grant that I may be forgotten and trodden underfoot as a grain of sand."

In these words Therese proved beyond a shadow of doubt that she was in deep earnest about desiring to love God as He had never yet been loved. Praying to be forgotten and esteemed as nothing, she proved that she stood ready to pay the full price for scaling the heights of Divine Love. For, indeed, to be treated with contempt and disdain is the last thing in this world that anyone wants. For this did Sister Therese ask, and after this did she seek. Studying the Face on the Veil, she concluded, logically, that this degrading suffering was the only thing that Christ longed for and embraced. It was destined to be the price of Redemption *itself*!

The writing done, the retreatant was interrupted by a gentle knock on her door. Opening it slightly, she noticed a Sister who came to hand her a note, an important-looking document. It was from Brother Simeon, Director of St. Joseph's College in Rome, whom her father had visited in the Holy City while they were on pilgrimage, and who had been instrumental in helping her enter Carmel at fifteen. The document was a special blessing from Pope Leo XIII on the occasion of her Religious Profession. Though she did not know it then, Sister Therese was to learn that she would have need of every ounce of the spiritual benefits of that Papal Blessing sent her by the faithful Brother Simeon.

The following night was to find her in a grave dilemma. It was the evening before her Profession. The sun had already waned and darkness began to overshadow her cell. A similar darkness came creeping into the Sister's thoughts. At first a lurking despondency stirred a chord of disunity. She was never very much inclined to ecstasy she admitted but, on the other hand, never had she had such a feeling of crowding gloom. Soon it was night in her soul and she could think of nothing else except that her whole religious life was as unreal as a dream . . . she had no vocation to Carmel . . . how could she have deemed such a life possible for her? — Surely, she had been deceiving not only herself but her superiors, all along.

Therese buried her face in her hands. She simply had to be a nun despite all these thoughts . . . . She *would* be one! Perhaps it would be best to say nothing to anyone and proceed with the ceremony of vows on the morrow? Yes, surely, that was the best thing! An hour passed and she felt herself being induced and prevailed upon to keep her silence — and go through the ceremony — rather than admit defeat.

Kneeling down, Therese took from her Breviary the small likeness of the Holy Face which she always kept there and prayed for help. It came like a flash of lightning . . . streaming from His Face into hers! Her temporary disturbance had been a ruse of the enemy of man and of God: for her to keep silence was the one thing he wanted. If he succeeded in forcing her to seal her lips and go through the ceremony without uncovering his assault against her — and bringing him out into the open — would he not be able then, ever after, to besiege her with remorse that she had done something in spite of her inclinations?

Pulling the veil down over her eyes, the Sister went at once into the choir to seek out the Novice Mistress and explain to her as best she could in her troubled state just what had happened.

"Nonsense! Absolute nonsense!" cried the enlightened Novice Mistress, adding to her protest a broad smile of encouragement. In a moment the turmoil vanished from her soul and Sister Therese was able to smile back at the Novice Mistress, who explained this ruse to her. She was no more concerned over it than she would be over a broken pin. By opening her heart thus to her superiors, the Sister had done the one perfect thing expected of her as a Novice. She resolved forever after to always be as simple as a dove. It rewarded her remarkably well.

The following morning Therese pronounced her vows:

"I, Sister Therese of the Child Jesus and of the Holy Face, promise to God, to the Blessed Virgin of Mount Carmel and to you, Reverend Mother Prioress, and to your successors, Poverty, Chastity and Obedience, according to the Primitive Rule of the Order of Our Lady of Mount Carmel, and its Constitutions, until death."

Lying face down on a black pall spread for this ceremony on the floor of the chapter room, and with her arms stretched out in the form of a cross, Sister Therese, as is the custom, made her silent private petitions to God. It was a solemn moment. Surely God hears the prayers of one who has just consecrated herself to Him until death, in a very special way. Sister Therese now asked that all the souls in purgatory be released from their pains and admitted to Heaven. Then she asked favors for all her family, particularly her sister Leonie:

"Grant that it be Your will for Leonie that she should become a Visitation nun; if she has no vocation, I beg you to give her one . . . . You cannot refuse me this favor . . . ."

Prostrated on the floor, Sister Therese was indeed doing violence to Heaven — daring, unheard-of violence. The Gospel said: *You have not chosen Me, but I have chosen you,* which seemed to indicate that in the realm of religious vocations the Divine Master reserved to himself the right of doing His own choosing. But, with the artlessness of a child, Therese, begging a religious vocation for her sister Leonie, admitted no Scriptural difficulties. He who wrote the Scriptures was above the Scriptures: Nothing was impossible with God. The Master could find a way to grant her request, and yet preserve the Scriptures whole. Indeed, the Sister prayed as one who had very rare powers over the Heart of the Bridegroom. Three of the five Martin daughters already were nuns. Celine, a fourth promised to enter for certain. But Leonie, attempting to be a Poor Clare nun, had returned home in failing health. Perhaps, too, she had no vocation? Therese had worried over this until the day of her own Profession, when in her hour of triumph she decided to wrest from Heaven the grace of a vocation for her sister.[12]

Now one more petition had yet to be made in behalf of her family: asking for a cure for her father. The Prioress had not only suggested this to her, but she had, in fact, ordered her to pray for this favor, though Therese felt this was out of her hands: her father had offered himself, and there was no recall-

___

12. Sister Therese was not to live to see Leonie settled in a convent, but, after her death, Leonie did enter the Visitation Sisterhood, and persevered there until death, some forty years later.

ing the sacred troth made to God. But, obedient to the Prioress, Therese lying prostrate on the floor, prayed:

"O my God, since Mother Prioress has told me to ask You, grant that Papa be cured if it be, indeed, Your will . . . ."

The ceremony was over. The entire conventual community now embraced the newly professed, singing: "Behold, how good and how joyous for brethren to dwell together in unity!"

There was special feast-day fare in the refectory, too: the gift of her Uncle Guerin and her Aunt, who had sent fish, cake, sweets, nuts and fruit. They were so generous to the convent that Therese had to remind them that delicacies in food were not the portion of the Discalced Carmelite on earth.

"Well, it is your feast, your great day," Uncle Guerin had told her, and she knew, indeed, that exceptions were not the rule, and was ever grateful to her relatives for their donations.

At recreation, her sister Marie asked her a question, puzzling over something she could not understand: "Why did you not decorate the Infant Jesus Altar in the chapter room with your new candles for the Profession ceremony, instead of using the old, half-burned-out ones, you saved from your Clothing nearly two years ago?"

"Because the old ones were given to me by Papa for my Clothing. Now he is not here but in that hospital. He could not come to my Profession, but his candles were there . . . ."

29

"You look as happy as a lark," said one of the professed choir nuns to Therese, who had just appeared at evening recreation. As usual, she was a full quarter-hour later than any of the other professed Sisters. The reason was that Therese had permission, as always, to remain behind for that week to help dry the dishes. It was something of an unwritten law that the novices offered their services for this kitchen duty, and so, for years, this custom had prevailed. However, when Sister Therese became a professed choir Sister, she managed — without in the least appearing unique — to obtain permission to continue helping to wipe dishes after meals, the same as she had always done before. The professed nuns paid no attention to this for it was generally taken for granted that the little, newly professed nun (who in reality was not little but quite tall) just naturally liked to be busy. It did not occur to them that Sister Therese, too, could have enjoyed a full hour's rest at recreation, not only as much as they did, but even more . . . . For the truth was, the numerous extra things she offered to do in the way of manual labor, at every turn, were beginning to tell on her health. But, then, Sister Therese would never let on that such was the case.

"If I look as happy as a lark, I'll admit it's because I really feel that way, Sister. I'm still under the spell of Father Alexis' wonderful sermons . . . ."

"I'm surprised to hear you say that."

"But why?" she asked.

"Didn't you know that everybody says Father Alexis is known as a preacher who converts hardened old sinners? If they hadn't been to Confession for fifteen years or more, then it's time to expose them to a few sermons by this prodigy, Father Alexis, and good results are sure to follow. He, himself, admits that contemplative nuns never invite him to preach!"

"Then, Sister, I must belong to the class of great sinners because, I assure you, I've yielded to his logic completely!" answered Therese smiling.

"Leave it to Sister Therese to make a good joke out of anything," chimed in another nun who overheard the conversation.

"But it isn't so funny after all," now offered Sister Agnes. "Any preacher who converts hardened sinners can appeal also to a youngster like Sister Therese. For, you see, it is a matter of the two opposites, the 'hot' and the 'cold.' With either of these two, any good preacher like Father Alexis is at home. It is the tepid ones that are hardest to move."

"I believe you are right at that, Sister Agnes."

"Of course, lukewarmness is the most dangerous state imaginable because you cannot appeal to the tepid by warnings about future punishment. Often they have no mortal sin. If you attempt to explain the Gospel to them, they will tell you that they believe . . . and that they can instruct you. And, often, they can. The very fact that they even go frequently to the Sacraments only makes it harder to approach them if you wish to show them how, in a hundred ways, they are offending continually — especially in charity toward their neighbors. A lifetime of such stubborn resistance to grace can bring them disaster in the hour of their death, when being appalled at their own past deliberate blindness, they can be tempted to despair."

The lay Sister crossed herself, a habit whenever she heard anything threatening someone's salvation. "Ah, Sister," she exclaimed, "tepidity is a fearful thing . . . especially in a religious." For the moment she had lost her gay expression.

"Oh, yes, tepid religious are compared to salt that has lost its savor, of whom Our Lord said that nothing remains but to discard it," further offered Sister Agnes. "I can understand that. Settled in their pattern of lukewarmness, they forget that there is no such thing as a standstill in the spiritual life. Since they do not move forward, they must be moving backward. Yet, just because they have no crimes to confess they think they can go along just as they are, nor would they ever think of changing by becoming charitable toward their neighbors. Oh, they themselves resent the slightest inattention shown to them, or to their own family members, but they openly and persistently refuse even a modicum of ordinary civility to others. In a religious, such conduct spells ruin . . . ." Sister Agnes ended.

"But there must be some cure for torpidity, I mean tepidity," said the lay Sister as they all suddenly broke out in smiles. But it did not matter, they soon agreed — torpidity, or tepidity, it was really one and the same thing. For surely the torpid and the tepid were numb, dormant and devoid of sensibilities. The inadvertent slip was a blessing in disguise, for, after all, this was recreation, and the spontaneous outburst of wholesome laughter was certainly in order.

"There is a cure for tepidity," now offered Sister Marie of the Sacred Heart as if anxious to press the topic of conversation to a logical conclusion.

"What is the cure?"

"The Sacred Heart!" answered Sister Marie in a tone of certitude.

"It is easy to tell that Sister Marie of the Sacred Heart is living up to her title. She could probably quote us all the Revelations Blessed Margaret Mary had at Paray-le-Monial, could you not?" asked Sister Therese.

"Not quite all, but I certainly do know that Sacred Heart Devotion has for its object the conversion of the tepid."

"A colossal task; sometimes considered quite impossible. That is why the conversion of the tepid is singularly reserved for the powers of the Sacred Heart *itself*!" again broke in Sister Agnes, the eldest nun in the small group. "Reparation to the Sacred Heart will undoubtedly win the grace of restoring the tepid to fervor."

"Oh, now that you mention Reparation, I suppose Devotion to the Sacred Heart really resembles Devotion to the Holy Face," casually remarked the lay Sister who continued to work on the mending of a worn alpargate.

"Oh, no, Sister," objected Therese. "If Reparation to the Holy Face as revealed to Sister Marie Pierre just a few years ago were the same as Reparation to the Sacred Heart, revealed about two hundred years ago to Blessed Margaret Mary, why would Rome erect two separate Societies, that of the Sacred Heart, and that of the Holy Face?"

"Oh, now it is easy to see that Sister Therese of the Holy Face is living up to her title," gently came from Sister Marie.

"Suppose you explain the difference between the two Devotions," said Sister Agnes, anxious to draw Sister Therese out on this important subject.

"Well, Reparation to the Sacred Heart is aimed at atoning for the coldness and indifference of those inside the fold who refuse to order their lives in accordance with charity. By doing this they wound the Saviour's Heart, because they already belong to Him," began Therese.

"So far so good. And now, how does it differ from Holy Face Reparation?"

"The object of Reparation to the Holy Face is to repair for the insults offered the Divine Majesty by those who through their own fault deliberately remain outside the Church; it is for avowed atheists, for blasphemers who scoff at all religion, and for all who out of hatred profane His Holy Name and hold in derision all that pertains to Divine Worship as, for example, atheistic communists. By these crimes, committed publicly, they strike the Saviour to His Face. These open outrages cause Him severe mental torture, for He created them all, and loves them, and died for them, and thirsts for their salvation. To convert them, the faithful are urged to become members of the Archconfraternity of the Holy Face, to venerate in their homes and churches the Vera Effigies and, especially on Sundays, to offer special prayers of Reparation for these unhappy people. You see, believers who are lukewarm do not strike at God, they only bruise the Heart of the Saviour by their lukewarmness and their indifference in His service. Reparation to the Sacred Heart on First Fridays, especially, has therefore been decreed, as we have learned from Blessed Margaret Mary. However, disbelievers who openly deny God and persecute religion, all commit crimes not only against the Son of God but against the Holy Trinity, God the Father, in particular. Therefore Reparation to the Holy Face, which is aimed at atoning for these crimes against God himself, is essentially a Sunday Devotion, Trinitarian in aspect. As Our Lord himself told Sister Marie Pierre, 'The Divine Head represents the Eternal Father who is unbegotten; the mouth of the Holy Face represents the Divine Word, begotten of the Father; the two eyes, finally, represent the reciprocal love of the Father and the Son, for the two eyes have but one light, one knowledge, and they produce the one same love, which typifies the Holy Ghost. The locks of His hair represent the infinite perfections of the Most Blessed Trinity . . . .' "

For a few moments there was silence and then the lay Sister asked: "Would you say, then, that Holy Face Devotion is higher than Sacred Heart Devotion?"

"It is not a matter of which is higher," explained Sister Therese. "The main thing to understand is that the object of these two special Devotions is to combat two particular evils of our day, very much as two different medicines might be prescribed for two different illnesses!"

"I like the way you put that!" said Sister Agnes encouragingly.

"Sister Marie Pierre tells us that Reparation to the Holy Face," explained Sister Therese, further "is particularly aimed at the evils of today, namely atheistic communism."

"Ah, Sister Marie Pierre, what a Carmelite she was!" exclaimed the lay Sister. "They were fortunate to have her at Tours. It is so close to Lisieux that she might easily have entered here . . . and been one of us . . . . And, since she lived at Tours, when our own Mother Genevieve was already here at Lisieux — and is now in the infirmary — she could be telling us first-hand stories about her . . . ." Then, after a moment's pause, she added, "It was wonderful, however, the way the Prioress at Tours was inspired to have Sister Marie Pierre write down every revelation about the Holy Face just as she received it, was it not?" she finished, looking up from her work.

"That, my dear Sister, was Providential. God rules His world and His Church."

"I wonder if she will be canonized?"

"Of course. She will be canonized some day," they all agreed.

"I've been told that pilgrims who go to Tours, where Mr. Leo Dupont spent so many years spreading Devotion to the Holy Face, came away very highly impressed. They say there is something so inexpressibly sublime in the very atmosphere of the Oratory of the Holy Face, at Tours, that it can be compared to only one other place in the world, Paray-le-Monial. No wonder! Our Lord himself sanctified Tours and Paray-le-Monial with His Presence, inaugurating there the two greatest Devotions to himself!"

Therese spoke so convincingly that the lay Sister asked: "But who told you that? It's most beautiful!"

"My father himself told me that before my Clothing, when I took the title 'of the Holy Face.' " Sister Therese sighed, thinking of her father. "He, you know, was very fond of making pilgrimages to holy places. He visited Tours and told us all about it."

"And how is your Papa now, Sister?" the lay Sister asked.

"He is no better. May God be praised!"

Just then the bell rang out the end of recreation, and the nuns, folding their handwork, filed into the chapel choir for Compline. On the way Therese smiled to herself. When she came to recreation that evening she had been as happy as a lark, to use the Sister's expression, but she was not able to tell the Sisters the real reason for her high spirits, because it had to do with something that had transpired in the Confessional. And of whatever takes place in the Tribunal of Penance, the

Sisters never speak at recreation, thus to safeguard the seal of Confession. While they freely chatted about the Saints and Devotions, they would never hint at what occurred during the Sacrament of Penance. But the fact was that Father Alexis had launched her full sail on the ocean of confidence in God and on love, which always attracted her so strongly. Nor was it his preaching alone that made her so jubilant, though she admired it. It was the encouragement received in the Confessional — which, indeed, she sorely needed.

The fact was that for the two years past she had gone on hoping and living her sacrificial life of penance, and done so without even a glimmer of encouragement that she was on the right road. During these two years she had constantly carried with her the memory of what Father Blino, a Jesuit, had told her, when she appealed to him in Confession.

"O Father, I desire so much to become a Saint!" Therese had said.

"Hush, hush! What pride and what presumption! Banish such ideas, Sister, and confine your efforts to overcoming your faults .... You must curb those rash desires!" answered Father Blino.

Today, however, she was jubilant. Father Alexis had reversed that verdict by encouraging her to trust she would reap the highest rewards for living her isolated life of penance. In view of this she would not mind the fasting, the abstaining from meat the whole year through, and the living in solitude and silence; not only denying herself all pleasures, but scourging her flesh with a discipline. No, she would not mind all this, for she was now allowed to hope that a reward awaited her. Moreover, she would not mind being forgotten and considered as nothing on earth. She would not mind kneeling from early dawn until almost midnight in endless prayer — tortured sometimes with an indescribable dryness which was most sure to come to those who pray continuously, since, at last, she could be allowed to trust, to know, that her heroism would win a rare reward after her death. When Father Blino had chided her for nourishing this hope, she felt quite abandoned. The harsh rebuke for her rashness, as though he were dealing with a worldling, rather than a monastic penitent, had gravely unsettled her peace. Now that Father Alexis had undone the unhappy reprimand, Therese beamed with joy. She could and she would be that Saint!

30

TWO MONTHS later, in December, Therese was to see the first death at Carmel. The aged Foundress, Mother Genevieve, passed away after a long and painful illness in the infirmary. She had established the Reparation to the Holy Face in her Monastery many years before, and as she now breathed her last sigh, and went to reap the rewards promised in behalf of those who gave themselves to this work, she most assuredly must have learned that her young daughter, Sister Therese, would soon cover her convent with world fame because she had embraced this very Devotion.

One night shortly after the death, Therese, who had always insisted that she paid no particular attention to her dreams, could, yet, not pass off unnoticed a very strange dream she had about the deceased Mother. In this dream, she beheld Mother Genevieve parceling out to each of the nuns something which had belonged to herself. When it was Sister Therese's turn to receive some token she noticed that the Mother's hands were empty: she had nothing left to give her. Then, looking at her lovingly, she whispered: "To you, Sister Therese, I leave my heart!" Three times over the sentence was repeated and then the dream vanished, and Sister Therese awoke. Was it the Work of the Reparation, dearest to Mother Genevieve's heart, the Devotion to the Holy Face, that she now confided to Therese by giving her her heart? The future alone would prove that.

᛫   ᛫

Hardly had the Foundress been buried when an epidemic of influenza spread through Lisieux and penetrated into the convent. Sister Therese, who suffered only a slight attack, and two other Sisters who escaped the contagion, had to nurse the entire community of some twenty nuns. Two nuns died. A third, whom Sister Therese was nursing, was on the point of death. Having a presentiment early one morning, as she woke from a few hours' rest that this nun was dead, Therese hurried toward the nun's cell. The corridors were still unlit and she had to make her way in the dark of the winter morning. She found the Sister dead. Unafraid, she went out to bring a blessed candle, and, arranging the dead Sister's habit, she then went to tell the infirmarian what had happened.

Besides attending to the convent of epidemic-stricken nuns and to burying the dead, Sister Therese was also attending to the Sacristy linens, by herself. Physicians, as also priests, among whom was Father Delatroette — who during the epidemic came into the enclosure to do their ministry — now had an opportunity to see to what degree of heroic action a nineteen-year-old nun could give herself, swiftly passing from one good work to another. She was, indeed, proving herself indispensable during that raging epidemic.

When the dread winter had passed and the stricken nuns were at their duties again Sister Therese was relieved of her office of assistant sacristan and for two months was allowed to try her hand at painting. As a child she had longed to take painting lessons along with her elder sister but had never expressed the desire, counting it a virtue to offer God this sacrifice. Now, taking to brush and easel, although she had had no training in art, Sister Therese painted several pictures so artistically that Mother Mary Gonzaga assigned her the task of painting a fresco in the oratory of the convent.

In the fall she was again called to additional manual labor, being assigned the office of portress. As such it was her chore to transact all of the convent business, carry in the provisions brought to the front door, and settle whatever business called for attention. Therese was now twenty and an experienced toiler, having overcome all her slow ways by dint of persevering effort. Her services were in demand everywhere, and she kept on from morning to night, serving and waiting on others.

This, however, did not interfere with her life of meditation. It is at this time, when particularly busy at every turn, and open to countless distractions incumbent on this office, that Sister Therese gives evidence of having never lost sight of the *one* important thing. Writing to one of her sisters, she says:

"Dear Celine — One day I was pondering over what I could do to save souls; a phrase from the Gospel showed me a clear light: *Lift up your eyes and see the countries, for they are already white to harvest. The harvest indeed is great, but the laborers are few. Pray, therefore, to the Lord of the harvest that He send forth laborers.*" Further developing the theme she says: "Our vocation is not to go harvesting the fields of ripe corn. Jesus does not say, *Go and reap them*; but says, *Ask Me for laborers and I shall send them . . . .*"

Therese had her eyes glued on the Scriptures and daily fulfilled their exactions.

Again she writes: "Celine, listen to what He tells us: *Make haste and come down for this day I must abide in thy house. The foxes have holes and the birds their nests but I have not where to lay my head . . . .*"

Applying the lesson to herself, she says: "How can this be done? Only by coming down to the lower levels." — By humbling herself to the dust, and allowing everybody else to triumph, while she makes haste continually to *come down*, is she able to make room in her heart for Him to come and dwell therein. This "coming down" must, then, have a twofold aspect, exterior and interior.

"Celine, you know the exterior one has already been brought to nothing by the painful affliction of Caen . . . in our dearest Father," she explains.

His isolation in the insane asylum among seventeen hundred other inmates continued to press down on Therese each day of her life. As for the interior "coming down," analyzing herself critically, Therese tells Celine: "Alas, I feel that my heart is not wholly empty of self, which is why Jesus tells me to come down . . . ." (She was not closing her eyes to what lay in her heart.) Sanctity was a progressive, grueling task, for which a full lifetime was needed. Therese was determined to go on ahead, daily. This could be done only by that critical analysis of self that opened to clear view those tendencies within her which she felt needed uplifting.

31

THE NUNS were tingling with suspense. Their monastery was to have a change of administration. The day was February 20 of 1893, a day of decisive moment to their convent. On this day a new Prioress would be voted into office — the term of Mother Mary Gonzaga having expired — and most of the nuns were anxious for this change.

In the parlor, before a gathering of important ecclesiastics, the secret voting was duly in progress. Therese was not among those voting, though she was eligible because she had been professed and this was her sixth year in the convent. But, because a special regulation prescribed that only two members of any given family were allowed to cast ballots for a Superioress, Therese, being the third and youngest from the Martin family, abstained. This, inwardly, was a source of comfort to her — who always wanted to go through life as one of no account.

The elections concluded, the nuns came from the parlor into the choir in procession, escorting the newly elected Reverend Mother Prioress. Therese, who in the meantime was kneeling, praying silently in the choir, looked up and saw that the newly elected Superioress was none other than her own sister, her own Pauline of childhood days, and now *Reverend Mother Agnes of Jesus.*

Although the elections ended smoothly enough, they nevertheless contained their share of contradictions. To begin with, the fact was that Mother Agnes was only thirty-three, [13] while

---

13. Before her death the Foundress, Mother Genevieve, once made the statement that an important position would be entrusted to Sister Agnes when she was in her thirties. Her election to office, as Prioress at thirty-three, indicates a rare and accurate prophetic gift.

the Rule stipulated forty as the required age for a Prioress, which called for a dispensation; besides, this overruling of her age had brought dissatisfaction from those opposing her. Moreover, some frowned upon the fact that the new Prioress had two sisters who were nuns in the same convent. There were other small pin pricks that stabbed with numbing pain, and these had all to be silently endured. At the day's end Therese, feeling it was up to her to write the new Prioress, her sister, a word of encouragement, quietly slipped a note into her cell late that night, without saying a word. The note read:

"My dearest Mother . . . . Oh! how lovely a day it is for your child! The veil Jesus has cast over the day makes it still more luminous to my eyes; it is the seal of the Adorable Face . . . . Surely, it will always be so. 'He whose look was hidden' will spread over the whole life of the beloved *Apostle of His Divine Face* a mysterious veil which only He can penetrate . . . ."

Here is a veritable climax of conclusive evidence that Sister Therese invariably and immediately, *before every decision made in her life*, was to turn to the humiliated Face on the Veil, to seek and find there the infallible clue that would resolve for her every difficulty. Waving the Banner of the Holy Face before the embarrassed and lowered eyes of her sister, she reminds her that all is well because this day of her election, otherwise so happy, was marked with the cross: "The veil Jesus has cast over the day makes it still more luminous to my eyes; it is the seal of the Adorable Face." Therese might have been afraid if her sister had been unanimously elected, and with acclaim. Even though she considered her the most perfect nun in the convent, and had selected her as her own model and guardian angel, yet Sister Therese might have been apprehensive had the day been without a shadow of contradiction. However, in view of the fact that the day had its share of bitterness, Therese rejoiced. Because there was a striking similarity between her dear sister and the Victim on the Veil, she exclaimed that "surely it would always be so" and, further, that "He whose look was hidden would spread over the whole life of the new prioress a mysterious veil since she had been the *Beloved Apostle of His Divine Face . . . ."*

Reverend Mother Agnes now realized that the lessons of perfection contained in the life and revelations of Sister Marie Pierre, to which she had introduced Sister Therese some six years earlier, had been mastered. As the years went by, Sister Therese understood ever more clearly that the road to true spiritual greatness was no superhighway. It was a muddy, grimy road filled with obstacles, and while treading it, one became sweated, bloodstained and murky. But then, when this happened, one also had, perforce, to rejoice, for there was, at the last, the one and only one desirable thing come true: a resemblance to the Outcast portrayed on the Veil.

1   1

Whoever could construe the spirituality of Sister Therese in any light less than that shining through the lowered eyes of the humiliated Face on Veronica's Veil would, indeed, have to do violence to the burden of documented history. But Sister Therese's note to Mother Agnes is not yet concluded. One more important observation is made on this decisive occasion, the election of her sister to the community's first office. This has to do with evaluating her sister's competency and talents regarding the office conferred on her that day. Isolating what she considered the culminating proof of why her sister, rather than any other nun, deserved this promotion to the office of Prioress, Therese writes in her note: "At thirty you have begun your public life; it was you *after all who wrote* the moving and poetic account of the life of our Holy Foundress [Mother Genevieve] which has been published and read by all our Carmels and by other pious persons. [14] But Jesus had cast a veiled look upon my dearest Mother and He did not let her

_____

14. *The Memoirs of Mother Genevieve,* the story of her saintly life and death, written by Sister Agnes of Jesus, though signed by the Prioress, Mother Mary Gonzaga, and duly circulated throughout France.

be recognized, for her look was hidden . . . . [Signed] Sister
Therese of the Child Jesus and of the Holy Face."

In the judgment of the Sister of twenty-one, it was Mother
Agnes' authorship of spiritual literature that deserved recognition, and therefore entitled her to the first place in the community. "It was you *after all who wrote* the moving and poetic
account of the Life of our Holy Foundress," are the words
Therese used, to prove the unrivaled distinction those hold in
her judgment whose talents and virtues combine to make them
writers of spiritual literature. Lauding her sister's achievement
in this field, by recalling that it was she, Mother Agnes, who
was the author of the Circular Letter comprising the memoirs
of Mother Genevieve, Therese feels that she has established
irrefutable proof of why it was her elder sister who deserved to
be elected. After all, the *Memoirs* had been published and
circulated, and had been read by many with interest and edifica-
tion. And, finally, the merits of her pen had won the Carmel
of Lisieux a place of honor.

The elections of the day were indeed to be decisive. Their
outcome was to be as far-reaching as revealing. For one, Therese,
who until now had continually stressed the value of the "little
things done for God," suddenly loomed on the horizon as
one stressing — and to no lesser degree — the value of "great
things done for God." In her twenty-first year, reaching out
toward a maturity of mind and heart, she refuses to lose sight
of Mother Agnes' literary achievements, and, placing a unique
value on them, openly declares that their greatness entitled
her sister to win acclaim in their midst. — "It was *you, after
all*, who wrote the moving account of the life of our Holy
Foundress which has been published and read . . . ."

And thus Sister Therese, the universal endorser of the value
of little things, is not to be confused with one despising rare
accomplishments, overlooking them deliberately or through
lack of vision, one setting no store on greatness, as the election
day note proves.

Unexpectedly the shrinking violet rises to the height of an

aggressive tall sunflower, one who, far from an unyielding attachment to a lowered gaze that refuses to admit reality, proves suddenly that she has been a keen observer of everything transpiring around her all along. A self-elected choice of the least position never made her shortsighted or a mistaken witness to what went on. And, surely, it is the only attitude to expect from such perspective as came from Sister Therese! And it was precisely because she did endorse the tremendous value "of even the *smallest* things . . ." that she was competent to evaluate and endorse, by the same logic, more convincingly "those greater things done in His service."

Immediately following the election the nuns braced themselves for a shift of minor offices and duties, for a newly elected Prioress can be counted on to make her own choices and adjustments so they will fit into her pattern of organization. Sister Therese, who till now had held the disconcerting office of errand nun — being the portress — unknowingly faced a change of office that nearly leveled her to the floor of the corridors she chased. Overnight, the Carmel of Lisieux had as a Prioress an unprecedented spiritual genius of thirty-three, one who recognized for a long time that neither the Ceremonial nor the Rule and Regulation Books were in themselves able to resolve the deep problems of salvation and of sanctification. Reverend Mother Agnes had just witnessed, for example in her own election to office, how the letter of the law had been set aside to allow her to become Prioress, when the age stipulated in the Book of Rules was no less than forty — one concrete example bringing Mother Agnes the conviction that the Holy Church orders its life not by a Rule Book alone but by the words of the Divine Saviour: "The letter killeth; but the Spirit giveth life."

The new Prioress of Lisieux became keenly conscious now of her responsibility for the affairs of the monastery in accordance with the highest exactions of conscience — no matter what price would be exacted for her brave convictions. One thing was clear: so that the spiritual and material welfare of the community could be assured a highest measure of prosperity, it was imperative to begin by distributing the various offices and positions of the convent according to the requirements of justice.

Those who through their talents and application had proved their merits would perforce have to be assigned preferred positions for the sake of the highest monastic well-being. If the letter of the law should in a particular instance seem to bar the way for an individual Sister to assume a position of importance, then the letter of the law would have to be set aside. The words of the Gospel were realistically clear on the point, and the conclusions they called for at first startled the thirty-three-year-old Superioress who had just assumed office. Going into the choir, she knelt, debating for a while the prudence of what was beginning to assert itself in her mind.

What would others say if she were actually to carry out the ideas now pounding in her heart . . . and which were demanding her complete consent in the hidden recesses of her mind? Surely, she would have to face a mountain of difficulties! It was just not done! And never at Lisieux! Then she remembered that the Rule Book had hundreds of small paragraphs explicitly proscribing just such an administrative gesture as the new Reverend Mother Prioress was now contemplating.

As she pondered the matter Mother Agnes felt cold perspiration on her fair brow. Already the first place in the Community had begun to exact a fearful toll from her.—If she could but appease the voice of conscience, if she could only allow herself to walk in the beaten path, there would be no toll to pay . . . . And everybody would be satisfied, yes, everybody except God! Mother Agnes had for too long and too seriously looked into the Face of that God as outlined on the Veil stained with red blotches to be able to disregard His essential demands. No matter whom she would displease, no matter how she would be made to pay, Mother Agnes was determined to do what she felt *God demanded.* And that is why, after several stiff debates within her heart she was, a few days later, on her way to her sister's cell, to inform the oldest in the family — Sister Marie of the Sacred Heart — about a matter vitally concerning the youngest, Sister Therese of the Child Jesus and of the Holy Face.

"Sister Marie, I have something of grave importance to discuss with you . . . ." Mother Agnes began.

"Yes, Reverend Mother," answered Sister Marie. "You seem worried."

"I am facing a trial, and the decision I must make is a very difficult one . . . ." she confessed.

"God will help you, Mother. Every Superior has difficulties, at the beginning especially . . . ."

"This is no ordinary difficulty, Sister Marie. And I know that God will help, but poor nature is so weak and it trembles to take a step knowing it will bring repercussions . . . ."

"But that is not like you, Reverend Mother. You are the strong one in our family, the first to have chosen Carmel, years before I did, although I was two years older than you. If I can help now, you know I'll be only too happy to do so."

"Well, Sister, as you already have seen, I've distributed all the offices in the convent except one," said Mother Agnes, steeling herself to the ordeal.

"Yes, I've noticed. You haven't yet chosen a Novice Mistress!"

"That is right!"

"Do you have someone in mind, Reverend Mother?"

"Yes, I have, definitely, which is the reason why I am troubled."

"But I don't understand. Whom have you chosen?"

"None other than Sister Therese of the Child Jesus and of the Holy Face!"

The small cell seemed to lose its limits of confinement and solitude. It loomed like a gigantic public stage on which a world heroine was expected to appear in a moment to be acclaimed by an enthusiastic audience breathlessly awaiting a singularly dramatic Command Performance which no lesser artist could attempt.

Ere she would finish her play in three acts — for which she had only three short years of life left, though nobody knew it then — the sublime actress was to reappear before the footlights of this stage to take her laurels as the unrivaled Heroine in the Greatest Drama of Real Life which the world had ever witnessed. Thence she was to ascend a higher stage, a heavenly one, never more to appear for a repeat performance. However, the memory of the three-act play would continue to uplift a world of tired and hopeless human beings to a new and fresh height of enthusiasm. Surely, the play of the superb heroine proved beyond a shadow of doubt one essential truth: that to spend one's life striving for supremacy was the only worthwhile aim in all human existence.

But the two nuns, the blood sisters of the Great Heroine, could for the moment share none of the enthusiasm reserved for the future. For the present there was only the grim realization that the performance of a duty would require courage and reap a harvest of thorns and thistles.

"I can well understand what you are suffering, Reverend Mother," Sister Marie said sympathetically, suddenly seeing her superior in religion as her younger sister at home, frighteningly in need of her elder sister's comforting presence.

"But, surely, Sister Marie, you do understand that I cannot shirk my responsibilities — I *must* make Sister Therese the Novice Mistress although I know beforehand what some among us and others outside will say of me."

"Oh, yes, Mother, they will surely say enough," agreed Sister Marie. She remembered too well the circumstances of the election casting suspicion on the three Martin nuns.

"Still, I *must* act on principle! The spiritual good of the novices is at stake, and the most perfect nun here should hold the office of instructing and molding those souls toward perfection. You and I both know well that Sister Therese answers that description, and she alone."

"It is true!"

"Very well, then, why should I shirk my duties just because I fear that others will accuse us of partiality? Six years ago I told our Therese to imitate Saint Veronica and brave the angry crowd of His executioners by offering Him a towel with which to wipe His bloody and tearful Face — and to disregard mere human respect. Better had I lecture myself, if I want to execute my office without blame! Is it not a flimsy excuse, for me to evade appointing Sister Therese to an office of distinction because others will falsely charge me with showing preference to a member of my family? And why should I fear them? Obviously, to escape criticism and be spared suffering! But, I ask you, Sister Marie, what sort of a Discalced Carmelite would I be if I planned my life with the view of escaping suffering? Surely, you would not admire such a trait in me, would you?"

"I know you too well to even suspect that you would compromise a principle to escape a bit of pain," Sister Marie answered, but her voice was devoid of enthusiasm. The hour called for every ounce of solemn determination.

"Surely, our life as Discalced Carmelites is meaningless unless it is lived in imitation of Christ. Can I say that it was quite proper for Our Lord to stand up to the magistracy in Pilate's courtroom, openly upholding a principle which He even knew in advance would cost Him not only a temporary annoyance but an agonizing death? Yet, for myself, Reverend Mother Agnes of Jesus, I must figure out a devious plan of conduct so as to be spared even a trace of annoyance . . . .

"Can I say that it was all very natural for Him openly to defend His claim to Divinity before enemies bent on destroying Him in a hall of justice the moment He would let fall the word that He was, indeed, the Son of the Living God? But when I, Mother Agnes, am confronted with the mere difficulty of upholding a principle — am I to be allowed to shun a conscientious duty to be spared a bit of pain?

"Indeed no man had more to lose than Christ did that Good Friday morning, when He was facing legal counsel in Pilate's hall of justice . . . and He was offered a final chance to deny or affirm His Divinity. We know that He chose to defend a principle by refusing to compromise the truth though it would cost Him his life before the sun of that day had set. Telling His contemporaries in the streets of Judea during the last three years of His public preaching that He was the Son of God, He said that if He did say that He was *not* the Son of God, then He would become, indeed, like His opponents, a liar. [15] Now, in Pilate's hall, He had a last opportunity to take back that testimony and save Himself untold woe. The whole legal case against Him resolved itself on this one and only issue: 'Is He or is He not the Only Begotten Son of the Eternal Father?' [16] Defending a principle — and the truth — He returned an affirmative answer, and then He took the consequences: a frightful Passion and a most disgraceful death on a cross . . . .[17]

"And here am I — Mother Agnes — momentarily confronted with the problem of defending a principle: Shall I do my duty as a Superioress unafraid? Or, compromising, shall I adopt a neutral course, one certain to procure for me the full endorsement of my neighbor — while I fail completely to ascertain if my action has or has *not* the endorsement of God! I know that Sister Therese is that one nun here who could give the novices true spiritual nourishment for their souls, and that this would give pleasure to Our Lord. As an act of justice and simplicity, it would wipe away some of that spittle from His cheeks. Must I have recourse to human respect, and, because I

---

15. Whom dost thou make thyself? Jesus answered, If I glorify myself, my glory is nothing. It is my Father that glorifies me, of whom you say that he is your God . . . . And if I shall say that I know him not, I shall be like to you, a liar . . . . JOHN 8 : 53-58.
16. The high priest asked him, and said to him: Art thou the Christ the Son of the blessed God? . . . And Jesus said to him: I am. MARK 14 : 61-62.
17. And they said, What need we any further testimony? for we ourselves have heard it from his own mouth. LUKE 22 : 17. And the whole multitude of them, rising up, led him to Pilate. And Pilate spoke to them, desiring to release Jesus. But they cried again, saying: Crucify him, crucify him. And Pilate gave sentence that it should be as they required. LUKE 23 : 1, 20, 21, 24.

do not relish being accused of partiality, must I leave Sister Therese at the turn attending to parcels, and appoint someone I know is altogether her inferior to attend to immortal souls? Well, I have made up my mind, Sister Marie! I shall appoint Sister Therese as the new Mistress of Novices. Let the reproaches fall upon me if they will. I am determined to see the Community at Lisieux have an opportunity to reach out to new heights of perfection, as the young ones in our midst under Sister Therese's direction will learn to scale new horizons."

"Reverend Mother, I agree with you completely. But, outside the difficulty in selecting your own sister for this prominent office, what shall you do about the regulations governing the age of a Novice Mistress? Sister Therese, you know, is not yet quite twenty-one."

"I thought that over already and I believe I have a good plan."

"It needs to be good, Mother. You know how they opposed your age at the elections last Monday."

"I know. And, believe me, I am as eager as anyone here to render fullest respect to the Rules and the Ceremonial, provided I can reconcile the Ceremonial with the Gospel. Sometimes, if the letter of the law conflicts, I feel I must invoke the spirit of the law. It was only last night that I prayed before the Holy Face asking for enlightenment. Do you know that as I knelt it seemed to me as if Our Saviour were addressing me from the picture. *Mother Agnes of Jesus,* He said, *tell Me where in the Ceremonial do you find outlined on what part of My Face should land the spittle of the mob? Is there a regulation, Mother Agnes, that designates where on My forehead the thorns should pierce Me? Does anybody consult a Rule Book before dealing Me a blow on My cheek? Right and left they struck me, hating Me without cause, and they spat upon Me as the tears and Blood mingled and fell down My face.*

"*It was then that I had My picture taken to leave you a portrait from which you would learn what to do and what not to do. My Face is the Book that will answer your deepest ques-*

tions. Look well at Me, Mother Agnes of Jesus, and then either make Sister Therese the Novice Mistress or reject her as a Novice Mistress. As for her, she will rise up to Me by either road, as portress or as Superioress; but you, Mother Agnes, will be judged by God and by man, for the way you discharge the duties of your office.

"You are now the Prioress. You have a free will to appoint whomever you decided to particular offices but, remember, your acts carry with them moral responsibility which will stretch with their consequences not only here below, but beyond the grave. You are, indeed, allowed to do as you will, but you must know that one particular person is meant for a particular office, and if you deliberately overlook the right choice, to escape annoyance, or to satisfy a personal liking, or whim, you will answer for this act of demerit. At present it is you, Mother Agnes, and not Sister Therese, who is on trial! It is you who are now being put to the test, and remember that your choice will lift or degrade you. How you use your authority, to whom you appoint particular offices, and on whom you confer privileges, will constitute the measure of your merit or your blame. Freedom to choose the right or the wrong is given to superiors as it is to all men, but no one, whatever his office, enjoys the liberty to choose the wrong arbitrarily, presuming that his office will protect him from blame or that he is immune from rendering a strict account for his wrong choice.

"Look well at Me, Mother Agnes of Jesus, and understand that My Kingdom on earth must spread and it can spread only if the right laborers, zealous and spiritually gifted, are assigned to offices of leadership. Look well at Me, Mother Agnes, and behold what a bloody price I have paid for establishing My Church on earth, and learn that I shall require a severe account from those who had it in their power to advance the growth of My Church by appointing enlightened and zealous laborers, who have proved their worth, to offices of importance, but who for any reason whatsoever refused to do the right thing.

"These zealous and gifted laborers are always available, for

I, myself, through My Divine Providence, supply these in every age. I count on them to spread My Church and bring peace to all men of good will, but when someone who has it in his power to appoint capable and proven laborers to important offices shuns this prime duty, and out of envy, out of a desire to himself outshine his fellow men, or to appease the ignoble, when such a superior of set purpose selects the mediocre to places of responsibility and demotes the deserving and the gifted, then disorder follows. Then the Church for which I died a most fearful death is impeded in her growth and stifled in helping the human race to attain to peace. For this travesty there shall be a serious reckoning.

"Look well at Me, Mother Agnes, and understand finally why this must be so. For, you see, this singular tragedy of being thrown over and discarded while the mediocre and faulty and envious triumphing over Me were preferred above Me, was My bitter lot in life. I, the Man who had done all things well, [18] *and of whom it is written that I have done the works that no man had ever done,* [19] *yet was singled out for the lowest demotion and then eliminated."*

A strange silence settled upon the small, dim cell in which two sisters, both Carmelite nuns, pondered the deep things of God.

"Reverend Mother, you have no choice. You must make Sister Therese the Novice Mistress. You can do nothing else. God certainly has some special designs for her, and you are His instrument to bring Sister Therese forward and into notice."

"That is all I wanted to hear you say, Sister," Mother Agnes replied.

As she walked away from her sister's cell she felt a deep peace settling in her heart. The storm was over. She knew where she

---

18. And so much the more did they wonder saying: He hath done all things well; he hath made both the deaf to hear, and the dumb to speak. MARK 7 : 37.

19. If I had not done among them the works that no other man hath done, they would not have sin; but now they have both seen and hated both me and my Father. JOHN 15: 24.

stood. "In the head of the book it is written of me that I should do Thy will; O my God." [20] Mother Agnes recognized that will of God and she was prepared to do its bidding regardless of the cost to her in misunderstanding and suffering. Going straight now to the cell of Mother Mary Gonzaga, the ex-Prioress, she addressed her as follows:

"Mother, I wish to appoint you Novice Mistress, but with a certain provision . . . ."

"And what is that provision?"

"I want Sister Therese to hold this office in conjunction with you. She is to be Assistant Novice Mistress. As she is too young to hold the title she will continue to be called Sister Therese. However, I want it understood that the novices shall all have full liberty to come to her for spiritual advice, and that she, Sister Therese, will be in full authority to watch over them, instruct them, and to call their attention to their faults . . . ."

"Yes, Reverend Mother," she answered in a reserved tone.

The next thing for Mother Agnes was to find Sister Therese to acquaint her with her new office. Opportunely, the Prioress found her also in her cell.

"Praised be Jesus Christ," greeted Therese cheerfully when she saw her sister at the door.

"Now and forever," replied the Prioress, entering the cell and closing the door behind her. "Sister, I came here to entrust an office of importance to you. You will be the new Assistant Novice Mistress, and as such you will help Mother Mary Gonzaga in the Novitiate. Your office as portress is hereby terminated!"

Therese swallowed. Such an announcement left her completely unprepared. Seeing her confusion Mother Agnes thought it best to leave her to herself, so she ended by saying:

"It would be advisable for you to read over carefully and study what Our Holy Rule prescribes regarding the duties of a Novice Mistress. Tomorrow I will introduce you to the Novitiate . . . ."

Mother Agnes did not realize, in entrusting her youngest sis-

---

20. PSALMS 39 : 8.

ter with the office of teaching the novices of Lisieux the Way
of perfection, that in a few short years the whole spiritual world
would pin its eyes on the inspired teacher of twenty-one, and be
forever grateful to the Superioress who had installed her in an
office of such prominence. Like the Saviour's, Therese's teaching career was to last but three short years, the novitiate was to
be her Palestine, her novices the eager crowds who listened.

32

Before the year ended Mother Agnes had ample opportunity to see what a severe burden she had placed on the shoulders of her sister by making her Assistant Novice Mistress. To begin with, there was the delicate matter of Sister Therese's working alongside Mother Mary Gonzaga, who had been in full authority over the convent for so many years.

Only a Saint could serve as intermediary in the way Sister Therese now served. Ready at one moment to disappear from the scene, and equally ready to reappear at the slightest indication that she was needed or wanted, Therese went on from day to day, never knowing just where she stood. What there was of self in her she now saw quickly being reduced to naught. But this was precisely what she desired and, therefore, she continued uncomplainingly in her office, being once called up for instant duty and again told to be off — if Mother Gonzaga wished to preside. Determined to preserve peace in this arrangement, in her new office, Therese discovered constant opportunities calling for self-effacement, that sped her swiftly on her road to sanctity.

In the meantime, like a sentry on the lookout from the highest turret of a fortified castle, she watched the novices, allowing nothing to escape her notice. To some who thought her too severe, she said: "A novice need not come to me for advice, if she is not prepared to hear the truth."

However, if she did continue ever on the alert to detect their faults, she never found it easy to correct them. The moment she noticed a novice fail in some point of rule or charity, Therese would sigh with regret, knowing that it now devolved on her to correct the erring Sister.

Particularly she was without mercy for signs of sloth, being convinced that a militant spiritual combat could not exist side by side with indolence in any form. Also she felt the futility of expecting a soul to fight interior battles courageously while exteriorly giving in to every inclination of ease and comfort. To a novice who one morning slowly sauntered toward the laundry on washday, pausing leisurely to smell the flowers on the way, the watchful Mistress said reprovingly:

"Ah, Sister, is that the way people hurry when they have children and are obliged to work to provide them food?" Therese was not one to endorse a system of spiritual perfection if it lacked zeal in God's service. Works, and works alone, proved the genuineness of one's love of God.

Herself very clean and tidy, Therese understood the irked feeling of a novice who came to her to complain of a companion's disorderly ways.

"But, Sister, you must learn to accept and put up with the annoying manners of others, for there will always be those who will never learn to appreciate neatness and order. As for myself, I made up my mind many years ago to rise above my natural feelings of repugnance against those who had what might be called 'sloppy habits.' Once, when washing clothes alongside a Sister who carelessly splashed dirty soapsuds so vigorously that they landed all over my face, I decided to return for some more of this until I was completely reconciled to it. You see, since we cannot change certain people, but must continue to live with them, we ought to learn to endure their annoying habits in silence, and without resentment. If everybody would have pleasant and proper habits, then we would have no opportunity to do penance. And since we know that we cannot endure such great lacerations as did the heroic Saints, let us take advantage of the small trials that come our way. Surely we can stand a splash of soapy water from a careless companion, or a trail of muddy prints in a corridor we have just cleaned, by someone who has just come from a rain-soaked garden. We are obliged to love our Sisters, and that means putting up with them cheerfully. It may take many years to learn this lesson, but I have come to embrace it as a sure way to Heaven."

If a novice occasionally began to show signs of self-complacence in her spiritual progress by speaking of her virtues in a way suggesting pride, Sister Therese would quickly bring the culprit down: "It is our nothingness that we should continually deplore, dear Sister!"

On the other hand, if a young postulant came to confess a fault, she was encouraged and highly commended. "The greatest grace we can have is to be able to see and acknowledge our failures. Keep on humbly owning up to your daily faults and you will soon become very, very dear to Our Lord!"

But if a Sister after repeated confessions became discouraged at her slow progress, she was soon warned against it: "You must accept your smallness and offer it to God. If we must be patient with others, we must be equally patient with ourselves. Perfection is a high goal. Do we expect to reach it in a few months of monastic enclosure? If we are proud, we will resent our slow ascent. If we are humble we will be glad to see ourselves so poor and yet tolerated by Our Merciful Spouse. That is being little."

One day a novice came to the young Mistress to ask pardon for having offended her. How would Therese treat with the erring novice, her subject? The straying little sheep was at once forgiven — and in words betraying the deepest emotion: "If a poor little creature like myself feels such tenderness for you when you come back to ask pardon, what must take place in God's heart when a sinner returns to Him. Even quicker than I, He forgives all our infidelities and never thinks of them again. He even goes further, for He loves us more than ever...."

Whether Sister Therese expected a great deal from those who aspired to become members of the strictest Order of women in the Church, she was also very anxious to lighten the burden of the conventual life, so, to instill an added measure of enjoyment to recreations, she at this time began to write verses which the Sisters sang to familiar tunes they knew. Soon pages and pages of beautiful verse, comparable to the poetry of outstanding French genius, came from her pen, which, along with her painting, began to win her much enthusiastic praise. Yet, Sister Therese would never write these verses except during the hours of free time, feeling that the hours allotted to remunerative manual labor could not be spent writing poetry, no matter how deeply spiritual it was.

But if there were those with unspoiled heart, who were glad to manifest praise for her accomplishments, there were also those who could not restrain their envy; and for these she felt genuinely sorry. Surely, it was not to triumph over them by any special skill that she gave herself to painting and poetry in her spare time, but to do good to them and be of service. It was not for her writing or her pictures that she ever cared to be known, since the only glory she came to Carmel to seek was eternal glory. Easily, the Sisters could well have imitated her in the endless round of small acts of virtue which they daily saw her practice.

She was the first to offer her services with a smile, never replying with a sarcastic word — and always eager to eat yesterday's leavings in the refectory and excuse any inattention or inconsiderateness shown her. Going out of her way at recreation, she sought to amuse those particular Sisters toward whom she felt a natural antipathy, to such an extent that on one occasion one such recipient of her warm, unrelenting affection expressed her surprise at being singled out for such particular attentions: "Sister Therese, how is it that you are so attached to me and show me so much preference?"

Certainly, there were hundreds of such obvious acts of virtue which Therese exhibited daily and which could readily and with great profit have been emulated by the other members of the community witnessing them. Yet, of these altogether imitable virtues they were never jealous — nor were they interested in emulating her in excelling in them for their hidden value. Only of her few paintings and her poetry were they openly envious. Yet these accomplishments they should have passed by: for themselves not being gifted with talents in this respect, they were not expected to achieve these particular works reserved for Sister Therese alone.

However, in a community such as are the Discalced Carmelites — never more than twenty-one members — it requires a singleness of purpose and spiritual vision not to lose sight of its goal, because, being isolated, they can come to live in a whorl of small, petty jealousies, constantly exposed as they are to the close proximity of only one group of a few nuns. Without any active works such as nursing or teaching to occupy them, they could readily become egotistical and fail completely in their interior vocation.

Observing this, the Mistress now realized how important it was to give this deadly outlook a crushing blow, and she therefore began to assert repeatedly the importance of examining the movements of the heart, in order to eradicate from them envy, guile, diplomacy and stratagem. *Unless you be converted and become as little children, you shall not enter the kingdom of heaven,* [21] she would exclaim, with ever greater vehemence. She saw that the adult human heart bent on guile, made man an enemy of God, and barred him from the gates of Heaven.

But soon the very Scriptural quotation she chose as most appropriate to deal envy a deathblow was exploited and used against her. — It was all right for Sister Therese to advocate being like a little child, and then, without any painting lessons, pick up brush and palette to execute such admirable oil paintings, and then the following month take up the pen and compose, practically without effort, page on page of spiritual verse proving her a gifted artist and a talented writer. So, overnight, everybody there wanted to be an artist and writer like Sister Therese, bent on achieving fame through the performance of these two intellectual feats. Or, else, they were bent on making

---

21. Matt. 18 : 3.

Sister Therese give up her high accomplishments on the pretext of being little. Surfeited with grief over these contradictions, the Mistress said to her novices:

"Believe me, the smallest act of self-denial is worth more than the writing of pious books or of beautiful poems!" And this she'd repeat again and again. But she saw that her admonitions provoked only a dubious reaction. "Very well," the facial expression of her hearers said in reply, "if smallest acts of self-denial are worth more than writing beautiful books, cease writing, and begin an endless round of those small acts of self-denial!"

How could she now explain that for her, Sister Therese, the very writing of these spiritual canticles was in itself an act of self-denial? How could she explain that for her it was the mainfest will of God that she give herself to this additional work, yet not for her own pleasure, but for the good of the others? To refuse to give herself to these higher tasks for which she was very singularly gifted, and to which she felt herself called, would have constituted a grave fault. But she saw the utter futility of trying to explain the contradiction. Still, in need of solace, she now went to her sister, the Reverend Mother Prioress, who, alone, always understood her.

"Reverend Mother, I sometimes wonder why it is that the novices keep telling me how much they desire to write poetry such as I write, and to paint pictures such as I paint. Yet they seem quite unconcerned about learning to practice the hidden virtues and sacrifices which I constantly stress, and regarding which I go to every limit to give them an example. Do you know what I mean, Mother?"

"Yes, Sister, I know exactly what you mean," Mother Agnes said, encouraging the young Novice Mistress not to give up. "Urged by pride, the novices want to imitate your accomplishments to gratify their craving to be noticed. They do not realize that it is the example of your *virtues* they should strive to imitate as Discalced Carmelites. To begin with, they were not made to paint or to write, yet that is the only thing they now seem to desire — to reap the bit of praise your verses and your pictures have won you. I see this every day, not only among the novices, dear Sister, but even among some of the older nuns who should certainly know better . . . ."

"There is only one obstacle I cannot as yet surmount. Since good example does not teach them, what will?" asked Sister Therese, and she knew instantly that someday she herself would be obliged to find the answer. A few weeks later she found it.

"Reverend Mother, I think I have discovered the one and only thing that finally can help . . . ." she announced smiling.

"What is that, Sister?" the Prioress asked, intrigued.

"Prayer! I'm praying for my novices to see the true light, Reverend Mother. Of course, I don't spare my voice, and I take the opportunity on every occasion to give them a good example, but I count mostly on the value of prayer. After all, that is our vocation, is it not, Mother?"

"Yes, Sister, you are absolutely right!" answered the Prioress, impressed.

In the fall, encouraged by the Prioress to pursue her painting, Therese took up brush and easel again and set herself to do an oil painting intended for her sister, the Prioress, as a feast-day gift on January 21. For so joyous an occasion, Sister Therese could not bring herself to painting anything less happy than a portrait of the Child Jesus with flowers in His hand. But a brief study of the picture revealed other objects in the background: the Image of the Holy Face on Veronica's Veil, a chalice surmounted by a Host, and the instruments of the Passion. When the Prioress' Feast Day arrived, and the painting was unveiled, there was attached to it a short note explaining its meaning, and the reason why the artist had titled it "The Dream of the Child Jesus."

"Night has come and the sweet Child Jesus sleeps and His heart goes on dreaming. He catches glimpses in the distance of strange objects bearing no resemblance to spring flowers.

A cross, a lance, a crown of thorns! His Childhood face is so beautiful, but now He sees it distorted and bleeding, out of all likeness. But Jesus knows that His spouse will always recognize Him, and that she will be at His side when all abandon Him, and therefore the Divine Child smiles although He looks at the blood-streaked image."

The painting was, indeed, one of those exquisite clues revealing her deep spirituality, with the ever-dominant Devotion to the Holy Face claiming her first and uppermost attention.

33

It was inevitable that as assistant Novice Mistress, training newcomers to monastic perfection, Sister Therese should often think of her sister Celine, and wish to have her among those privileged ones who belonged to Carmel. It was July again, the month of the Precious Blood, which invariably drew her to ponder those biblical passages that related to this mystery. Writing to Celine, she says: "Often we can say with the Spouse (of the Canticles) that our Beloved is a 'bundle of myrrh' for He is for us a 'Betrothed in Blood.' Often He treads the winepress alone. He seeks for those who may give Him aid and finds none. Who, then, will be willing to serve Jesus for himself? Ah, it must be you and I, Celine and Therese . . . . And what does the Trinity want to see in our heart except 'choirs of music in the camp of an army.' "

Here, indeed, is Sister Therese a poet laureate behind Carmel's wall, caressing the Face of her Beloved through the surpassingly exquisite verses of the Canticle of Canticles. Mingling her own incomparable poetic language with verses from the loftiest tracts of Holy Scripture, she goes on: "How shall we sing the songs of Sion in a strange land? For a long time now we have hung up our harps on the willows by the river for we cannot play on them . . . . Our God, our heart's Guest . . . comes within us to find a dwelling place . . . . How great must a soul be to contain a God! Since the soul of a day-old child is for Him a paradise of delights; what then will our souls be that have fought and suffered to ravish the Heart of their Beloved!" [22]

---

22. *Collected Letters.*

Surely, here is no shrinking violet, but a full-blown red rose on the tallest stem of a giant rosebush hurling her own splendor against the dazzling brilliance of a sun-blazing sky at high noon! "What then will *our* souls be who have fought and suffered to ravish the heart of their Beloved?" Let him, who will, be taken aback by the open disclosure of her place in the sun, but Sister Therese, recognizing it, was unafraid to clothe the fact with words. A soul that had fought and suffered to ravish the heart of God was, indeed, something exquisite, and Therese was beside herself with joy beholding the spectacle, even though the soul happened to be her very own! She had now attained a degree of humility which resembled that of the Blessed Virgin of Nazareth, when she said of herself: "For He who is mighty had done great things to me. Behold, from henceforth all generations shall call me blessed."

It is a logical characteristic of the saints to recognize themselves. This is inevitable for saints do not become saints through a surprise gesture played on them by the benevolent planning of third parties. By no stroke of luck, nor even through the opportune demise of a rich relative, have they come into possession of the oil well of sanctity, yielding the golden liquid of charity, the *Love of God*.

Only in one way can title to the well of sanctity ever be acquired. The land has to be paid for in full, and in advance, with coins self-earned. Moreover, the digging below cannot be done by hired help, though, indeed, there is never a shortage of those who are only too willing to contribute that gentle push downward that accelerates one's speed in reaching the bottom.

By personally undergoing the grueling ordeal of plumbing the depths — digging ever lower — it is inevitable for the saint to recognize step by step what progress downward has been made in the way of finally removing that crust of rock that will make the golden oil of charity gush forth. And since humiliations, ignominy and suffering, alone, can bring one down to that last place deep below the surface, is it any wonder that, scarred until non-recognition from the ordeal, the saint at last comes forth clutching his gory riches in his heart, since his hands cannot contain them? The riches are *charity*, and the heart alone can contain them!

Sister Therese had not stumbled unexpectedly upon her mine of golden liquid. Remembering the price she paid when she willingly accepted and sought the last place (which she had noticed nobody else wanted), she came away with those battle scars on her humbled brow that told her all too eloquently that she had become fabulously wealthy.

Before the end of July, she had news that her father passed away. Celine, now twenty-five, felt it was now opportune to apply for entrance into the convent. At the last moment, however, Therese learned that several nuns had vigorous objections to housing four members of the same family in one Carmel. Discounting the virtues of their Prioress, Mother Agnes, and of Sister Therese, who was such a striking model of detachment, and also of Sister Marie, who went about her convent duties giving no anxiety, the opposition prevailed.

After a few days, however, most of the objectors relented, and only one nun remained adamant in her stand.

Therese sought to break down this nun's resistance by prayer. "Dearest Jesus, you know how earnestly I desired that the trials my dear father endured should serve as his purgatory. I long to know if my wish has been granted. Since one of our community is strongly opposed to Celine's entrance here, if she withdraw her opposition I shall consider it as a sign from You that my father went straight to Heaven."

What was her surprise when leaving choir but that the first person she met in the corridor was the protesting Sister who with tears now assured her that she would no longer stand in the way, and was most anxious to see Celine in their midst as early as possible. This was indeed a sign that the Martins' father had gone straight to Heaven!

Shortly after, on September 14, 1894, Celine joined her three sisters in the Carmelite enclosure. "Since you are the Assistant Novice Mistress," suggested the Prioress, "take Celine upstairs and introduce her to her cell."

Delighted beyond words, Therese escorted Celine to the second floor. Opening the door of the bare room, both sisters stepped inside. "You will soon be Celine no longer, but will be called Sister Marie of the Holy Face — as we had planned for years. What a beautiful name yours will be and what a royal title. But hold on, before telling you anything else, let me instruct you in a simple but holy custom. It is this," said Therese. Then kneeling and bending her head forward, she reverently kissed the floor. Then, rising again to her full height, she said: "Each time you enter your cell, and each time you leave it, no matter whether it be ten or twenty or forty times a day, you must always first kiss the floor as I showed you. What this exercise of humility will do to your soul, only years of unremitting practice — which I now have — will prove that our Carmel has all the secrets of perfection. This is something I have learned."

Celine was wise enough to know that she did not as yet understand in the least what her younger sister was trying to convey to her. But obey she would.

"Now here is this card on which I wrote the Order of the Day. If you keep it in your cell and refer to it, you will gradually become acquainted with the various exercises making up the Carmelite day," Therese said pleasantly.

"Thank you, Sister," Celine replied genially.

"Ah, and now I must correct you for the first time," the youthful Novice Mistress said with a smile.

"What for?" asked Celine with interest.

"For saying 'thank you.' In Carmel, remember, we never merely say 'thank you,' but 'may God reward you.' "

"I should know that by now from the many visits in the parlor, but . . . ."

"By no means. You are not expected to be able to practice

the Carmelite Rule and customs in the world. But from now, in the enclosure, you will have every advantage of reaching to the heights. And just think, Celine, each time you perform the smallest service toward any nun you will always be told, 'God reward you,' and not given a mere 'thanks,' which is, after all, meaningless. Similarly, every time a Sister does you a service, you must implore God's blessing for her by saying, 'May God reward you, Sister.' Here at Carmel every act has a meaning in relation to God; and that alone is what counts. Here we are bound to charity for our neighbor, not for narrow humanitarianism, but for the sake of God, who commands us to love each other. We prove this by being of service to one another, and for this He will reward us eternally . . . ."

"Oh, that's wonderful, Sister," said Celine enthusiastically. The new postulant could not help but feel inspired. She was being initiated into the way of Perfection by one who was to become the outstanding spiritual genius of the century.

The day sped by. Then, after evening recreation, Celine was instructed to retire for the day.

"Do you like Carmel?" asked the Novice Mistress confidentially.

"Oh, yes, I do. I particularly love our cell . . . ." Celine answered.

"I am happy to note that you did not say 'my cell' but 'our cell' — and on the very first day too!" Therese praised encouragingly.

"That much I do remember from my visits to the parlor: that a Carmelite never refers to anything as 'mine,' but as 'ours,' " she finished.

"That is correct. Never, never use the word 'my' unless you are referring to your faults, or your aspirations. But when speaking of material possessions, we always say 'our' instead of 'my.' "

"I'll try not to forget," was the humble reply.

"You mustn't fret about forgetting, Celine. You are expected to forget ever so many times during your novitiate, but if you're careful, by the time you are professed you will never say 'my,' but in a spirit of complete detachment from all created things you will always refer to material objects as 'our cell' and 'our prayerbook' and 'our bench.' And how logical this holy custom is! Why call anything 'mine' when we know that tomorrow we may be dead, and the objects claimed as 'mine' are held by another? Moreover, by the Vow of Poverty taken on our Profession, we relinquish claim to all possessions in this world, and, hence, never allude to anything as 'mine.' If you drill yourself to call everything 'ours' *instead* of 'mine,' by the end of your novitiate, you will never make such a slip . . . ."

"But should it take that long, Sister?"

"Ah, how much you have to learn, dear Celine. And don't be too disillusioned when you see how hard self-love dies. Just close your eyes when you hear an older nun slipping again and again, even in this trivial self-denial — . . . 'A benefactor gave *me* this' or 'I received that' — when it should be 'a benefactor gave *us*' and '*we* received that.' Yes, self-attachment is so dominant it requires real heroism to just not satisfy it at least in some trivial thing."

"But should this be so difficult, for a Carmelite?" incredulously asked Celine, feeling a trifle like this should cost nothing.

"It is particularly difficult for a Carmelite, or, rather, it is singularly so, because, dear Celine, a Carmelite, cut off from every chance of appropriating things of material value, is left only the means of satisfying self in trivial non-essentials at which the world would laugh indeed. You see, by entering enclosure, a Carmelite cuts herself off wisely, and with one stroke, from all occasion of temptation. The result is she is then reduced to satisfaction in trifling, insignificant things. Her test is to either forego, generously, a petty indulgence or, foolishly, to satisfy self if only by clinging to possessions by the use of such forbidden terms as 'mine' and 'my,' and the like."

Alone in her cell, the postulant reflected on the lessons received her first day at Carmel. She did not pretend to her sister's advancement in things spiritual, but felt an inclination toward its appealing reasonableness. Suddenly her eyes fell on the ORDER OF THE DAY which Therese had given her that morning. Taking it up, she read it slowly and solemnly, dwelling on every exercise listed on the card:

ORDER OF THE DAY

rising hour	4:45 A.M.
mental prayer in chapel-choir	5:00 to 6:00
Holy Mass and Thanksgiving	6:00 to 7:00
10-minute interim for partaking of slice of dry bread and cup of coffee	
recitation aloud of Divine office in choir: as follows, Prime, Tierce, Sext, and None	7:00 to 8:00
manual labor	8:00 to 11:00
dinner	11:00 to 12:00
recreation in common during which nuns are permitted to converse, do needle-work, etc.	12:00 to 1:00
free time	1:00 to 2:00
recitation of Vespers and spiritual reading	2:00 to 3:00
manual labor	3:00 to 5:00
mental prayer in choir	5:00 to 6:00
collation or small supper	6:00 to 6:30
evening recreation (same as at noon)	6:30 to 7:30
recitation of Compline	7:30 to 8:00
free time	8:00 to 9:00
recitation of Matins and Lauds of the Divine office, examination of conscience, and reading of points for meditation	9:00 to 10:45
retiring hour	11:00 P.M.

Long after Celine had gone to bed, she thought about what her sister had told her, and also what the Order of the Day prescribed for a Carmelite. Twenty-two of the day's hours had to be spent in complete silence. At least eight hours were daily spent in prayer, kneeling before the Blessed Sacrament, or standing in alternate choirs reciting the long offices, the prayers of the Church. About five hours were devoted to ordinary manual labor. And only about six hours were left each night for sleep. What she saw of the meals even on her first day in the cloister indicated that a lifetime of similar, unexciting meatless meals would brook no indulgence of one's appetite. In addition, the impenetrable enclosure, the confinement to one house in one given place for the rest of one's earthly life, offered no prospect of diversion, or any change of scenery.

Finally, as she began to surrender to sleep, unconsciously turning on her side, she also acknowledged that the hard boards would be unrelenting in their stiffness. Who could possibly embrace a life like this and then refuse the smaller sacrifices which her sister had mentioned to her? It was unlikely that such logical inconsistency could even exist side by side!

She was to learn, as the years went on, however, that all rebellion to God, whether in things small or in those great is logically inconsistent. Also, that the great part of humanity not only tolerates it, but is bent on perpetuating the inconsistency to its last breath. When Celine recognized that in her sister Therese this contradiction was not tolerated, she asked by what method one arrived at the summit where such logical congruity was finally sovereign.

"Persevering self-analysis and the constant study of Christ, Celine, in an effort to become like Him, is the answer," said the Novice Mistress. Then, quietly, she gave her a picture of the Holy Face and, pointing to the Sacred Scriptures, assured her that in the dual combination was to be discovered the key to truth and sanctity.

34

THREE MONTHS later came Christmas. Sister Therese was happier than ever. One evening surrounded by her sisters during recreation, she found herself suddenly recalling childhood incidents at home. Her three sisters simply marveled (not suspecting that the gay and unrehearsed story-telling was to be climaxed by an outstanding autobiography).

"Reverend Mother, do you realize what wonderfully interesting stories Sister Therese is telling us, and all of them true?" exclaimed Sister Marie of the Sacred Heart.

"Yes, I do marvel at her," replied the Prioress. "She remembers almost everything that ever happened at home."

Therese only laughed, then quickly recalled another incident which she began cheerfully to narrate.

"Let me tell you — when I was about three, Mama was very anxious to break some of my strong will and pride. Once she said, with a smile, of course: 'Therese, if you will kiss the floor I will give you a *sou* . . . .' In those days, you know, that sum was a staggering fortune. — What I could do with it — And to gain it I did not have very far to stoop . . . . So tiny, there was not much distance between my lips and the ground. But my *pride* was up in arms and, holding myself very erect, I said: 'No, thank you, Mama, I would rather go *without* the money!'"

"Do you actually remember all those things? They happened to you when you were only three!" broke in the Prioress.

"Oh, yes, I remember my childhood so vividly, it seems to have happened only last week," Therese replied.

"Now tell us another story," urged Sister Marie, pressing for more which brought back their happy home life. Then, at last, turning to her sister the Prioress, she stated frankly:

"Reverend Mother, really, I think you ought to make Sister Therese write up all those childhood incidents. They would make delightful reading even if they were only made-up stories. That they're actually true makes them simply enchanting!"

"Oh, really, they are nothing much," Therese protested laughing, but the older nun was not to be brushed off.

Several days later Sister Marie still pressed for action, urging that with her authority as Prioress their sister should *order* Therese to write her childhood memories.

Mother Agnes, while of the same mind, might well have put the matter off, owing to the pressing work of her office, but thus gently constrained to action by her own sister, one evening she sought out the young Novice Mistress and ordered her to write all those things of which she had spoken that Christmas recreation period, and to add any other of her childhood incidents which might come to mind.

"I shall leave you complete liberty of spirit to write about whatever comes to you. There's only one thing, since my office as Prioress is to end in one year, finish your writing by then. I do not know who will succeed me and I want to be sure that while you are under obedience to me these memoirs will be written . . . ."

With a pen and a simple school-exercise notebook, Therese began. And soon there fell from her pen those rapturous pages revealing the story of her soul. It was not a book of mystical revelation, as was written by her predecessor in Tours, Sister Marie Pierre, but it emphasized the identical message.

"How are you getting along with your writing?" Sister Marie asked one evening at recreation.

"Not too rapidly. What with all my other duties I have to be content to note down only a few pages by the end of a week," she confessed.

"Well, you have time. Reverend Mother said you could take until her feast-day next January. That gives you a full year."

"Yes, I know," Therese replied.

"Have you heard that Celine is not to be allowed to keep the religious name you both had planned for her?" asked Sister Marie.

"You mean she will not be called Sister Marie of the Holy Face?"

"That's what I mean. But you had better wait for Reverend Mother to announce it. She will tell us all this evening."

Presently Mother Agnes of Jesus was speaking.

"Sisters," she quietly announced, "as you know, our postulant is to receive the Holy Habit next week, that is, February 5. And we had all decided to call her Sister Marie of the Holy Face; but Father Delatroette has objected. He said he thought she should be named after our deceased Mother Foundress. So her name will be Sister Genevieve of Saint Teresa."

The announcement caused a strange tumult inside Therese as she listened. Every inch of the way up toward the Holy Face seemed barred by unexpected obstacles. (Father Delatroette intervening! Well, no matter. What was there in a name!) But, notwithstanding her efforts to be resigned, she was unable to shake off the disappointment. Later she was somewhat relieved when Mother Agnes assured her that the title "of the Holy Face" would also be added to Celine's religious name.

The next four months sped by for Sister Therese, whose already crowded daily program was now increased by the memoir writing. In the meantime, she was still far from experiencing anything new. There was only the unbroken monotony of her holy penitential life. She had quite finished the glowing story of her childhood; now she was already describing her first months as a Carmelite. She looked longingly at the page she had finished, then she read it over to herself with a strange deliberation:

> *Until then I had not appreciated the beauties of the Holy Face, and it was you, my little Mother, who unveiled them to me . . . . I wished, that like the Face of Jesus, mine should be as it were hidden and despised . . . .*

The words reread, she turned poignantly away, dwelling on her memory of those days when she had first entered the convent and first learned of the compelling theology contained in the Devotion to the Holy Face through her sister here. More than seven years had elapsed since the day she had surrendered to the revelations of Sister Marie Pierre. Where was she now? What had the persevering study of the abused countenance of Jesus done to her?

The following morning, during the hour of mental prayer and all through Mass, she found herself wondering if there had been anything that she could yet give God that she had not given Him. A plan slowly unfolded itself to her mental gaze. Yes, there was still something she could do. She remembered that the generosity of certain religious impelled them to consecrate themselves to God in a special manner, as *"victims."* Through this deliberate offering of self they sealed their destiny for good, in a most concrete way, just as did Sister Marie Pierre whose picture and relic she always carried pinned on her breast, and whose revelations on the Holy Face had become her own! Compellingly, this particular, this "victim" phase of the Carmelite of Tours now claimed all Sister Therese's attention. This was the act of complete, willful self-surrender God had demanded of the Carmelite of Tours *almost immediately* on her entering the cloister. After Holy Communion one morning, showing her a multitude of souls falling into hell, the Saviour had mystically desired that Sister Marie Pierre offer herself entirely to Him as a *victim* — for the furtherance of His designs. The Superiors of Tours had waited four long years before granting the nun permission for this complete offering of herself for God's unknown purpose. She had asked for this permission in writing on Christmas Day of 1843. Sister Therese had read this often:

Act of Perfect Donation — I offer myself entirely to You, O God, on the flaming altar of Thy Sacred Heart, consumed with love; I there make to You the entire sacrifice of myself for the fulfillment of Your designs to the glory

*of God's Holy Name. I renounce myself and I give myself
entirely to You. Do with me and in me what will be
pleasing to You; I am Your property, take sovereign possession of me. Yes, most gladly for love of You do I
divest myself of all things forever . . . .*

[*Signed*] SISTER MARIE PIERRE

Shortly after this complete oblation of the mystic of Tours to
God, she was vouchsafed a series of exalted communications
wherein the Saviour disclosed that the crimes of Communism,
blasphemy and profanation of the Sabbath, all of them sins
against the First Three Commandments of God, and which irri-
tated Divine Justice. Then He explicitly commended Sister Marie
to work for the establishment of a Confraternity of Reparation
to the Holy Face. This, then, was the special design which God
had had on the soul of Sister Marie Pierre: To use her as an
instrument to establish within the Church a Devotion of Reparation for the outrages against Him of the modern growth of
infidelity and of militant atheism and Communism. The *Holy
Face of Christ* was to be that portion of the Sacred Humanity
to be offered to the Eternal Father as the price of atonement for
the blasphemies and crimes of this age.

For a cloistered nun to bring this message to the attention of
the world was obviously a mission requiring courage and sacrifice beyond that exacted even from Carmelite contemplatives.
It went beyond the call of duty. For that reason it was imperative that the nun of Tours volunteer, before God would send
her into the storm of indescribable torments and humiliations
on a mission of such colossal importance. And it was only *after*
Sister Marie Pierre presented herself, as a *victim*, reflected Sister
Therese, that He condescended to use her as His special instrument.

It was now time for Therese to receive Holy Communion,
but she was unable to dispel this compelling thought of offering
herself, as did Sister Marie Pierre. After receiving the Blessed
Sacrament she returned to her place in choir. There, as she

knelt, she knew that the hour had come. She was ready for a complete oblation of her self to God . . . . But how, and in what manner?

Therese knew she had no mission as had Sister Marie Pierre, and had never seen or heard the Saviour as did her predecessor, so to offer herself exactly in the same way could not be God's plan. What then? Therese had often admired those brave and noble souls who took upon themselves the punishment due to sinners, in order to save them from perishing. However, she did not feel drawn to imitate them. In glowing humility she felt too small to take on what seemed a giant's undertaking: the balancing of the scales of Divine justice!

Original in her sweet schemes to constrain the Mercy of God, Therese arrived at a striking conclusion: "O my Divine Master, shall Your justice alone find atoning victims? Has not Your merciful love need of them also? On every side Your love is ignored and rejected . . . . Those hearts on which You would lavish Your love turn to creatures! O my God, must that *Love* which is disdained lie hidden in Your heart?"

Sister Therese, the courageous thinker, was now on the verge of a decisive resolution. She was *determined*. She would be a victim to God's merciful love! After Mass, therefore, she motioned to her newly clothed sister, Sister Genevieve, to accompany her to the cell of the Prioress, where with a face transfigured with emotion she related her desire to become a victim of God's merciful love. Her two hearers, both of them blood sisters, listened to Therese with grave attention. The Prioress was so impressed with her ardor, she willingly approved her seraphic plan.

"I give you full permission to make your Act of Oblation. I further suggest that you write it down so I can submit it to a theologian for approval," the Prioress said solemnly.

On Trinity Sunday, June 8, 1895, Sister Therese, volunteering for the select army of "Victim Souls," offered herself unreservedly as a sacrifice to the merciful love of God!

In a transport of joy, she addressed her prayer of self-sacrifice:

In order that my life may be one act of perfect love, I offer myself as a holocaust to Your merciful love, imploring You to consume me unceasingly, so that I may become a martyr of Your love. I desire at every beat of my heart to renew this oblation until the shadows retire and everlastingly I can tell You of my love face to face . . . .

[*Signed*] SISTER THERESE OF THE CHILD JESUS
AND OF THE HOLY FACE

It was inevitable that, destined to become the model saint of Reparation to the Holy Face in the twentieth century, she should, with striking deliberateness, have chosen the Feast of the Most Blessed Trinity as a day appropriate to surrender herself as a sacrificial offering. Indeed, Devotion to the Holy Face, aimed at repairing the crimes committed against the first Three Commandments of God, had for its object the Adorable Trinity Itself. Not a Friday Devotion but a glorious Sunday Devotion! Since *the Head of Christ is God* [23] worship of the Holy Face was essentially Trinitarian in aspect . . . .

Following her special Act of Oblation, Therese saw a transformation take place in her soul. If she complained during a recent retreat that though she was completely detached from creatures, and that she yet found that her heart was not completely "empty of self," now, at last, that self-emptiness had become a reality. Permeated with fervor, she now went through the cloisters during those following weeks a new creature. Meditating on the Passion in choir one evening, she felt her heart pierced with a dart of love. She could find no words able to describe it.

But even as St. Thomas Aquinas teaches, that as flames show the presence of fire, so, similarly, does zeal prove the burning ardor of true love, Therese now gave herself even more earnestly to her duties than ever, particularly those incident to her office

---

23. I COR. 11 : 3.

as Assistant Novice Mistress. Determined to help her cousin Marie Guerin make up her mind to join their Carmelite Monastery, she wrote a month after her Act of Oblation to Marie's mother, her own aunt, stressing the importance of being energetic: "Ah, what virtue your little Marie has. Her self-control is astonishing, yet she has enough energy to become a saint! And *energy* is the *most necessary* virtue, for with energy one can easily arrive at the summit of perfection . . . ." Then drawing a contrast between her own sister Leonie, who alone of the family of five still remained in the world, and the energetic cousin Marie, Therese added: "If Marie could only give a little of her energy to Leonie! In the meantime, Marie would still have enough for herself . . . ."

From now on Sister Therese was on a victim's hunt for generous religious, wanting to see zeal and action and energy, not indifference, sloth, apathy, passivity, the letting of others do things, and the leaving of well enough alone. In her new love as a victim, she was insatiable to give of herself and see others imitate her in the giving. And Marie Guerin, unable to resist the compelling example, entered the Carmelite Convent August 15 that same year and was enrolled as one of her novices.

What spare time was now to be found was still given to finishing the pages of her memoirs. There remained less than five months in 1895, and she had still to record several events. At last she was close to the end. She had reached the point of telling of her Act of Oblation as a Victim (made in June), and when this was finally recorded suddenly she fell short of anything more to say.

So when January 21, 1896, dawned, and this was the Prioress' feast-day, the last in her three-year term of office, Sister Therese quietly walked up to her during prayertime, and handed her the school notebook, not aware that she had surrendered a manuscript of such world-shattering importance that it was destined to reach the four quarters of the earth. The last page spoke eloquently of the victim state to which she had now been raised:

Dear Mother . . . You know the flames of love which filled my soul when I made that Act of Oblation on June 8, 1895, Since that day, love surrounds and penetrates me. This is all I can tell you of the story of your little Therese . . . . So you will forgive her for having greatly abridged the account of her religious life.

The Prioress took the notebook to her cell and laid it safely away. This was no time to peruse her young sister's authorship. There would be elections within a month, and it was important to put many things in order against any possible shifting of office.

On March 21, the secret balloting was again in progress before the ecclesiastics in the small Carmelite parlor. Sister Therese was again conspicuous by her absence, for she abstained again. But her two elder sisters participated. The election proved a long-drawn-out matter, and when, after six rounds of vote-casting, no nominee had gained the necessary majority to be elected, a seventh ballot was proposed. On this ballot, Mother Agnes of Jesus was defeated [24] and Mother Mary Gonzaga, prior to this past term the Prioress for sixteen successive years, was once more reinstated to the community's first place after a lapse of three years. How the elderly Reverend Mother Mary Gonzaga managed her election victory that day was based more on intrigue of questionable character, than on monastic simplicity.

Inasmuch as Sister Therese, to become the outstanding saint of the age, was, through no fault of hers, strangely drawn into this intrigue, the incident, otherwise better left unmentioned, must be brought out into the full light of day. — For the history of heroism ceases to be such if the heroine, at the climax of her victory, has to be removed from sight in order to spare the parties opposing her the embarrassment of testimony revealing them in uncomplimentary shadows.

---

24. At the time of Sister Therese's Beatification, the Pope, by special rescript, confirmed Mother Agnes of Jesus as Prioress until death.

Election day over, Mother Agnes of Jesus, the one person deserving credit if only for her unique distinction in molding, guiding and leading her youngest sister to perfection to her final emergence as the greatest saint of her era, after one short term of three years was removed from office as Superioress.

Night had fallen on Lisieux, and Therese, alone in her cell, reflecting on the day's doings, felt grateful that as the third family member to enter the cloister, she was spared from even having a voice in the voting. To her everything hinting of a desire for the first place, or of any form of asserting self, was to be avoided at all cost.

Obviously, *someone* must be installed to govern a community and it seemed only reasonable that the person most gifted and accomplished should be chosen. It was just as simple in its working as one person's getting the highest grade for the best examination paper at school. That anyone should pursue or initiate such reprehensible methods as cunning or strategy in order to win first place for herself — or confer it, unmerited, on another, presented a grave dereliction, with seriously immoral concomitants.

Eyes relentlessly riveted on the Gospel, Therese, while in her cell, could almost see those things which happened nineteen centuries before — which bore a striking resemblance to what was enacted that day. The contemporaries of Jesus had for a long time been searching the horizon for a leader. Surely, there would never be another who could even remotely resemble Him in accomplishments and stature. But did He receive their votes? *"Get thee hence! Don't you know that Herod has a mind to kill you?"* Not only was the Son of God voted out of *any* office, but His contemporaries voted Him out of His duty; of even *teaching* the ignorant and poor for which labor His recompense in gain or prestige was nil! "Get thee hence! Don't you know that Herod has a mind to kill you?" To stand His ground, the Saviour was forced into humiliating self-defense. He replied: *"Go tell that fox that I intend to work while it is day. For the night will come when no man can work!"* Reflecting on the

Gospel incident Therese was instant in her love toward the outcast, the un-elected Saviour who made no bid for power but only for fatiguing labor — and a Baptism in Blood for which He thirsted.

It was a sad waste of time to even consider that day's elections, she concluded. As for her darling Pauline of childhood days, now the defeated, un-reelected Mother Agnes of Jesus, no fear troubled Therese that her sister was to lose her office as Prioress and come away with any scars. She had observed Mother Agnes too long, and for too many years had taken spiritual nourishment from her to have any fear that her loss would have any other effect than send her on an undiscovered trail toward perfection. Kneeling in her cell, Therese whispered a prayer that she be delivered always from any network of play and counterplay in the fearful game of winning distinctions and offices, or of even conferring them.

At that moment she was startled by a knock on her door. She was soon to learn, and suddenly, that if she had had any hope that the elections and their decisive results were over — and that *she* had been spared from participating in them — it was not to be so at all!

In a moment she was thrust into a situation so unpredictable, that it would engulf her deeper in the intrigues of that day than any other Sister in the convent, notwithstanding she was a classified absentee from the balloting.

While the Carmelites are forbidden to discuss what takes place at any election, Therese was unwittingly drawn into such conversation by none other than the veteran Prioress of sixteen years, the reelected Mother Mary Gonzaga, who having knocked, now entered the cell unceremoniously. Upset and visibly perturbed, the old Superioress unfolded a series of remarks revealing her reactions to all that took place in the parlor that day.

At first the story seemed incoherent, but Therese soon put the events together piece by piece. The root of the matter was that being reelected was not sufficiently comforting to the Reverend Mother, because the nuns took seven ballots before finally deciding to confer this distinction on her. Was she not right to feel hurt at not being reelected on the first ballot — and unanimously? She, Mother Mary Gonzaga, had actually to wait for seven ballots before she was installed as Prioress that day!

Therese grew pale, then flushed, and then pale again. What was she supposed to do? Here was an experienced Superioress of veteran standing crying on the shoulders of a twenty-three-year-old nun, bitterly deploring her loss of prestige. Despite the fact that she was, after all, elected! And considering that Therese's own sister, Mother Agnes of Jesus, had lost out to this Prioress, this only added to the dilemma. Anyone less than a saint would have thrown up her hands and called a halt to what now loomed as an absurd, ironical comedy.

Sister Therese, who since entering the cloister at fifteen had desired to be esteemed as nothing, and, as a victim of love, longed for nothing greater than to be reduced to ashes, or less, as a holocaust to ravish the meek, love-stricken Saviour, now had to take it on herself to find some way to soothe a Prioress who could not bear having not been unanimously voted into office on the very first ballot.

Descending from her heights of detachment and her love of the least place, Sister Therese began soothing the elderly nun with quieting words of comfort and understanding. If Mother Mary Gonzaga had never learned the first thing about the value of seeking the last place, she did understand most clearly that no matter what sorrow encompassed her, she could always seek consolation from the young nun. Therefore, it was to her that she went that eventful day to weep, and indeed before the day gave up its last hour, she did leave comforted. Therese gave sympathy as a big sister gives to a younger one. That the big one was twenty-three, and the little sister a veteran of sixty-two offers that thrilling parallel of contradictions so singularly revealed only in the careers of saints.

Having soothed the Prioress the best she could for the time, Therese promised more later, after praying, when some further words of consolation would come to her. Soon enough, the thought-out solace took the form of a long letter, in the third person, representing a little lamb speaking to a shepherdess. Therese assumed the role of the lamb, with the Prioress appearing in the role of shepherdess. Defending most delicately, yet daringly and adroitly the position of the offended Superioress, the Sister's letter reaches a climax of charity.

"It was not that the Saint actually saw things in this manner, which was very far from the reality. She merely used this means to bring Mother Mary Gonzaga to judge the facts more supernaturally, and to detach herself from whatever was too human in her feelings" — is the official explanation behind the Letter of the Shepherdess and the Lamb, as officially given from Lisieux, in the volume of *Collected Letters of Saint Therese*, published fifty years after her death.

The truth is that Sister Therese had so surrendered to love at this point of her spiritual career that she could do nothing but sympathize with every form of human sorrow — even that born of moral weakness and the less noble promptings of the fallen human heart. This was none the less real suffering, and her heart went out, with real pity, to the old Prioress hoping only to console her whom she saw as a small, groping child, wanting something insignificant and grasping at it as if it were Heaven itself.

Surely, this gesture must have won the heart of God. How could He resist one who resisted not even those diametrically opposed to her, one giving love for even sham, and ardent devotion for a sorry imitation?

Sister Therese had never been blind to the irregularities and faults in her Superior's makeup from her very entrance into the cloister. She remembered all too well that day when the Prioress ordered her to prepare a night-lamp for Mother Mary Gonzaga's married sister and little nephew who were expected as guests in an outer building of the convent. She clearly saw that Mother Mary Gonzaga ordered things done which would never be allowed to the relatives of any other nun. Inwardly resentful at being ordered to serve the Prioress' relatives, Therese nevertheless resolved to perform the service asked of her. If so many years in religion could not make the Prioress see any irregularity in her own conduct, then nothing remained but to submit. Therese was too much a spiritual economist to lose time attempting the impossible. "I got the lamp," says Sister Therese, "as if it were going to serve the Blessed Virgin and the Child Jesus, and I began polishing it with infinite care so that not a spot of dust was left on it. Soon I grew calm and felt myself ready, in all sincerity, to attend to the wants of Mother Mary Gonzaga's relatives throughout the whole night if I had been asked to." [25]

Now, many years later, on the night of the seven ballots, Therese in a letter, portraying a lamb speaking to a shepherdess, appeased the wounded Prioress and calmed her upset nerves.

But the Mother did not yield to the sublime and tender requests of the lamb to rise above such human considerations. Quickly the following week, distributing the offices of the community, she, alas, revealed to open view her deep attachment for the paltry glimmer of honors. Monopolizing all authority, she did not even appoint a regular Novice Mistress to succeed herself, now that she was Prioress again. To bridge the gap, she simply assigned Therese the role of acting assistant to the Novice Mistress, but without the honor of the official title. In short, the Sister was to perform the duties of this difficult office, but the Prioress also reserved to herself this honorary title.

"I shall be both Reverend Mother Prioress and the Mother Mistress of Novices, as well," she told Therese.

It was very embarrassing. Sister Therese was now a nun of some eight years' standing, and not a mere novice. She might have been given the title, especially since she performed all the duties incumbent on a Novice Mistress, yet here she was clearly told there would be no change whatever in her status. Too happy to be retained as an ordinary Sister, of ordinary title, Therese was quick to express her delight over this arrange-

_____

25. *Storm of Glory,* by John Beevers, p. 115.

ment, adding a suggestion of her own, so as to remove herself to a further position of remoteness.

"Reverend Mother, I was thinking that it would work out quite well if I could just continue to be in the Novitiate as one of the novices, and act merely as a sort of 'elder sister' to them, and nothing more," she said, straining each brain-cell for that last place of obscurity that by now had become a veritable passion.

"Yes, yes, Sister, I think that should work out very well!" agreed the Superioress.

"Then, in that case, since I will continue as a novice, you could arrange it so that I would not have to become a member of the Chapter, couldn't you?" pressed Sister Therese further, determined to seal her destiny in anonymity until the end.

"Well, that could be arranged. Of course, you know, you have a right to be a Chapter member, yet, if you prefer to be considered a novice, I see no reason for objecting. It is a good plan, and I approve your humility, Sister," the Prioress concluded, not ascertaining her own lack of this exalted quality, which had been so strikingly exposed by her eagerness to claim two titles of honor simultaneously.

As for Mother Agnes of Jesus, now ex-Prioress, Mother Mary Gonzaga appointed her Depositary Sister, entitling her to supervise the stock room containing the yard goods used for sewing, and other miscellaneous merchandise. And looking on, Therese noted with gratification how her elder sister, the Apostle of the Holy Face, relegated to quite the lowest post despite her qualities and capabilities, set about fulfilling her humble chores.

But Mother Agnes had reasons of her own for optimism and cheerfulness. She alone knew that among the less valuable objects on the cupboard shelves of her insignificant depositary, was a certain item of inestimable worth. That treasure was a certain school copybook filled with neat writing by one whom she had always deemed a saint.

For the time being, however, she was not disposed to peruse these pages of her sister's autobiography. Laying the manuscript away, she closed the cupboard carefully and left. It was Thursday in Holy Week, when every spare moment was to be spent in adoration before the Repository. There would be ample opportunity in the future to go through those memoirs. Besides, her sister, both author and subject of the writing, was still so very young, and these memoirs, intended for publication after death, would not likely be called into use for decades. Of course, Mother Agnes could not know that ere that very night of Holy Thursday ended, Sister Therese, in her cell, at the hour of midnight, would receive her first warning of death's swift approach.

It is the custom at Carmelite convents to extend Holy Thursday's adoration throughout the night. Having finished her two-hour watch before the Altar of Repose from ten until midnight, Therese departed silently to her cell. And hardly had she laid herself to rest, a few minutes later — it being now Good Friday — when she felt a warm stream rise to her lips. Undoubtedly this was a hemorrhage, she thought, and, as such, foreshadowing fatal tuberculosis.

Her first reaction was a spontaneous lurch of interior joy. Death was in the offing and Heaven with its unending joy would be hers forever, in the oh so near future! What should she do now? Get up and determine if it really *was* blood? It took just a second to decide. Since her lamp was already put out, it was best to mortify her curiosity and wait for morning to investigate. Therefore, reaching into her tunic sleeve for a handkerchief, Sister Therese calmly wiped her lips in the darkness and went quietly to sleep.

This act of mortification had nothing in it of stoicism, for as Pope Benedict xv declared, the Way of St. Therese was not one of "presumption, of hoping to attain a supernatural end by a purely natural means." Stoic pride, manifested in acts of self-will, in an effort to become known as a dominant, superior being, in an effort to be singular, certainly had no part in the makeup of one desiring only to be unknown, unrecognized, and who chose to give God the small acts of mortifying her self-will to show her love for Him.

The truth was that she had done this so consistently since the age of three, that mortification in things small or great had long become habitual. After twenty years of consistent self-denial, it was inevitable that Sister Therese, confronted with settling a crisis of a hemorrhage that presaged her early death, should delay its investigation until the morning. Besides, she had been convinced for a long time that curbing curiosity contributed invariably to the greater well-being of all concerned.

For instance, what purpose would it serve to relight her lamp, discover the blood in her handkerchief, and then proceed to waken the nuns, who due to the rigorous exercises of Holy Week were already more than normally exhausted? Then, too, she herself was completely worn out now. In addition to the strictest Lenten fasting, Holy Week calls for added penitential works. The Divine Office on Wednesday, Thursday and Friday of Holy Week, instead of recited, is solemnly chanted, requiring hours of fatiguing voice rendition which the Sister never stinted.

It was no wonder then that when the discipline of cords, lasting ordinarily the space of one Miserere, is during this time extended to last the space of the Miserere chanted three times over, Sister Therese, finishing lashing herself with merciless abandon, should feel exhausted. Yet, not realizing that she was on the verge of a tubercular hemorrhage, she ascribed her fatigue to the flesh being weak and forced her spirit to take the ascendency.

At the first sound of the clapper, just before five in the morning, Therese, on rising, immediately remembered and, examining the handkerchief, saw it was crimson with blood. Dressing she went to choir as usual, and, finally, when the bell after Prime rang out the end of the period of strict silence, she felt this was the proper time to inform the Prioress of the occurrence. In Mother Mary Gonzaga's cell, she spoke about the happening almost laughingly.

"Reverend Mother, I do not want you to be concerned, for really, I feel no pain," she said.

"Are you sure?"

"Oh, yes, quite sure," she answered promptly. "That is why I want to get permission to finish out Lent as I had begun, especially since this is Good Friday."

The Mother Superior, herself robust and strong, did not realize that such a hemorrhage as Sister Therese had suffered the night before, though painless at the time, can prove fatal. She easily granted the permission asked.

"Very well, Sister, since you say you feel no pain, you may finish out Lent as you began. Tell me tomorrow how you feel."

At the end of day, on retiring to bed, again Therese felt the surge of blood rushing to her mouth. So this was not a freak, one-time occurrence. Its repetition, on the succeeding night, indicated a serious lung condition, Therese now knew, and she could not repress her delight at the thought of a swift transition into eternity.

For this she lived, for this she sacrificed each earthly joy and pleasure; for this she kept vigils and recited long prayers; for this she left the world to bury herself in a cloister; and now, at the age of twenty-three years and three months, having had two hemorrhages, she felt the hour of her deliverance at hand, and, therefore, could do naught but give herself to joy.

Then came Easter Sunday, and special rejoicing for the Community, and Sister Therese, mingling at recreation with the others, was as gay as ever; no one yet suspected her dread malady. One of the novices noticing Therese grouped for the moment with her sisters, Mother Agnes, and Sisters Marie and Genevieve, exclaimed excitedly:

"Since all four of you, belonging to one family, are here, let me ask you, don't you agree with me that Sister Therese is looking unusually well at the end of Lent? Look at her pink cheeks!"

Therese winced when she felt her sisters' eyes upon her, especially Mother Agnes'. Surely she would guess the heightened color in her cheeks was no health glow, but a fever she was feeling now every afternoon. Only two weeks before, her own blood sister, Mother Agnes, was still the Prioress, and had Therese then suffered her hemorrhages she would have gone straight to her to acquaint her with the symptom. But Mother Agnes had been rejected a fortnight since, and now that Mother Mary Gonzaga was Superioress the Sister felt perfection required her to advise none other than the Prioress alone.

For a moment, as the three nuns scrutinized their youngest sister's falsely glowing cheeks, Therese stirred uneasily. She was overcome with a deep sympathy for them, and would have liked to tell them everything. Especially did she long to confide to Mother Agnes, her beloved Pauline of childhood days, that her hemorrhages had begun on Good Friday! At home, since she was five, she had come to Pauline to acquaint her with the smallest pin pricks; but now, having suffered two lung hemorrhages, she was obliged as a Discalced Carmelite to speak of this disastrous sign to no one but the Prioress. Undoubtedly the greatest act of self-denial she could be called on to perform, yet Therese performed it unflinchingly.

As the three nuns, tied to her by religious bonds and family blood, stared at her flushed cheeks that Easter Sunday, they were not to learn, even indirectly, what the cause of the high color was. As a Novice Mistress she had counseled the Sisters not to be cowards but to endure the hardships that came their way, particularly in silence.

"It is indeed a very natural feeling, this desire that people should know of our aches and pains, but in giving way to this we play the coward," [26] she told a novice on a certain occasion.

---

26. *Autobiography,* p. 303:
"One day a novice complained of being more tired than other Sisters since, besides ordinary duties, she had other work unknown to the rest. Saint Therese replied: 'I should like always to see you a brave soldier. You feel this fatigue so much because no one is aware of it. Now, Blessed Margaret Mary (one of our greatest saints, since she was chosen to inaugurate the Devotion to the Sacred Heart all over the world) tells us that she had two painful whitlows, but confessed that she really only suffered from the hidden one. The other, which she was unable to hide, excited pity and made her an object of compassion.' "

Sister Therese never preached any doctrine of self-mortification which she had not first practiced.

That hers was not an ordinary case of acquainting "people" but her nearest kin with her deadly malady did not, nevertheless, incline her to grant herself leniency. She kept silent. Someday when Mother Agnes found out she would simply have to understand that this was the only course she could possibly take, and remain consistent. There was one consolation now stirring Sister Therese: perhaps the Prioress would, herself, tell her sisters the details. Surely, she would tell them soon, so her family would be acquainted with the state of her health. This Therese felt they had a right to know. But until this happened Therese felt bound to silence.

A month went by. Pursuing all the exercises of her monastic routine, together with the multiple duties of a Novice Mistress, Therese was seen going on as usual. Indeed, like any perfectly healthy person. Then came the day for the regular Chapter Meeting. Since, through her own choice, she never was a Chapter member to which she was entitled by seniority, having heard the bell announce this exercise, she proceeded to assemble the novices as usual. Having entered the Chapter room, Therese made her customary honest confession of faults; then she prepared to withdraw, while the other Chapter nuns remained to discuss the business matters of the monastery.

Mother Mary Gonzaga lost no chance to publicly humiliate Sister Therese on these occasions to such an extent that even the reticent Mother Agnes felt obliged to intervene. Entering the Prioress' cell, she told her privately: "Really, Reverend Mother, I must in all conscience tell you that it makes me very unhappy to see my sister Therese continually being humiliated for no reason whatsoever." [27]

But Mother Mary Gonzaga was instant with a retort that cut through like cold steel: "Well, if it makes you unhappy to see your sister humiliated, I am afraid you will have to accept that

---

27. *Storm of Glory,* p. 101.

as one of the disadvantages of having sisters of your own in the cloister. No doubt, you would like Sister Therese to be made a fuss of, but I must do exactly the opposite!"

"No, it is not that at all," explained Mother Agnes. "I don't ask anyone to favor my sister. I only object to her being continually humiliated without cause . . . ." Now Mother Agnes was determined to use her prestige, after all, as an ex-Prioress in order to register her voice in a case involving a matter of conscience.

"Humiliated without cause, did you say? Well, let me tell you, Mother Agnes, Sister Therese has far more pride than you imagine, and she needs to be constantly humiliated!" [28] ruled the Prioress.

Had Therese herself witnessed this, she would have realized how naive she was ever to hope that Mother Mary Gonzaga might soon take steps to acquaint her family, and particularly Mother Agnes, with the news of her hemorrhages, to make it easier for them to endure the trial of her death later on. The Prioress was far more concerned with carrying out a certain program, one she seems expressly to have outlined for herself. This was none other than singling out Sister Therese for a series of relentless humiliations, in a desperate effort to unseat the deadly sin of pride. In the meantime, she ignored completely even mentioning the fatal symptoms of which she had been told.

But even this knowledge would have come as no surprise to Therese. The truth was that for years she endured the "contradictions" of behavior which defied all effort of logical explanation. This was to be her particular trial to the very end.

Herself consistent, refusing to tolerate in herself even the shadow of a judgment or opinion incompatible with the sovereign rules of logic, yet Therese was doomed to suffer from those whose lives were a pattern of inconsistencies which no amount of generosity or charity of viewpoint could ever reconcile.

For instance, as early as 1890, one day after Therese had made

---

28. *Ibid.*

her Profession, Mother Mary Gonzaga took formal occasion to highly extol the virtues of the Sister. Writing a letter to the Carmel of Tours, with whom she kept up a correspondence on the Devotion to the Holy Face, Mother Mary Gonzaga wrote the following words of praise in favor of the newly professed nun: "This angelic child is only seventeen and one half but she is as mature as a nun of thirty . . . . She is a perfect religious." [29]

About three years later, the Mother Superior endorsed the Sister by telling a Retreat-master several times: "Sister Therese is a little angel. If a Prioress had to be chosen I should select Sister Therese out of the whole community in spite of her youthfulness. She is perfection itself!" [30]

Finally, bridging the period between 1890, when she wrote such glowing eulogies, and 1893, the Prioress shows explicit evidence of the same tribute, in 1896, when she selected her, though so young, to act as Assistant Novice Mistress. In her memoirs, Therese records this distinction accorded by Mother Mary Gonzaga: *I walk in the dangerous path of honor. If I were looked upon as incapable and wanting in judgment, you, Reverend Mother, could not employ me to help you in the office of Novice Mistress . . . .* [31]

But diametrically opposing her own testimony is suddenly the unexpected attack — by the same Prioress — when she declares to Mother Agnes: "No doubt, you would like Sister Therese to be made a fuss of, but I must do exactly the opposite. Sister Therese has far more pride than you imagine, and she needs to be constantly humiliated." [32]

Of course, if Therese remained unaware of this she could yet not be described as going through life without realizing her position. "The life of a Carmelite is largely one of thought." [33] Hence mental tardiness in not noticing what went around her could never be attributed to her.

---

29. *The Rose Unpetaled,* p. 142.
30. *Storm of Glory,* p. 83.
31. *Autobiography,* p. 338.
32. *Storm of Glory,* p. 101.
33. *Autobiography,* p. 189.

It belonged to the nun's caliber of clear vision to note almost every instance of incongruous reasoning in the way of *contradictory action and speech* occurring in her environment, and this precisely was what constituted one of her deepest tragedies. To her *nothing could at the same time possess and be without the same reality*, because contradictions are incompatible. It struck dread in her heart to realize that it was obvious that those around her were never troubled by any such logical principle. She was alarmed at the overwhelming tendency to cling to *that which was convenient and not which was the truth!*

Entering Carmel at an early age, without any technical specialization in the science of logic, it would yet be rash to consider her lacking in any erudition. She understood the basic truth that a person cannot think correctly without thinking logically. From earliest childhood she grappled with problems at the very root of consciousness, *thinking*.

"When I was a little girl staying with our aunt," Therese told her sisters one day, "I read a story in which a schoolmistress was highly praised for her tact in settling difficulties without hurting anyone. She would say to the one party: 'You are quite right,' and to the other: 'You are not in the wrong.' And I reflected as I read: 'Now, I *never* could believe like that because one must always tell the *truth*.' And I always do tell the truth, though I admit that it is often more unpleasant for me to do so. It would be far less trouble, when a novice comes with a grievance to cast the blame upon the absent. Less trouble . . . yet, I always say just what I mean, and if it makes people dislike me, that cannot be helped." [34]

Even as a child her primary law forbade contradictions. Nothing can be true and false at the same time. Such a system, which did tolerate contradictions, could bring nothing less than intellectual frustration. And to a Carmelite, whose vocation was irrevocably rooted in thought and contemplation, and not a career of active works, Therese ascribed the duty of examining one's thought processes as of prime importance.

---

34. *Ibid.*, p. 324.

With her remaining strength she made a final gesture to impart these convictions to the Novices entrusted to her. She had an innate trust in youth. They could be made to learn her doctrines, having as yet no vested interest in serious errors made in the past, since for them life had just opened up. For that reason they had no temptation to defend, as the aged did often, the ignoble deeds of their past, in an attempt to escape censure. With the young there was only the question of the present and the future, and this promised a lifetime of hopeful endeavors.

Therese was especially alert to reprove any young Sister attempting to avoid work. Pursuing a culprit who had retired to her cell to escape certain chores, she said: "Do you know what will happen to you if you shut yourself in like this? *Your soul will dry up, if you close yourself up.*" Warning her to keep busy, Sister Therese urged the novice not only to follow, but to *run quickly* to perform the works of charity.

If any novice thought that marking up her Divine Office and attending the community's various spiritual exercises sufficed for her perfection, so that manual labor could be done or left undone, or that this could be accomplished in a shiftless manner, she was to unlearn this false view. Entering the cell of a novice who had jut finished making her bed badly, Sister Therese said: "Is that how you would have made the bed of the Child Jesus What have you come to Carmel for if you are not going to live an interior life? It would have been much better for you to have stayed in the world!" [35]

The superb Novice Mistress was, indeed, pursuing her convictions to a final logical conclusion. Not only did prayer matter, but the way one made one's bed, and the way one kept one's room, and the way one sat up in a chair, and clothed one's body, *what* one ate, and how much one ate, and how one helped defray the cost of one's board — all these things entered into one's spiritual makeup. An easy, shiftless and slothful life had nothing in common with sainthood.

---

35. *Storm of Glory,* p. 102.

Consistent to the end, Sister Therese refused to let kindness degenerate into weakness. "When we have had good reason for finding fault, we must not allow ourselves to worry over having given pain," she said, explaining her position.

Another month soon passed. Still no one in the convent suspected her of having been attacked with a mortal illness. Mother Mary Gonzaga kept this knowledge to herself. Therese pursuing her ordinary life, seemed strikingly imbued with the conviction that all must be endured for God, every humiliation tolerated, save such as might be an offense against God. [36] In this, she reached the heights of St. Thomas, who also taught this doctrine.

But what humiliation could be an offense to God? Obviously, one submitted to at the price of detraction, calumny or lying! Therefore, it was no virtue to accept or relish such humiliations where one's Christian name is detracted, one's character is slandered and one's charitable works so lied about that they appeared as wicked deeds.

Since God is Truth, He cannot delight in any act of untruth. Furthermore, it is inevitable that from such calumny a righteous Christian would emerge as one giving scandal, which cannot in any way benefit the cause of God's Church. "Woe to the world because of scandals. For it must needs be that scandals come, but nevertheless, woe to that man by whom the scandal comes." [37]

Discerning the greater importance of evaluating Truth, above any other pursuit, Therese declared: "I do not know whether I am humble, but I do know that I see the truth in all things." [38] She had long been thirsting for this, pinning a steadfast gaze on the Sacred Brow of the Holy Face, the very seat of Truth, and now her burning thirst was beginning to be slaked. This thirst became her deepest preoccupation. She had surmounted the last obstacle on her quest for sanctity

---

36. *The Rose Unpetaled*, p. 166.
37. MATT. 18 : 7.
38. *Autobiography*, p. 297.

and found herself on a mountaintop, searching for nothing else and nothing less than the stark, the unadorned, the naked *Truth*!

Looking back she saw, at their face value, the vast store of spiritual ingenuities cultivated and acquired in the relentless effort to abase herself for the sake of becoming humble. In her attempt to escape notice and favor she had for many years resorted to various noble contrivances, well-intentioned and heroically executed, which certainly earned her their share of merit, but she now realized that these had to give way to something higher. Now *all* artifice, regardless of purpose, had outlived its usefulness. She was on the trail of the noblest of pursuits, the quest of Truth. More, the quest was reaching fruition. "I do not know whether I am humble, but I do know *that I see the truth in all things!*"

Fired with new zeal, she now saw herself in the role of one who had something good to give his neighbor, and was most eager to give it: "I compare myself to a little bowl filled by God with good things. I am willing you should feed from this little bowl . . . ."

But even in her role as assistant, to which she held no title whatsoever, Therese hastens to insist that she did not allow herself to bid for the approval or affection of those in her charge: "I am ready to lay down my life for my novices, though my affection is so disinterested that I would not have them know it. By God's help, I have never tried to draw their hearts to myself. I have always known that my mission was to lead them to God . . . ." [39]

Then she points out that though she is an instructor she holds no official rank, adding that because God keeps her on the ground without titles of prestige she suffers no great dangers to her soul. But she who said that she discerns the profound Truth and its purposes in all things could not brook an abuse which, without warning, she now records.

---

39. *Ibid.*, p. 177.

Inveighing against a realm from which she consistently kept aloof, Sister Therese exclaims: "This is *not* so with *Prioresses*! They are set upon tables, as it were, and therefore they run many risks. Honors are *always* dangerous." Lashing out with the accumulated spiritual logic of eight years in Carmel, she fearlessly discloses her stand, oblivious that her words might provoke resentful reaction. Decrying what loomed as the greatest scandal of the religious life — personal catering to superiors for the mean and ignoble ends of selfish gain — the Sister exclaims: "*What poisonous food is served daily to those in high positions! What deadly fumes of incense!*" [40]

In all of Sister Therese's prodigious writings, nowhere does she reach a climax of such heated rage against any other single vice. In an all-out effort to combat this evil, and stem the scandal that results in great losses to souls, she does not hesitate to use terms hardly in keeping with her gentle, girlish personality, her twenty-three years, and her innocent background of spiritual childhood. "*What poisonous food is served daily to those in high positions! What deadly fumes of incense!*" declares the soft-spoken Sister.

Perhaps the word "daily" is the most dangerous threat. From this "daily" serving of the poison of flattery to superiors, she concludes that there arise "deadly fumes of incense."

Baffled and frustrated, the humble Sister seems at a loss to find any remedy for this evil. She simply concludes: "A soul must be well detached to pass unscathed through it all!"

---

40. *Ibid.*, p. 300.

35

ANOTHER MONTH passed. Sister Therese was now coughing noticeably. Dr. de Cornieres, the convent's physician, was consulted. Moreover, since the Sister had a cousin whose husband, Dr. La Neele, was a physician, he also was called in. But neither her family nor the physicians were told of the hemorrhages, which accounted for their verdict that nothing serious was the matter. Their diagnosis left the nun unmoved. "That will not prevent Our Lord from taking me to himself," she wrote at this time in a letter.

The ensuing fall and winter she continued to fail in her strength. In the spring she was so weak, that on reaching her cell at night it took her fully an hour to prepare for bed. Yet, obedient to the infirmarian, Therese could be seen taking a walk every afternoon in the garden, though she knew that what she needed was complete rest in bed, instead of this fatiguing exercise. Her sister coming upon her one day and seeing her exhausted from the outdoor strolling, objected, but forcing a smile, Therese replied: "I am offering my fatigue to gain grace for some missionary . . . ."

Although it grew more obvious each week that she was steadily growing weaker, yet there was no real alarm. Since she was still up and about there was hope that she might rally and recover.

It was not until the month of May that Mother Agnes and the two other sisters first learned about the hemorrhages Therese had suffered in April of the previous year.

"You had hemorrhages thirteen months ago? And we never knew it until now?" cried Mother Agnes. "All this time we never dreamed you were so grievously ill. Why have you kept silent? Why didn't you tell us?"

"It was not up to me to tell. Surely, you know that," replied the invalid.

But Mother Agnes was inconsolable. What conspiracy of silence could have thrust this cross upon her? She tried to fathom the enigma, woefully shaking her head in near desperation. At least their cousin's husband, Dr. La Neele, should have been told of the hemorrhages when he examined her. There would probably still have been time to do something then. The answer to their puzzlement, however, was so simple no one would have thought of stumbling on it.

For one thing, Therese was certainly not to blame: acting as always on principle she had at once reported it to the Prioress on Good Friday morning a year before. It was then up to her to report this fearful symptom to the physician, but this she failed to do. When, three months later, a persistent cough developed, and physicians *were* summoned, Mother Mary Gonzaga, realizing her error in not at once reporting so grave a symptom as a hemorrhage, and, alas, wishing to escape blame for her negligence, decided to keep this symptom hidden. Sister Therese, the perfect religious, could be relied upon to keep her lips sealed. This the Prioress knew. As the months passed it grew increasingly difficult for the Mother to own up to her former blunder. In the meantime the Sister increasingly succumbed, a victim of the suppression of the true facts. When, finally, thirteen months later, the hemorrhage history did trickle out, it was too late for remedies. Procrastination in righting a wrong had woven its fearful fate; Mother Agnes looking at her sister who was wasted with illness shook with grief and tears.

"Don't weep so much, I beg you," said Therese consolingly. "You really should not fret because you weren't told about the hemorrhages. Instead, you ought to thank God that He spared you this. For, really, had you been aware and seen me so little cared for, your heart would have been very sore."

Having settled in these short words the whole matter of her lengthy illness, Sister Therese seemed anxious now to speak of something much higher, growing ever more eloquent on the topic of her career after death. From her lips now began falling those sublime sentences which spoke of the glory to follow her beyond the grave. Her death should not be mourned, she warned her sisters, for her mission was really only to begin *after* she passed away.

Mother Agnes, discerning her sister's rare sanctity, began daily to note down whatever words were spoken by her. As the month of May wore on Mother Agnes' notebook was being filled with her sister's prophetic utterances (soon to be read by the whole world). Then, on May 27, Sister Therese, though wasted more than ever with disease, was jubilant:

"I am very glad," she said enthusiastically to Mother Agnes, "that I shall have a Circular Letter after my death." On returning to her own cell, Mother Agnes copied the sentence into her notebook. Then she found herself staring at the words with stark realism. A *Circular Letter* after her death? But of course! Therese had been alluding to the memoirs she had finished writing more than a year ago, when she was well, and when no one dreamed she would so soon be stricken with a fatal malady.

Quietly going to the cupboard where she kept Therese's reminiscences written in obedience to her own order, Mother Agnes took the manuscript and began to read. During the next four days she studied it and prayed over it secretly. The fact was that she had never told Mother Mary Gonzaga that while she, Mother Agnes, was Prioress, she had had Sister Therese write the memoirs. What should she do?

In light of Therese's prophetic utterances regarding her mission on earth after death, Mother Agnes recognized more than ever the value of these pages. The world would be the sufferer if the *Autobiography* were not carefully preserved. Finally, on the fifth day, about midnight of June 2, urged deeply by a Divine inspiration, she took the manuscript, and went with it to the cell of the Prioress. Using every ounce of prudence to win that hour for God, she told the Prioress about it, humbly suggesting that it might prove useful after Sister Therese's death. Mother Mary Gonzaga seemed interested, even sympathetic.

Grateful for this, Mother Agnes felt encouraged to press the case further: "There is one small drawback, Mother. The manuscript I have is still rather incomplete. It says little of Sister Therese's life inside the cloister. However, if you ordered her to finish writing these memoirs, we would then have a more complete Circular Letter to publish after she passes . . . ."

The Prioress thought for a moment. Perhaps it would be advisable to heed Mother Agnes' suggestion. After all, it was Mother Agnes who wrote the Circular Letter when the Foundress passed away some five years before, and that publication was widely read and praised, and it had brought the Carmel of Lisieux a good measure of favor in the public eye . . . .

"Very well, Mother Agnes. I will tell Sister Therese to finish writing her memoirs . . . ." came the answer.

The next day, having been ordered to resume writing the story of her life, Therese set herself to the task. She was weak, suffering, and writing was no small assignment. But, whenever the weather allowed, she was to be seen under the chestnut trees in the garden, seated in her invalid chair, writing the final pages of her life.

Meanwhile, throughout June, Mother Agnes, as in the month previous, continued to write down the sayings of her baby sister. Notebook and pencil in hand, she approached the invalid for a visit in the garden. Therese noticed this, but refrained from any objections; on the contrary, she was perfectly tranquil, and even seemed eager to have her words preserved.

As has been said, she had long realized that the devices she had employed for years to escape notice and hide her virtues for humility's sake, sweet as they had become, would have to be replaced by the noblest of pursuits, that of Truth! At first it cost her something to break down this gray-walled abode of humbleness, and emerge before her neighbors in her true light. And she who had not refused God anything since the age of three was not likely to falter in the climax of her spiritual career. Dispensing with those noble stratagems called "acts of humility," Therese proved her complete detachment from all created things by choosing to cling with her whole will to the Uncreated Truth alone.

To impart this light to others, it became clear that she could no longer hope to hide it under a bushel. Steeling herself to practice what many spiritual writers recommend as "holy indifference to praise," she once did say: "I compare myself to a little bowl filled by God with good things. I am willing that you should feed from this little bowl . . . ."

Once having made this open avowal, Therese had embarked on a new career, that of holy indifference to praise. She learned how good it was to declare the works of God, even if these did happen to be wrought inside *her* own soul.

The good things she possessed, of teaching a new short method to sanctity by performing the small ordinary acts of charity, attracted the novices. Even some of the older nuns now sought her out for counsel. Looking back on this last phase of her development, Sister Therese felt encouraged. Noticing the benefits others derived from her teaching, she decided never again to hide her gifts. She was, indeed, proving herself in every way a true daughter of the great reformer of Discalced Carmelites, Saint Teresa of Avila, who had written centuries before:

> *Let those souls who have reached to a perfect union with God hold themselves in high esteem, with a humble and holy presumption. Let them keep unceasingly before their eyes the remembrance of the good things they have received, and beware of the thought that they are practicing humility in not recognizing the gifts of God. Is it not clear that the constant remembrance of gifts bestowed serves to increase the love for the giver? How can he who*

ignores the riches he possesses spend them generously upon others?

Now, three months before her death, resting in the garden and observing her eldest sister in religion, Mother Agnes, noting down the sentences which fell from her lips, Sister Therese marveled at her own indifference to this sign of esteem. The truth was that in her invalid chair in the garden she recognized that she had traveled even beyond that signpost of perfection referred to as "holy indifference."

There was no longer anything indifferent about her attitude! The word *indifference* repelled her with its implication of chilly and callous aloofness. It was obvious that Sister Therese was on fire with Divine Love, and anything savoring of passivity could not hold the slightest attraction for her. These final months she lived on a mountaintop from where she viewed all things below her in a true perspective, and she was now ready to swoop down upon the whole world of souls so as to ignite them with the same fire of love burning inside her.

Indifference? Even holy indifference? Never! Recognizing the unrivaled advantage of being the challenger, Therese was eager to launch an offensive war in order to win souls for God. Any defensive or neutral position, or a cold war resulting in stalemates, was unworthy of the crusading, fighting entity known as the Church Militant.

Sister Therese, the modern heroine, was clamoring for ACTION! Why not? One by one she had taken on the archenemies of God and man, and one by one she had defeated them.

Out from childhood, on through nine years of conventual retirement, always seeking the last place — lonely, in tears, misunderstood; in the dingy atmosphere of a wash-house, where for a whole day she stooped over a tub of laundry, or in her cell at night, her pen dripping with exotic poetry whose excellence rivaled the best French literature — Sister Therese emerged, ready to exchange this role for that of conqueror!

[299]

Girding herself with holy indifference, she sang a song of praise in favor of her method of perfection. On the very eve of her departure she had discovered that something vastly more energetic than the attitude of "holy indifference" was essential if one would win the world for God! She who had sought obscurity in life, revealed a vehement desire to be known and followed.

Sitting in the garden, while Mother Agnes sat with pencil suspended, Therese now said, with due deliberation: "*You shall see. After my death I will let fall a shower of roses . . . .*"

The Mother looked up. Never was her sister more outspoken. Her future glory was like an open book to her.

The following month, after several fresh hemorrhages, Therese was removed to the infirmary of the cloister. Continuing to press her notebook into service, Mother Agnes recorded sentences never uttered by a saint before.

"I feel that my mission is about to begin. This mission of mine is to make others love God as I love Him, and to teach souls my Little Way."

The eagle atop the mountain peak was ready for the powerful plunge to earth, to perform a twofold spiritual mission: to ignite souls with the fire of Divine Love; and to extricate man from error and pitfalls by teaching him her simple way of perfection.

But even this did not satisfy her! Realizing that humanity was in endless need also of temporal gifts as health, shelter, employment, food and peace, Sister Therese now promised to reach forth these benefits *to all who would invoke her after death*!

I desire to spend my Heaven in doing good upon earth. No one will invoke me without obtaining an answer. There will be abundant graces for all . . . . For me there cannot be any rest until the end of the world. When the Angel shall have said: "Time is no more," then I shall take

*my rest. Then indeed shall I be able to rejoice, because
the number of the elect will be complete . . . !* [41]

In one leap, the contemplative of Carmel had become the
superb Catholic Actionist of the era — "I desire to spend
my Heaven in doing good upon earth." She who chose to
spend her life on earth in prayer and retirement had surprisingly elected for herself a career of virile activity as her
sphere after death.

That evening in her cell, her notebook before her, Mother
Agnes marveled at the boundless confidence burning in the
heart of her sister. Indeed, one must dwell on heights of consolation bordering on beatific vision to be able to make such
lofty pronouncements about one's glory beyond the grave,
she reflected.

There was a knock on the door. It was the Prioress.

"I brought you the memoirs which Sister Therese finished
writing last month. Look them over when you have time and
keep them together with the other parts," Mother Mary Gonzaga said. Then she left.

Examining it, Mother Agnes saw some fifty written sheets,
which when set in print would be condensed into a dozen
pages. It was definitely a very curtailed autobiography, she
told herself. Then, sitting down, Mother Agnes began reading.
Scarcely able to believe that this was no dream but a reality,
the Mother stared at the words before her. Page after page
spoke of Therese's desolation of soul. Not only was her sister
bereft of enjoying any feeling of God's comforting presence,
but she was deeply immersed in the most frightful temptations
against Faith itself, as evidenced by her writing:

*When my heart tries to find some rest and strength in the
thought of an everlasting life to come, my anguish only in-
creases. It seems to me that the darkness, borrowing the
voice of the unbeliever, cries mockingly: "You dream of a
land of light and fragrance, you believe that the Creator of*

41. *Autobiography,* p. 231.

these wonders will be forever yours, and you think that you will escape one day from the mists in which you now languish. Hope on . . . . Hope on . . . . Look forward to death! It will give you not what you hope for but a night darker still, the night of utter nothingness."

This description of what I suffer is as far removed from reality as the painter's rough outline from the model he copies. But to write more might be to blaspheme. Even now I may have said too much. May God forgive me. He knows how I try to live by faith even though it affords me no consolation. I have made more acts of faith during the past year than in all the rest of my life . . . . Hastening to my Saviour, I tell Him that I am ready to shed my blood as a witness to my belief in Heaven. I tell Him that if He will deign to open Heaven for eternity to poor unbelievers I am content to sacrifice during my life all joyous thoughts of the Home that awaits me . . . .

You may think that I am exaggerating the night of my soul. If one judged by the poems I have composed this year, it might seem that I have been inundated with consolation, that I am a child for whom the veil of faith is almost rent asunder. But it is not a veil. It is a wall which reaches to the very heavens, shutting out the starry sky.

And yet I have never experienced more fully the sweetness and mercy of the Lord. I believe He did not send me this heavy cross when it would have discouraged me, but chose a time when I was able to bear it. Now this cross does no more than deprive me of all natural satisfaction *in my longing for Heaven . . . .* [42]

Mother Agnes closed the manuscript. She realized with striking clarity that a saint is not one who is above temptation. On the contrary, a saint is a saint precisely because, enduring the fiercest temptations, he grapples with and triumphs over them.

---

42. *Ibid.,* pp. 156-58.

On her visit to the infirmary that evening, she said sympathetically: "I've been reading the manuscript you wrote for Mother Mary Gonzaga. Really, Sister, I must own up that even I thought you to be one of those favored persons whose faith never suffers a shadow of doubt . . . ."

Sister Therese smiled wanly.

Two weeks later, on July 30, Sister Therese received Extreme Unction. Consoling her three sisters, she said: "Do not grieve. I should like you rather to rejoice, my dearest sisters, because God makes me very happy."

A few days later, alone with Mother Agnes, she said: "Oh, I know, *the whole world will love me!* [43] I repeat, *I will spend my Heaven in doing good upon earth.*" After a pause, she added, "Would God give me this ever-increasing desire to do good on earth after my death unless He wished to fulfill it? No, He would give me rather the longing to take my repose in Himself." [44]

Then, not waiting for a reply, she reached for the manuscript of her memoirs, which she had been asked to reread, and declared, emphatically: "I urge you again to do all in your power to have this story of my life published after I die."

"You are still that hopeful about the future?" asked Mother Agnes.

"Oh, yes! I have the strongest confidence that these pages will do a great deal of good. Those who read my life will be better able to understand God's goodness." After a short pause she said, "Having reread my manuscript, I want to assure you also that every word I have written is true." [45]

But even while soaring to such heights of supernatural faith, hope and charity, and voicing exalted prophecies of her glory beyond the grave, her whole being was plunged into fearful doubts. Her body racked with pain, her head burning

---

43. *Message of St. Thérèse of Lisieux* (taken from her Last Confidences, August 1, 1897), by M. M. Philipon, O.P., Introduction, p. ix.
44. *Autobiography*, p. 231.
45. *The Rose Unpetaled*, p. 220.

with fever, she confided to her sister in a voice of pitiful anguish: "I feel completely submerged, as if I were thrust into a dark hole. Doubts press upon me day and night. I am given no relief. Although I have never wished to serve God for the sake of enjoying His presence here below, and of dryness of spirit I endured much during my life at Carmel, yet it was nothing like this. My faith in God, and my belief in a life hereafter, were always lively and vivid realities. But now all is darkness."

Reaching for her notebook, she opened it and said: "As I wrote here, having had my first two hemorrhages on Good Friday and on Holy Saturday, I was full of joy at this sign which indicated my speedy entrance into eternal life. Let me read you, word by word, how I felt at that time."

In a soft voice she began to read:

My faith at that time was so clear and so lively that the thought of Heaven was my greatest delight; I could not believe it possible that there should be wicked men without faith, *and I was sure that those who deny the existence of another world belie their convictions. But during the Paschal days, that time so full of light, Our Lord made me understand that there are really souls bereft of faith and hope, which through the abuse of grace have lost these precious gifts, the only source of pure and lasting joy. He allowed my own soul to be plunged in thickest gloom, and the thought of Heaven, so sweet from my earliest years, to become for me a subject of torture. Nor did the trial last merely for days or weeks; months have passed in this agony and I still await relief . . . .*

Looking up at her sister, she added, "To be exact, it is now a year and a half that I've endured this." Then, taking the manuscript, she continued reading:

But, dear Jesus, Your child believes firmly that You are the Light Divine; she asks pardon for her unbelieving breth-

*ren and is willing to eat the bread of sorrow as long as You
shall will it so. For love of You she will sit at that table of
bitterness where these poor sinners take their food and will
not rise from it until You give the sign. But may she not
say in her own name and in the name of her guilty brethren:
— "O God, be merciful to us sinners?" Send us away justified. May all those on whom faith does not shine, at last
see the light! My God, if that table which they profane
must be purified by one who loves You, I am willing to
remain there alone to eat the bread of tears until the day
when it shall please You to bring me to Your Kingdom of
light. I ask no other favor beyond that of never offending
You . . . .* [46]

Sister Therese closed the notebook. For a while neither
spoke. Then Mother Agnes suddenly brightened. "Tomorrow," she said, "is the Eve of the Feast of the Transfiguration
of Our Lord, the special feast of all adorers of the Holy Face.
Perhaps Our Lord will bring you some comfort . . . ."

Finding the Prioress, Mother Agnes obtained permission
to place a large picture of the true Image of Our Lord's Face,
adorned with flowers, in her sister's sickroom. Therese spent
the whole night of the Feast of the Transfiguration contemplating the Bruised Countenance of the Saviour, before which
burned a vigil lamp. When Mother Agnes came to see her in
the morning, Therese announced:

"I had hoped Our Lord would call me from earth on this
wondrous Feast. I have waited for Him all night . . . ." Then,
after a moment she added: "Never have I suffered more from
temptations against faith than on this night of the Feast. But
I never stopped looking at the Holy Face and making acts of
faith!"

Sister Therese did not know it then, but she had spent her

---

46. *Autobiography,* pp. 155-156.

worst night on earth. She had fought the decisive battle of her life and while scarred beyond recognition from the ordeal, she had risen to her feet — the victor. Nor did Mother Agnes know to what extent she had helped her youngest sister overcome the fearful enemy on that night of temptation by placing before her the miraculous Image of Christ on the Veil. The historic fact remains that from this battle of the *intellects* in which the foe of the spirit fired his relentless blasts of materialistic thinking at her throughout the night of the Feast of the Transfiguration, Sister Therese did come forth the winner. "Never have I suffered more from temptations against faith than on this night of the Feast," she declared. For the following seven weeks — her last on earth — she was never to retract that statement. How, then, had it happened that that decisive battle had to take place at all?

Obviously it was no surprise attack, though coming under cover of the night. The enemy had long since given up hope of ever coming on Sister Therese unawares. His secret desire for years had been to catch her off guard someday, and to launch a surprise attack. To his complete discomfiture he discovered that Therese, who claimed that the life of a Carmelite was largely one of thought, did live up to her contemplative vocation. She never allowed her mental alertness to wane.

When the hemorrhages of Good Friday and Holy Saturday indicated an early death the enemy became unwilling to brook further delays. This might rob him of his chance of winning against her. In the full and brilliant light of Easter Sunday he opened fire, besieging her with doubts about God's very existence and of a life hereafter.

At once she recognized the foe assailing her. It was the spirit of blasphemy and infidelity. That he disguised himself as an intellectual and proposed disbelief in God as rational, did not for a moment deceive the Sister. The logical thinker in her proved capable of drawing a perfectly straight line between reasonable deductions and intellectual farces. And for every round of ammunition the enemy fired from his perverted angelic intellect, she replied with shellfire from her enlightened human intelligence, which beat him to the ground.

For one year and a half she continued this barrage, as she admits in her memoirs:

> *The darkness, borrowing the voice of the unbeliever, cries mockingly:* "*You believe that the Creator will be yours forever. Hope on . . . . Look forward to death . . . . It will give you not what you hope for but a night of utter nothingness . . . ."* *I have made more acts of faith during the past year than in all the rest of my life. I tell God that if He will open heaven for eternity to poor unbelievers I am content to sacrifice during my life all joyous thoughts of the Home that awaits me . . . .* May all those on whom faith does not shine at last see the light!

And now a year and a half of this fearful conflict was to culminate in a decisive battle during the entire night of the Feast of the Transfiguration. Pounding at the walls of her intellect with his atheism and blasphemy, the foe was confident. The strength of his army lay in its name which was Legion. Alone in her sickroom Therese as always waged a heroic counter-offensive by answering back with her WILL, making acts of faith in God.

Finally her solitary voice of prayer, "I believe in God," began to be drowned out by the enemy's concerted screaming of disguised rationalism. Clothed in the garb of a modern educational pundit, the shrewd enemy, donning cap and gown, now proposed blasphemy and outright disbelief in a life hereafter, with doctrinal sophistry and ultra-intellectualism.

How did the Sister answer on this night of nights when he hurled the full force of his rationalistic might against her? It is recorded that unable, even, to form a prayer, Therese had recourse to the Holy Face of Christ, by gazing steadfastly at the "Vera Effigies" Mother Agnes had placed in her room. So overpowering was the effect of the Image of the Holy Face, that, by merely gazing at it, she managed successfully to repel the foe. It was a military maneuver worthy of a brilliant spiritual mind, belonging to one who knew when to be as cunning as a serpent and when as simple as a dove. She had constrained the Divine Wisdom corporeally contained in the Head of Christ to come to her rescue in the fearful battle, and so she had won the balance of power.

This worship of the Holy Face, embraced as the highest expression of her soul, had in the short space of nine years at Carmel won her complete union with the Blessed Trinity. On the occasion of her decisive conflict fought before her passing, during the awesome night of the Feast of the Transfiguration, that worship of the Holy Face of Christ had rebuked and repelled with devastating power the spirit of blasphemy and infidelity, reducing that spirit's dark kingdom to a fearful waste. *"I never stopped looking at the Holy Face . . . ."*

36

"I AM GLAD we are alone for a while. I want to speak to you again most urgently about my memoirs," said Therese to Mother Agnes. "When I'm dead the manuscript must be published without delay."

Hearing her sister speak of this, Mother Agnes grew quite distressed. The publication of her sister's life would involve tremendous problems, about which it was difficult even to speak. Certainly, it was one thing to publish a biographical circular about a Mother Foundress, as that written when Mother Genevieve died, but it was altogether another thing to get to publish the life story of her own sister, one of the convent's youngest members, and in the form of an autobiography!

Had she been the Prioress, at least the matter might have been resolved more easily, but without official authority this loomed like an impossible feat for Mother Agnes to accomplish. Not that the matter posed financial difficulties: the Martin estate could cover the expenditure of publication ten times over without suffering any sizable diminution. Besides, there were Uncle and Aunt Guerin, whose wealth and charity could be relied upon in any matter concerning their niece Therese. So material difficulties were not the problem. There was the opposition of those inside the convent to be feared. Those who would frown at seeing Sister Therese brought forward in any way — even after death. No stranger to what went on, Therese calmed her sister's anxieties:

"Do not worry. My mission will be accomplished like that of Joan of Arc. In spite of the jealousy of men, God's will shall be done." [47] Then, looking up, she said hopefully: "What joy to think that in Heaven there will be no looks of indifference, that there no envious glances will be cast! For just as the members of one family are proud of each other, so without the least jealousy shall we take pride in our Heavenly brothers and sisters!" [48] Then, returning to the subject of her manuscript, she said: "*Regardless* of what happens, you must take the initiative and work toward getting the story of my life published after my death, and without delay."

"But to publish it immediately may be somewhat difficult," replied Mother Agnes.

"It is the only way. And one more thing; be very discreet and speak of it to no one. For I warn you that if there is any delay, or if you should be so imprudent as to speak of my *Autobiography* to anyone, the Devil will set a thousand snares to prevent its publication." [49]

"But how am I to set about getting the manuscript published, if I speak to no one about it?" asked Mother Agnes puzzled.

"You shall, of course, be obliged to speak about it to the Prioress. When doing so, make her realize that it is of great and urgent importance that the story of my life be published. It will help all kinds of souls."

Mother Agnes promised to do her utmost. The invalid lying back on her pillow seemed relieved. "Don't grieve about my passing, dearest sister. When I am gone you will find consolation through the mail box," she finished, smiling.

A couple of days later one of the nuns who always admired Sister Therese visited her in the infirmary. "Because your sister, Mother Agnes is so devoted to you, she will be heartbroken when you leave us."

"Don't worry about that," Therese replied, her face lighting up with joy. "My sister won't have time to think of her grief."

---

47. *The Rose Unpetaled*, p. 220.
48. *Autobiography*, p. 301.
49. *Les Annales*, November, 1951, p. 14.

"What do you mean?" asked the visitor.

"I mean that Mother Agnes will be so busy on my account until the end of her life that she won't be able to dwell on losing me."

These utterances, though not spread throughout the convent, were shared among the few who held the dying Sister in high esteem. Several days later another nun who visited her asked confidentially:

"You will look down on us from Heaven, will you not?"

"No," replied Therese. "I shall *come* down."

Though continuing to endure the dark trial of temptations against her faith, the dying Sister nevertheless proved that at the same time, in the highest regions of her soul, the clearness of her spiritual vision remained unimpaired. To the very end she spoke with certainty about the glory to follow her after death.

Then dawned September 30, 1897, her last day on earth.

Asked by her sister for some parting word, she answered:

"I have said all I ever had to say. All is accomplished. It is Love alone that counts."

Then at about three in the afternoon it appeared that she would enter upon her agony.

"Mother," she said to the Prioress, "I could never have believed it possible to suffer so intensely. I can explain it only by my great longing to save souls." After a moment she added: "Mother, prepare me to die a good death."

"My child," the Prioress answered, "you are quite ready to appear before God because you have always understood the virtue of humility."

"Yes," uttered the expiring Sister, making her final striking testimonial, "my soul has never sought anything but the Truth!"

She then repeated several times over, as if in an effort to sum up her whole religious life in one sentence:

"I have no regret for having surrendered myself a victim to God's Love. I have no regret for making my Act of Oblation to God, offering myself a victim to His Love!"

It was a synopsis of her spiritual career which was to end within an hour or two. Her whole life of penance in the cloister, and all her anguish from the trial of temptations against faith that besieged her for a year and a half seemed, somehow, connected with one and only one link — her Oblation to God made on Trinity Sunday a year before she was stricken by disease. In that solemn Act of Oblation as a sacrifice offering, a victim to God, she gave herself out of love for Him, leaving Him full choice to do with her as He would. Her surrender was so willful, her intention so upright that God had taken her at her word . . . .

She did not know it then nor did she know it now as she lay dying, but when she had offered herself a victim to appease His scorned Love, God had decreed that she become a Victim of Reparation for the blasphemers and modern infidels.

It was inevitable that Sister Therese should climax her career as did her model and predecessor, the Carmelite of Tours, Sister Marie Pierre, who a few years before had died also a victim of reparation for the crimes of modern atheism. During her entire hidden life at Carmel, Sister Therese had consistently applied herself to penetrating the secrets contained in the Face of Christ, pondering His unspeakable mental anguish. Imitating her model, who gave the world the incomparable revelations on the efficacy of Devotion to the Holy Face of Christ as the weapon with which to fight blasphemy and to defeat atheistic Communism, Therese was unerringly carving her own exalted destiny, not realizing herself how ultimate her mission was. *"It is impossible to understand this trial,"* she declared, referring to the darkness of the temptations she had endured in her illness.

The very nature of this cross, being darkness, prevented her from recognizing the perfect similarity she bore in death to Sister Marie Pierre, whom she so perfectly imitated in life. Both modern heroines were destined to repair for the crimes of the present era.

At the time of offering herself a victim, she openly said that she was but a little soul, and shrank from offering herself to appease God's justice. Such a task was too difficult; she surmised that an undertaking of such magnitude had, perforce, to be reserved only for the greatest saints. She never held herself capable to that extent and declared it was not her aim to appease His justice by *atoning for the sins of men*, but by offering herself a victim to His love, so violently scorned on every side.

Manifestly, these were one and the same thing. If Divine justice was being outraged by blasphemers and infidels as by no other crime, then also was Divine love spurned by these excesses of the present century. It, therefore, fell to the lot of Sister Therese to repair these worst outrages: Atheistic Communism denying existence of an All-loving God. For, alas, having proclaimed that God does not exist, the next step of the Bolshevik Regime was the launching of a world-wide campaign to annihilate God. From the cradle to the grave the unhappy subjects of Communist states were being drilled to fight the Person of God.

And so, when it came to be that this violent abuse spread so that it had assumed world proportions and became a national statedom, disaster stalked the path of mankind. Someone had to be found to do reparation and point out a path of rescue to those still preserving their reasoning inviolate; as also their faith in God unimpaired; and who stood ready to fight for their convictions.

Now Sister Therese in her humility never counted on assuming this burden. Yet, when God allowed the arch-enemy to besiege her with his most destructive weapons during her entire illness of eighteen months and she drove off the foe and defeated him, the nun had actually performed this unique service in behalf of her guilty brethren.

It was part of the price she was expected to pay for knowing that she was performing this service of reparation. In her desolation, surrounded by the mocking voice of the evil spirit, she was willing to endure her darkness to the hour of her death, if, through it, unbelievers could be granted pardon.

[313]

And now this hour had come. It was seven o'clock in the evening. The shadows of night began gathering in the sickroom where the Saint of Reparation was dying. In about fifteen minutes she would be no more.

Would she learn before she died the Divine secret behind her trial of darkness? Would she understand before she expired the reason why the All-loving God had laid upon her this trial of darkness? Or would she die in the same desolation that she had endured during her entire illness of eighteen months? Certainly, nothing in her exterior expression or attitude indicated that her trial was in any way being lightened. The very manner in which she now clasped her Crucifix betrayed tremendous struggle. Moments of severe anguish passed slowly by. No relief was in sight. The end seemed near, and Sister Therese, in one final effort to defeat the formidable foe, seizing her Crucifix, cried out:

"Oh, I love Him! . . . My God, I love You!"

Having said this, the Sister fell gently back. Her last words were more a protest of her love of God, rendered in the darkness, than an affectionate avowal of tender emotion. She had, in fact, conquered with a final act of Love of God an unseen enemy, who to the very end refused to admit defeat.

To those looking on it seemed that Sister Therese had passed away. But, suddenly, to the surprise of all the Sisters gathered in the infirmary, Sister Therese revived.

Raising herself, as though summoned by a mysterious call, she opened her eyes wide, and looked upward with a face transfixed with indescribable joy. As if in a rapture of ecstatic delight, with a smile illuminating her, she remained thus for the space of about three minutes, gazing steadily up on some object which she alone could see, and contemplating something that was being revealed to her for the first time.

Could she but speak, could she but tell! Eighteen months of uninterrupted darkness was now being dispelled by a light so dazzling that no earthly language could describe it. As the

Sisters looked on the dying nun beaming with happiness, they became struck with wonder.

The three-minute rapture of ecstatic joy upon which they had gazed in silence aroused in them a feeling of such happiness that they would have wished it prolonged indefinitely. But suddenly this ended. Sister Therese was seen falling back on her pillow, dead. Only the smile on her face remained, to testify that Sister Therese expired in an ecstasy of delight, thrilling with Divine Love.

37

Hardly had Mother Agnes and Sister Marie finished enshrouding the remains of their youngest sister, when the convent rang with the joyous message of a sudden miraculous cure.

"What is this you're saying?" asked Mother Mary Gonzaga of the lay Sister who, weeping with joy, hastened to tell her what had happened.

"I realized," she explained to the Prioress, "that I never wanted to own up that Sister Therese was a saintly nun, and, then, seeing her laid out, I suddenly felt that if I were to press my forehead to her feet, that she would cure my cerebral anemia. I did it, and I am well . . . ."

"Are you sure?" the Prioress, asked bewildered.

"Oh, but of course," the lay Sister said.

Four days later, on October 4, when Sister Therese was buried in the little cemetery on the outskirts of Lisieux, most of the nuns in the convent were convinced that she had begun her shower of roses. In addition to the lay Sister's cure, there were reported several other expressible signs of wonderful things to come, which permeated the atmosphere of the entire cloister. Mother Agnes, logical and practical, pressed at once for a first gesture of esteem to be rendered in behalf of her dead sister for restoring the lay Sister's health.

"I suggest we inscribe some suitable words on the wooden cross that will mark Sister Therese's grave," she told the Prioress before the funeral.

"It seems fitting," the older nun agreed, impressed by the miraculous cure. "What shall it be?"

"*I desire to spend my Heaven in doing good upon earth,*"

replied Mother Agnes, quoting the prophetic statement her sister made before her death.

"Very well. Attend to it, Mother," the Prioress assented.

With this small beginning Mother Agnes won her first victory toward making Sister Therese known and loved. When the cortege prepared to leave the cemetery after burial, many of the priests and religious turned back to read for a second time the inscription on the simple wooden cross:

I DESIRE TO SPEND MY HEAVEN
IN DOING GOOD UPON EARTH.

They had never read anything like it before. Somehow, the words had the power of God behind them. Silently the mourners traced their way back. But they would remember when they were in need, they told themselves, to have recourse to this Sister Therese who volunteered of her own accord to spend her Heaven in doing good on earth.

In the days that followed, Mother Agnes, intent on carrying out her sister's wishes regarding publication of the *Autobiography,* could be seen in endless conferences with the Prioress. It was no easy matter to surmount the various objections presenting themselves. In certain ways the memoirs were quite outspoken; publishing them was to lay open to public view many things which some in the convent preferred definitely to keep suppressed.

Mother Agnes discreetly suggested deleting or reconstructing any passage to which objections might be raised, saying that Sister Therese had herself suggested this before she died. The bulk of it must be published, however, Mother Agnes insisted, since it was for the good of souls. Finally the Prioress felt obliged to accede, whereupon Mother Agnes hastened at once to prepare the manuscript, under the title *The Story of a Soul.*

"I think we should ask Father Godefroy-Madelaine to examine it first and request him to secure Bishop Hugonin's 'imprimatur' to publish it," she told the Prioress.

"So soon? It isn't even ninety days since Sister Therese passed away," was the reply. She was surprised that Mother Agnes had all the papers ready for examination.

"But that is what Sister Therese pressed me to do. She told me not to delay. Besides, Sister Therese did not wait even ninety days to cure our lay Sister, but hastened to shower her first rose on the day she died . . . ."

"Very well. Give the papers to Father Godefroy-Madelaine. We will see what he says."

After reading it, the priest was so enthusiastic that, taking the manuscript, he went at once to Bayeux to obtain the Bishop's 'imprimatur.' But when a month later the manuscript was returned, Father Godefroy-Madelaine was speechless with disappointment. The 'imprimatur' had been refused! It was sad news to bring to Mother Agnes, but he had a suggestion.

"Mother Agnes, all is not lost. I will try again, if you allow me to. The canons of the Church protect us. If there are any statements in the memoirs contrary to Catholic morals or dogma, these should be pointed out to us by the Diocesan Office of Censorship, and we shall willingly submit to corrections; but to be denied permission to go to print without cause is not the way the Church works."

"Oh, by all means, Father. Will you try again?" encouraged Mother Agnes.

The priest, whose character and erudition were to bring him the Abbacy of the Premonstratensian Monastery at Frigolet in a few years, armed to the attack and went back to Bayeux with Sister Therese's manuscript under his arm, thus by his determination saving one of the priceless contributions to Catholic literature.

Two months later, March 7, 1898, the Carmel of Lisieux had the coveted 'imprimatur' of Bishop Hugonin, and *The Story of a Soul* went to press, only five months after the author's death.

In October, when the books were ready, they arrived at the Carmel. Mother Agnes was optimistic indeed, since she ordered two thousand copies in the first edition.

When the Sisters saw the immense quantity, one of them exclaimed, "How are we going to dispose of all these books?"

"That's what I say," added another. "Surely, we're going to be left with them on our hands!"

And for a while they were left with the books on their hands. The fact was that when Mother Agnes finished sending single copies of *The Story of a Soul* to the various Carmels in France, in place of the usual Circular Letter generally distributed among Carmelite Monasteries on the death of one of their nuns, only a very small dent was made in the two thousand, because Carmelite convents even in Catholic France are few in number.

"Now what do you propose to do with all the rest?" Mother Agnes was asked as the first few weeks passed and the stack of books was undiminished.

The nun had no ready answer. The truth was that she had no plan whatever by which to bring *The Story* to public notice or promote its further distribution. She had been urged by her dying sister merely to get the book published and send copies to the Carmelite Monasteries in France. Beyond that she was given no further responsibility. From the very beginning the whole project rested on blind faith answering in the voice of some Divine inspiration. Mother Agnes had done her part, all that was asked; now she willingly surrendered the project to Divine Providence. For if she did not underestimate the importance of doing her share as a human agent to advance the works of God, she also had the humility to know the limits of merely human agency, and to depend on God alone to crown His works.

Thus three months went by. The stack of books remained practically untouched. Their promoter, Mother Agnes, seemed a failure. By now the instantaneous cure of the lay Sister's ailment following directly on Sister Therese's death had somehow lost its pristine glory.

Then things began to happen. Various Carmelite Monasteries, having had sufficient time to read the book and discuss its merits, began to react favorably to it. Mail trickled into Lisieux recommending it. Ever more and more orders kept coming in for it. Many wanted *The Story of a Soul* for friends and relatives, for a prospective postulant, a seminarian, a missionary, for a priest, a bishop.

Letters also arrived attesting to favors received through the intercession of Sister Therese. No book had had less publicity build-up than did *The Story of a Soul*, yet by the time the year ran out, the Sisters who had worried over the vast amount of unsold books, only a short time before, were struck speechless. The supply was exhausted. Mother Agnes had to ask for a second printing. This was not all.

A year after that, the fame of Sister Therese had reached beyond France, penetrating into England. In that year, 1900, Professor Dziewicki translated *The Story* into English, and the life of the French Carmelite began to win over the English-speaking world. Other translations followed in rapid succession: *The Story of a Soul* was rendered into Polish, Italian, Dutch, German and Portuguese.

There was no stopping the conflagration of her glory sweeping the world. Sister Therese was accomplishing on a colossal scale just what she proposed to do after her death — she was spending her Heaven in doing good on earth. No place was too distant for her to reach. She needed no one's financial backing, nor any magisterial patronage, to come down to help the thousands who invoked her. Consequently, grateful beyond measure for the favors she showered on men all over the world, the Sister in a few short years had won thousands of ardent admirers. No voice could prevail against her as her clients, now certain of her intercession, became loud and insistent with praise, spreading the book telling of her life, and asking for her speedy Beatification.

Not only the outside world showed its gratitude and response to *The Story of a Soul*, but the Carmel of Lisieux was no less generous. It was now ready to lay its laurels at the feet of the zealous promoter of the *Autobiography*, Mother Agnes of Jesus, whom they now elected their Superioress.

Guided by the spiritual genius of Mother Agnes, who assumed her office as Prioress in 1902, the Carmel of Lisieux was to emerge as the first Carmel in the world. Under her direction the true spirituality of Sister Therese, as taught in *The Story of a Soul*, was now applied in all its beauty and spirit of sacrifice, with the result that perfection among the Sisters grew by steady and rapid strides. One after another, each false notion and each unidealistic movement of the heart gave way to the truth which Sister Therese had so lovingly taught. Tepidity and unkindness were steadily replaced by fervor and by charity. But most difficult of all, the spirit of envy was being crushed in one concerted effort to assign credit where credit was due, joyously acknowledging that which was praiseworthy.

Within the year that she assumed office, Mother Agnes had so completely instilled the spirit of the *Autobiography* into the Sisters, that even Mother Mary Gonzaga surrendered unreservedly as a client of Sister Therese. On her deathbed, in October 1904, she whispered to Mother Agnes, her Prioress: "I have offended God more than anyone else in the community. I should not hope to be saved if I did not have my little Therese to intercede for me. I feel that I shall owe my salvation to her . . . ."

Sister Therese was indeed winning souls for God, inside and outside the cloister — through her life story. Nor was she backward in replenishing her own convent with new novices. About this time, Mother Agnes was particularly struck by a postulant who had been recently admitted. The newcomer was one of Sister Therese's followers, who had read *The Story* outside the cloister and surrendered to its logic and entered Carmel, although before then she was very fond of the world and no one would have suspected the possibility of her ever becoming a nun. Having received the habit, she was given the name Sister Marie-Ange of the Child Jesus. Applying all the lessons of the *Autobiography*, this novice strode rapidly in the path of per-

THE WHOLE WORLD WILL LOVE ME

fection, carrying out in the letter and the spirit all the counsels contained in *The Story of a Soul*.

Came the year 1908 which was destined to bring striking evidence that Sister Therese was achieving a unique conquest inside her own beloved Carmel of Lisieux. Mother Agnes was just completing her second successive term in office and it was again time for elections. Who would be the new Prioress? Some outsiders felt that because of the prestige of the Martin name, now known throughout the world, one of Therese's other two sisters, either Sister Marie or Sister Genevieve might be chosen. Again, others thought that some nun particularly devoted to Sister Therese during her lifetime might be selected.

Having gone into the small parlor to cast the vote, and deeply imbued with Sister Therese's spirit as continuously taught to them by Mother Agnes, their Prioress for the past six years, the nuns knew what was expected of them. Voting for a Superioress was an act involving very serious moral responsibility. Owing to its newly won fame, moreover, the Sisterhood realized that the eyes of the world were upon their particular cloister. She who was to be their Prioress must perforce possess not only genuine interior perfection, but had to have an outstanding personality, be able to represent monasticism to the various high ranking personages visiting Lisieux and, to an unusual degree, acquit herself socially, intellectually and even economically of problems which seldom confronted a Superioress. There was no room whatever for petty considerations, was the dominant conviction Mother Agnes had left on the nuns as her last official advice.

A surprise was in store for them, proving how completely Sister Therese had won over the Community, with whom she had once lived, to her way of thinking

When the ballots were cast and the votes counted, the new Prioress was found to be none other than the recently admitted novice, Sister Marie-Ange of the Child Jesus. [50] She was only

---

50. *Ibid.*, p. 16.

twenty-eight years old, and not as yet a Professed Sister! As a a novice, she did not even have a voice in the elections. Yet, summoned from the novices' hall into the parlor, she was told that the Sisters, all her seniors, had elected her to the office of Prioress!

Choosing a novice to rule them, the Carmel of Lisieux had scored a spiritual victory that was to make them immortal. For the fact was that the nuns of the Lisieux Community, following a high ideal proposed to them by Mother Agnes, and over-coming all petty, human considerations, had chosen for their Superioress her whom they felt to be the most competent in every way.

No doubt, this conquest of supernatural virtue over mere natural feelings had won for the Community of Lisieux that store *of graces which they sorely needed* to complete the work for which they were destined. Undoubtedly, one from their Community, the late Sister Therese, was scheduled for the honors of the Altar. To achieve such triumph posed colossal difficulties, tireless work, the bulk of which would naturally fall to their Community, and particularly on the shoulders of their Prioress.

The youthful Mother, Marie-Ange, assuming her difficult office, at once began to prove that the confidence reposed in her was justified beyond measure. Losing no time, the newly in-stalled Prioress, on the very day of her election, appealed for-mally to Bishop Lemonnier, the new Ordinary of Bayeux and Lisieux, to submit the Cause for Sister Therese's Beatification to the Holy See.

The Bishop knew this was no small task. However, Mother Marie-Ange was so convincing, her prudence and piety became so evident, that the Bishop was deeply moved. Mother Marie-Ange's eloquence and her grasp of basic problems proved to him that her motives for action in Rome on Sister Therese's Cause were dictated by her burning zeal for the glory of God. Before he left the parlor that election day, he promised the young Mother Prioress to do what he could to open the Process for Beatification.

Accordingly, soon after, the Ordinary, together with Mother Agnes and Mother Marie-Ange, requested that the Very Reverend Father Rodrigo, a Discalced Carmelite, be appointed the Postulator, and Monsignor Roger de Teil of Paris, Vice-Postulator of Sister Therese's Process. The Vatican sanctioned these appointments and the Process was ready to get under way.

Accepting office, Monsignor de Teil hastened to Lisieux. No stranger to Beatification Processes, Monsignor de Teil exclaimed: "My experience has proved to me that Carmelite Causes are hopeless in Rome. The Congregation of Rites is weary of Causes in which it is all very easy to prove that virtue had been heroically practiced, but where actual miracles of authenticated cures are invariably wanting. The last canonization of a Carmelite happened centuries ago."

However, after a careful examination of only some of the voluminous medical evidence testifying to various outstanding cures attributed to Sister Therese, he was overwhelmed. Taking the documents with him, he lost no time in bringing them to the attention of the Sacred Congregation of Rites. "Look," he said, "here, at last, we have something substantial from the Carmelites. This case has real prospects."

There still remained the *one* problem, which they all knew was invariably encountered; but the Vice-Postulator solved this quickly. With a smile, he agreed.

"Yes, yes, I know," he said, "a Process is a very costly affair, you will tell me. And besides miracles, we also need money. Well, have no worry. Sister Therese is supplying both — "

Monsignor de Teil should have known. As Vice-Postulator of her Cause in Paris, he was in full possession of all the facts and data.

Everything was running smoothly. The unprecedented was actually happening. Sister Therese was literally storming the world with her glory; stupendous favors were granted to countless persons everywhere; there was no impeding her spreading fame. No sooner had the Official Process been opened, in her diocese, in 1909, than a veritable torrent of wonders began sweeping the world. Fresh reports of cures and favors were now pouring steadily into Lisieux.

When, in the following spring of 1910, the diocesan authorities had collected all the writings of Sister Therese with a view to examining them, and also the various reports of miracles in order to pass on them, there was one incident that came up to claim particular attention.

This was the famous Gallipoli story. It had roused the curiosity not only of the general public and the Lisieux diocesan Tribunal in session, but also some of the authorities connected with the Sacred Congregation in Rome, undoubtedly because the events reported had taken place in Italy itself.

It was essentially what modern journalism terms a "human interest story" with a generous suspense build-up, and, as such, it was bound to catch and to hold the public's imagination. Almost overnight everyone was discussing the small Italian town of Gallipoli, the scene of unusual happenings.

The story ran that a small convent of Discalced Carmelite nuns in the town, stricken with poverty so that at times they went without food, had decided to invoke the help of Sister Therese whose *Autobiography* they had just finished reading. Outlining for themselves a program of prayers, which they offered for three consecutive days to the Blessed Trinity, they asked for material assistance through the intercession of the famous Sister of Lisieux.

The day was January 15, 1910, and the Prioress of the Gallipoli convent, Mother Carmela, besides the worries she had over unpaid bills and the scarcity of food for the nuns, had contracted a cold, and went to bed that night with fever and chills. In the early morning hours she thought she dreamed that a gentle hand was covering her up with her blankets. Without opening her eyes, thinking that it was one of the Sisters, Mother Carmela whispered that she was quite comfortable, but: "I am in perspiration and your movement only stirs the air . . . ."

"But, no," replied the other, "it is a good act that I am doing. Almighty God makes use of the inhabitants of Heaven as well as of the inhabitants of the earth to help His servants." The voice paused for a moment, then it went on: "Here are five hundred francs which I give you so that with this money you can pay the debt of the Community . . . ."

"But," replied the Prioress, defending her economic dignity "the debt of the Community is *not* five hundred francs. It is only about three hundred francs."

"Very well, then, the rest will be over and above. However, since you are not allowed to keep money in your cell, come with me," the voice answered. This was in allusion to the Carmelite custom which provides that neither the Prioress nor any of the Sisters should keep any possessions, particularly money, in their cells, since, through *voluntary* poverty, they should be completely detached from earthly things. Money, therefore, is kept in a community strongbox and never held privately in the cell of any Sister, under pain of serious fault.

But, how can I get up now, thought the Prioress, since I am covered with perspiration? Reading the thoughts of the Prioress, the voice replied pleasantly:

"In that case bilocation will help."

What was that about bilocation? As a member of a contemplative order, Mother Carmela understood that the phenomenon of bilocation belonged in the realm of the mystical, and that it implied being present in two places at the same time. Catholic theology, moreover, treating God's omnipresence, clearly demonstrated that there was no contradiction in this sphere proposing the possibility of dual presence. It explained that the greater the spirit, the higher its inherent powers of penetration and subtlety, and, consequently, the more numerous are the points at which such a spirit can be present at one and the same time. God, the Infinitely Perfect Spirit, is present, therefore, at all points of the universe continually, every point in the universe craving His sustaining power, so that were God to remove himself from any such point in the universe at any given time, it would instantly disintegrate into nothingness.

But even while Mother Carmela wondered why the voice had proposed bilocation, she found herself, without any effort on her part, walking down the cloister corridor. She was following a young Carmelite nun whose habit and veil shone with a silvery brightness which served as a lamp to light their way in the dark. The nun with the shining, bright habit led the way to a small room on the ground floor, where there was a bureau in which the monastery's documents and papers were kept, and a cash box, which was now quite empty.

Going straight to the bureau, the nun, without the aid of a key, opened the cash box which was concealed in a drawer. It contained seven little copper coins and a stack of unpaid bills. As the Prioress looked on, the nun with the radiant habit deposited five hundred francs she had in her hands. Seeing this, Mother Carmela dropped to her knees and thinking that she had been visited by the great sixteenth century reformer of Carmel, Saint Teresa of Avila — known as the Holy Mother of the Order — she exclaimed:

"Oh, you are our Holy Mother!'

"No, I am not our Holy Mother," replied the Sister of the silvery light. "I am the Servant of God, Sister Therese of Lisieux. Today, in Heaven as also upon earth, we celebrate the Feast of the Holy Name of Jesus."

Then, intimately touching the veil of the Prioress, as if to smooth it gently, the visiting Sister embraced her, and was about to withdraw.

"But wait," cried Mother Carmela. "You don't know the way. You might make a mistake . . . ."

"No, no," replied the Sister. "*My way is sure*. I am not mistaken in following it . . . ." and she disappeared.

When the Prioress rose in the morning, she remembered the happenings of the night, and she wondered if it was all only a dream. She then told two of the Sisters. They were all puzzled, but they had a solution:

"Let us go to the cash box and see if it was a dream or not." they decided.

Fitting a key into the small strongbox they opened it and there they saw the sum of five hundred francs, made up in a roll of ten fifty-franc notes on the Bank of Naples.

During the following months, of February, March, April and May, the Carmelites of Gallipoli found additional mysterious contributions in their strongbox. Where did the help come from? Sister Therese finally assured the Community, herself, that the help they received had come from God, through her intercession.

When news of this spread, people began to send in alms to the Gallipoli convent and so the urgent, basic needs of the poorest Carmel in Italy were supplied, after which Sister Therese stopped her personal donation. For the time being.

A month passed by and the Gallipoli story, which thrilled all of France, the Carmel of Lisieux, and the Diocesan Tribunal at Bayeux then working on the Process, also trickled into Rome, straight into the Office of Monsignor La Fontaine, Secretary of the Sacred Congregation of Rites. He was a man of prudence, with grave regard for rigid adherence to all the laws and rules governing the Sacred Congregation.

To his mind, the Gallipoli story had assumed a tone of sensationalism, to say the least, and he was distressed because of this. To be sure, his Office had sanctioned the appointment of a Postulator and Vice-Postulator to open the Process of Sister Therese's Cause, but, to his way of thinking, the way the matter was being handled was quite out of bounds and he felt it was up to him to resolve the case into more discreet channels. Consequently, the Vice-Postulator, Monsignor de Teil of Paris, was informed in no indefinite terms that the whole Process of the Beatification was in serious peril at the Vatican as a result of evident mishandling and sensational build-up.

Monsignor de Teil was alarmed. Gathering only the most pertinent records, he boarded a train for Rome that very night. As soon as he arrived before the Secretary of the Sacred Congregation of Rites, he knew, from the frigid reception given him, that the worst possible turn had taken place. He waited for the verdict.

"Monsignor de Teil, I want to tell you, the Vice-Postulator of this Process of Beatification," began Monsignor La Fontaine in a grave voice, "that entirely too much fuss is being made over this young Carmelite nun! I, therefore, want to make it clearly understood right now that unless you do something to *stop* this fuss, the whole Cause for Beatification will be suspended."

"Suspended?" asked Monsignor de Teil, stunned.

"Yes, suspended! Now you take this Gallipoli matter," went on the Secretary, "it has grown out of bounds. Everybody is talking about Sister Therese paying personal visits and filling up the nuns' cashbox with actual greenbacks, *and on the Bank of Naples!*" he added with special emphasis.

"But it's all absolutely true," managed the Vice-Postulator meekly, to which the Secretary, caught up in the logic of his own argument, paid no attention, but went on:

"Surely, Monsignor de Teil, you will agree with me that it is one thing to discuss incontestable cures of fatal maladies with due dignity, but this . . . this matter of Sister Therese's banking endeavors, well, indeed, it is quite embarrassing to say the least. I understand that not only in January, but that every month for the past four or five months there is a fresh report that she's been supplying added greenbacks for the benefit of Gallipoli. Everywhere I turn it's Gallipoli, Gallipoli, and more greenbacks. Do you know that they're asking me whether there isn't a mint of some kind in Heaven to which Sister Therese has access? And even newspaper articles, speculating on this unusual financing, are asking where Sister Therese gets her supply of ready cash . . . ."

"I am asked the same questions, and in answer I quote a splendid article I read in the press which explained that everybody knows there is no circulation of currency in Heaven and that everybody also knows that a given amount of currency is lost, burned, or otherwise destroyed. Surely, without upsetting the numerical, systematic order of world banking, it is altogether possible for Sister Therese to have recourse to a small number of these 'lost greenbacks' — and so help a convent of impoverished nuns buy bread for their table."

The Secretary remained unimpressed.

"I repeat, Monsignor, all this publicity about Gallipoli has simply got to stop!"

"Am I to understand, Monsignor La Fontaine, that you question the veracity of these reports about Gallipoli?" asked the Vice-Postulator.

"Of course not. I am not *authorized* to question their veracity, nor to pronounce on them one way or another. That is up to your Diocesan Tribunal in Bayaeux to settle. After that, that will be up to the Apostolic Tribunal to worry about, if the Cause ever gets that far. As Secretary of the Congregation of Rites, I am interested only in one thing. And that is to keep the Process of Beatification on a dignified level, without all this fuss and undue publicity. We have rigid rules to keep. Fifty years is the space of time required for launching a Beatification. Do you want these wise laws disregarded? It is only about twelve years since Sister Therese died. There is no need to rush things so much. That is why this Gallipoli story simply has got to be hushed up. There is entirely too much sensationalism about it."

"But, Monsignor, what can *I* do to stop Sister Therese from advertising herself, as she insists on doing in this Gallipoli matter?" the Vice-Postulator asked, distressed.

"What do you mean, Monsignor de Teil?"

"Didn't you hear the latest news about Gallipoli?"

"Is there something new? Again?"

"Well, yes, there is," the Vice-Postulator answered. "It comes from one of our French Carmelite nuns, who has sent in a signed statement about it to Lisieux. In it she declares that on

July 20 she was writing a letter to a nun in Belgium, to acquaint her with the latest favors received from Sister Therese by Mother Carmela. Suddenly, realizing that she forgot the name of the quaint Italian town, she paused in her writing and whispered a prayer to Sister Therese to remind her of it, when at once she heard a soft voice say, 'Gallipoli.' "

Monsignor La Fontaine sat down.

"But that is not all," continued Monsignor de Teil. "The voice went on to encourage the Sister to continue writing letters spreading the report of the favors and miracles which God was working through her intercession. 'You must continue to write the kind of letters you are now writing. I desire very earnestly to do good on earth. *You must make me known everywhere,*' said the voice. Such is the latest development on the Gallipoli story, Monsignor. You can see for yourself, therefore, that although we cease all efforts on our part to make her known, we cannot hinder Sister Therese from advertising herself."

Before ending his interview, the Vice-Postulator gave full details of another incident attesting to the power of the Lisieux Carmelite. At this the Secretary decided to put the candidate to a test. He needed a rare favor. If the Carmelites of Lisieux prayed to their Sister Therese, and if he *were* to receive the exceptional favor he wanted, well, then he would yield.

"Pray for this intention as you never yet prayed," wrote Monsignor de Teil to Mother Agnes at Lisieux. "The whole cause of her Beatification is at stake."

Two days later the Secretary called on Monsignor de Teil, his face beaming with joy. The favor he sought had been unexpectedly conferred! — There was no more question in Rome about too much fuss being made over Sister Therese.

The next month the Diocesan Tribunal ordered the first exhumation of Sister Therese's remains, to take place on September 5, 1910. Surprisingly, Gallipoli was again to come in for a share of prominence. On the eve of September 5, Sister

Therese appeared again to Mother Carmela at Gallipoli, who knew nothing of the proposed exhumation, and informed her of it. Her face shining with extraordinary beauty and her garments glittering with a light as of transparent silver, Sister Therese announced: "Only my bones will be found in my grave."

With these words she confirmed the prophecy she made when she was alive. To the Sisters who asked her if she would be incorrupt after death, she declared that this would not be so in her case since she was just an ordinary soul, one whom *everybody* ought to be able to imitate. Therefore, the extraordinary favor of incorruptibility of body after death, granted to certain saints, she said, was not to be expected in her.

All these wonders helped to accelerate the Process. But, because the Church provides for devious and exhaustive inquiries, a Beatification Process inevitably does stretch over many years. During this period of investigation, no public worship — such as scheduled devotions in Church — may be given to the person proposed for beatification. Private devotion, however, is not only allowed but must be proven to exist to an extensive degree, if successful culmination of the Process is to be expected.

About five years after the opening of her Cause, while the investigation was in progress, World War I broke out. Sister Therese proved so powerful with aid to soldiers in the trenches that the Holy See granted a dispensation, allowing medals of her to be struck even before she was beatified. That same year, circulation of the complete French edition of *The Story of a Soul* reached 200,000 copies. An additional 700,000 of an abridged French edition had appeared, to say nothing of the numberless versions of the foreign translations of the *Autobiography*.

The Holy See, satisfied with the evidence submitted by the Diocesan Tribunal at Bayeux, authorized, in 1915, the introduction of the Cause in Rome, and an Apostolic Tribunal was set up. Three years later so widespread was the fame of Sister Therese, both among Catholics and non-Catholics, that Mother Agnes wrote to the Vice-Postulator, Monsignor de Teil, on December 30, 1918:

> *I take this occasion also to tell the Holy Father that our Community remains fervent and regular in spite of the enormous work imposed on it by the mailman, who brings us between three hundred and five hundred letters daily. Also I wish to note that what gives us the greatest hope for the success of the Cause is the fact that we receive approximately fifteen thousand requests for Masses each month, either to obtain favors or in thanksgiving for favors granted.* [51]

And thus the prophetic words of Sister Therese, who during her illness declared that her sister Mother Agnes would find consolation after her death through the mail box, have been realized.

Further inquiries into the life of this Sister, and the veracity of the miracles attributed to her intercession, continued until 1923, when Pope Pius XI announced that it was safe to proceed with the Ceremonies of Beatification.

Dispensing with the regulation providing that fifty years should elapse before a Beatification, Sister Therese of the Child Jesus and of the Holy Face was solemnly beatified in Rome, on April 29, 1923, about twenty-five years after her death. Two years later, on May 17, 1925, she was canonized a Saint of the Universal Church.

On the solemn occasion of her Canonization, the Supreme Pontiff declared that the whole world ought to study Saint Therese. Calling her not a little Saint, but a great Saint, the Pope emphatically and explicitly declared that Saint Therese was entrusted with a special mission in modern times:

> *A glance at the times in which she lived almost enables us to assert that it was, indeed, her mission that* the enemy and the avenger might be destroyed. *However, without the*

---

51. *Ibid.,* February 1952, p. 203.

world-wide circulation of the book, *"The Story of a Soul,"* it *would not have been possible for this mission to have been fulfilled.* [52]

It was inevitable to expect that a saint so strikingly modern in all her outlooks on life as Saint Therese, who on noting the benefits accruing from the invention of an elevator said that she decided to find also an easier way of ascending to Heaven, should achieve her mission through a modern means, namely, the press as Pope Pius XI pointed out in his Papal Document. For, obviously, without the worldwide circulation of the book, it would not have been possible for Saint Therese to fulfill her mission that *the enemy and the avenger might be destroyed.*

*   *

It was inevitable also to expect that this greatest saint of modern times should achieve her sanctity in accomplishing a modern mission, one singularly engendered by the turmoil of the present century. Explaining the nature of this twentieth-century mission of the Saint, the Supreme Pontiff declared that is what it essentially was: that THE ENEMY AND THE AVENGER MIGHT BE DESTROYED.

Today, that *Enemy* and *Avenger*, presumptuously establishing himself in the high places of world statedom, under the banner of *Atheistic Communism*, is threatening the survival of civilization itself. Unmasked, this *Enemy* and *Avenger* is the evil spirit of atheism and blasphemy, who made *Irreligion* the prime object of a political system known the world over as the *Red Menace*. Disbelief in God has actually assumed the form of a militant system of government. Simultaneously, the struggle of the two opposing parties has become the struggle over one and only one issue: GOD OR NO GOD! Compulsory World Atheism, shackled on every human being, or Freedom of Divine Worship, conceded to man who has been created in the Image of God!

---

52. *Autobiography,* "The Papal Documents," p. 265.

Happily for the modern world, Saint Therese has faced that enemy and avenger, the evil spirit of Atheism, and, challenging him, has brought from beyond the grave a message of hope. The century in which she lived and offered herself a victim, praying that all those on whom faith does not shine may at last see the light, proved to be a century of rampant disbelief in God never yet envisaged on earth. Communism, in a well-advanced stage, began threatening doom to men of every creed and nationality, imposing itself as the arbitrary lord and master, dictating terms of tyranny and serfdom. And society, unwilling to face the reality and repel the foe at the offset, alas, unwittingly hastened his despotic growth. In addition, a lukewarm spirituality, unmindful of the place prayer holds in the scheme of balancing the power — of evil let loose in the world — remained aloof, refusing to admit that *God Demands Reparation*!

Saint Therese, in one generous gesture of love, taking on herself the task of appeasing God, spent nine years in a cloister adoring the Outraged Countenance of the Saviour and her last year and a half enduring, in behalf of her guilty brethren, the fierce attacks of the enemy and avenger — who flaunted his atheistic boasts before her. Enduring the fearful struggle, the Saint declared: "I tell God that if He will open Heaven for eternity to poor unbelievers, I am content to sacrifice during my life all joyous thoughts of the Home that awaits me. *May all those on whom faith does not shine at last see the light!*"

Saint Therese has found the surest way to peace; taking upon herself the duty of repairing for the guilt of her brethren; as the strong one, she made up for the weak. Seeing the futility of trying to convert those who were visibly beyond the pale of logical entreaty, she established herself before the Image of the Sacred Face; it was there she made reparation for the guilty brethren whom she loved beyond words, and whose souls she was determined to see safely in eternal bliss beyond the grave.

Love drove her to Reparation. It was the only way left to achieve a goal otherwise impossible to reach. For indeed,

Christ, having spent himself in teaching and in miracles, alas, also ascended the gibbet on Calvary in one sacrificial stroke, and, thus, He sealed the destiny of erring mankind by His Divine Reparation in Blood.

"Father, forgive them for they know not what they do . . ." was that last prayer of the Divine Victim who recognized that He had no time left to convert, but only to make Reparation. That Reparation in His last hour on the cross took on the form of a prayer for atheists and blasphemers, the sinners of obstinacy to the end.

Thus Christ became the Divine Model of Reparation, relying in His last agonizing hour on prayer and vicarious suffering alone as a means of reconciling unbelievers to God. Reparation became, thus, the Saviour's last resort in His rescuing of souls.

Similarly, in her last months on earth, it became the destiny of Saint Therese to *imitate* the Divine Model of Reparation. Attacked during her last illness by the spirit of darkness who hurled at her his propaganda of disbelief, Saint Therese had fought, suffered and prayed that the enemy who had begun his reign of terror under the name of atheistic Communism might be destroyed.

History has proved her equal to the combat. It has proved her victorious in battle. But, then, the Saint had a *secret weapon!* That weapon was made known to the world by her sister, Mother Agnes of Jesus, who testifying before the Apostolic Tribunal during the Process for her Canonization, declared under oath:

> *However tender was her devotion to the Child Jesus, it cannot be compared to the devotion which she had for the Holy Face.*

BIBLIOGRAPHY

Les Annales de Sainte Therese de Lisieux, November 1951, February 1952.

Collected Letters of St. Therese of Lisieux (*Lettres de Sainte Therese de l'Enfant-Jesus, Carmel de Lisieux*), translated by FRANK J. SHEED.

God Demands Reparation: The Life of Leo Dupont, Rev. EMERIC B. SCALLAN, 1953.

Histoire d'une Ame, SAINTE THERESE DE L'ENFANT-JESUS.

Life of Leo Dupont, edited by EDWARD H. THOMPSON, 1882.

Life of Sister Marie Pierre, PETER JANVIER, translated from the French by HENRI LE MERCIER DE POMBIRAY, 1884.

Life of Sister Marie de St. Pierre of the Holy Family, SISTER M. EMMANUEL, O.S.B., 1938.

The Memoirs of Mother Genevieve, SISTER AGNES OF JESUS.

Message of St. Therese of Lisieux (taken from her Last Confidences, August 1, 1897), M. M. PHILIPON, O. P.

Personality of Christ, ANSCAR VONIER, Abbot of Buckfast.

The Rose Unpetaled, BLANCHE MORTEVEILLE.

St. Therese of Lisieux (revised translation of Definitive Carmelite Edition of Autobiography and Letters), Rev. THOMAS N. TAYLOR.

The Spirit and the Bride, ANSCAR VONIER, Abbot of Buckfast.

Storm of Glory, JOHN BEEVERS.

Victory of Christ, ANSCAR VONIER, Abbot of Buckfast.

Vie de M. Dupont, tome I, II, ABBE JANVIER.

If you have enjoyed this book, consider making your next selection from among the following . . .

Discover the other two books in this trilogy!! . . .

THE GOLDEN ARROW
THE LIFE AND REVELATIONS OF SISTER MARY OF ST. PETER (1816-1848) ON DEVOTION TO THE HOLY FACE OF JESUS

Edited by Dorothy Scallan

Translated by Fr. Emeric B. Scallan, S.T.B.

No. 1123. 232 Pp. PB. Imprimatur. ISBN 0-89555-389-9

15.00

This is the story of the Carmelite nun who was chosen by Our Lord to spread the devotion to His Holy Face—a devotion specially revealed by God to make reparation for blasphemy and Communism.

THE HOLY MAN OF TOURS
THE LIFE OF LEO DUPONT, APOSTLE OF THE HOLY FACE DEVOTION (1797-1876)

By Dorothy Scallan

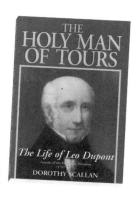

This is the fascinating story of a Catholic man who was given a unique vocation after his wife and young son died. Pope Pius IX declared that Leo Dupont was perhaps the greatest miracle-worker in Church history! These miracles occurred through oil from a lamp that he kept burning before an image of Veronica's Veil. Unique, surprising and encouraging!

No. 1124. 212 Pp. PB. Imprimatur. ISBN 0-89555-390-2

15.00

TAN BOOKS AND PUBLISHERS, INC.
P.O. Box 424 · Rockford, Illinois 61105

Toll Free 1-800-437-5876
Tel 815-226-7777

Fax 815-226-7770
www.tanbooks.com

About the Author

Dorothy Scallan, whose pen name was Doris Sheridan, wrote extensively and uninterruptedly for the Catholic Press over a period of many years. She contributed hundreds of articles dealing with almost every phase of Catholic life, including editorials, short stories, essays, analyses of world news and affairs, poetry, full-length biographies and, last but certainly not least, multiple and deeply analytical book reviews of contemporary Catholic literature.

Deeply concerned about the moral tone of modern books which are recommended to the faithful as Catholic literature, Miss Scallan spent years writing many book reviews, which won her warm and enthusiastic commendation from many members of the American Catholic hierarchy in the U. S.

While writing for the Catholic Press was Miss Scallan's chief occupation, she also contributed her efforts to promoting Catholic Action in yet another field. Permeated with the conviction that a Catholic Information Center located in the most prominent commercial district of large cities could be of invaluable service to the Church, Miss Scallan in 1942 founded THE GUILD. Located in the heart of downtown New Orleans, THE GUILD served for many years as a center from which the public could readily procure good Catholic books and devotional articles.

In the wake of rapidly developing world crisis—regarding which Pope Pius XII went so far as to say, "There persists a condition which may explode at any time"—Miss Scallan felt the need of concentrating entirely on the impending social upheaval. Heeding the voice of that Holy Father, who called on every "individual to do what he can and must do personally as his own contribution to the saving power of God, to help a world which is started, as it is today, on the road to ruin," she turned her pen exclusively to making known the optimistic means of winning happiness, peace and unity for men.

Dorothy Scallan and her brother, Fr. Emeric Scallan, shared a home on Canal Blvd. in New Orleans in their later years. Father went to his reward in 1990, and Miss Scallan moved to a home run by the Little Sisters of the Poor; she passed away a few years later. Near the end of their lives, Fr. Scallan and Dorothy Scallan wrote to the Publisher of TAN Books and Publishers, Inc. expressing their wish that TAN republish all three of their books: *The Golden Arrow*, *The Holy Man of Tours*, and *The Whole World Will Love Me*. The first two of these books were reprinted by TAN in 1990, to the joy of Miss Scallan; the present book completes the series. Father and Dorothy Scallan saw these three books as a trilogy setting forth the crucial importance of reparation to the Holy Face of Jesus as the God-given means of overcoming the blasphemy of the modern world, especially in the form of Communism.